Also by Deirdre Stanforth

The New Orleans Restaurant Cookbook
Creole!

Buying and
Renovating a House
in the City

Buying and
Renovating a House
in the City

A PRACTICAL GUIDE

Deirdre Stanforth
and Martha Stamm

Alfred A. Knopf · New York · 1972

PHOTO CREDITS: *Niels Thorsen:* pages 4 (A) , 13 (F) , 18, 19 (B & C) , 22 (A & B) , 24(A & B), 25, 26, 63, 151, 160, 182, 302. *Philadelphia Redevelopment Authority:* pages 8(A & B), 16, 73, 74, 75, 76, 77, 186, 187. *Brooklyn Union Gas Co.:* pages 13(D), 67, 177, 298, 299, 303. *Charlotte La Rue:* pages 12(C), 48(A, B & C), 49(D & E), 52. *Historic Savannah Foundation:* pages 9(A & B), 12(B). *Providence Preservation Society:* pages 39, 40, 41. *Operation Clapboard, Inc.:* pages 13(E), 44. *San Francisco Redevelopment Agency:* page 118. *Virginia State Library:* page 139. *Pittsburgh Post Gazette:* page 102. *Pittsburgh History and Landmarks Foundation:* page 103. *Walter Lowrey:* pages 122, 123, 190, 191. *Towne Properties, Inc.:* page 105. *Louis Reens:* page 5(C). *John T. Hill:* pages 20, 21. *Martha Stamm:* pages 5(B), 132, 133. *Deirdre Stanforth:* pages 12(A), 13(G), 66, 85, 91, 94, 95, 162, 163, 168, 169. Floor plans by *Arnie Hecht.*

Hardcover ISBN: 0-394-47424-4

Paperback ISBN: 0-394-70759-1

Library of Congress Catalog Card Number: 71-173774

Manufactured in the United States of America

Published March 15, 1972

Second Printing, May 1972

This book is dedicated to all those who have rescued and restored old houses.

Contents

List of Illustrations   *ix*

Acknowledgments   *xiii*

1   Rediscovery of the City House   3

2   The Infinite Possibilities of Old Houses   15

3   A Tour of Renovation Neighborhoods   29

The East: Boston 30, Providence 37, Newport 43,
Schenectady 45, New Haven 46, New York City 46,
Philadelphia 70, Baltimore 82, Washington 91
The Midwest and West: Pittsburgh 99, Columbus 104,
Cincinnati 105, Chicago 106, San Francisco 112
The South: New Orleans 121, Savannah 129, Atlanta
135, Charleston 136, Richmond 138

4   Living in Renovation Neighborhoods   143

5   The Story of Two Renovations: The Stamms' Story
and the Stanforths' Story   148

6   What Kind of House Suits Your Needs?   171

7   Finding a House   183

8   Is It a Good Buy and Can You Afford It?   194

9   Financing   218

10   Purchasing a House   248

11   The Basic Elements of a Renovation 262

12   Drawing the Plans   311

13   How the Work Will Be Done   333

14   The Renovation   352

15   Being a Landlord and the Alternatives to
        Renting   381

    Appendix   389

    Index   follows page 400

List of Illustrations

Photographs

The living room of the Stanforths' 1881 Manhattan
    brownstone 4

A city garden 5

Interior of Gerard Cugini's home in Boston's North
    End 5

C. Jared Ingersoll's house in Philadelphia's Society
    Hill: before and after 8

A house in Savannah's Marshall Row: before
    and after 9

The doorways of seven city houses 12–13

Village atmosphere in downtown Philadelphia 16

Wide moldings used in a typical inner front door of
    a Brooklyn house 18

Two mantels in Brooklyn and Manhattan 19

Exterior and interior of Caswell Cooke's nineteenth-
century brownstone in New Haven   20–21

Parquet and wide plank flooring   22

Nineteenth-century hardware   24

Pier mirror and valance in the Stamos nineteenth-
century Manhattan house   25

Original details of the Stanforths' front parlor   26

Benefit Street, Providence: before and after   39

Eighteenth-century Providence clapboard house:
before and after   40–41

A double house in Newport   44

A variety of Manhattan houses   48–49

Fanciful details of Upper West Side brownstone
façades in Manhattan   52

L. J. Davis' house after restoration   63

Carroll Gardens brownstone   66

Park Slope brownstones   67

Center city Philadelphia   73

The Ingersolls' elegant eighteenth-century dining
room before and after renovation   74–75

Two houses in Society Hill, Philadelphia: before and
after   76–77

Houses in Bolton Hill, Baltimore   85

Houses in Dickeyville, Baltimore   91

Some typical façades in Capitol Hill,
Washington   94–95

Pittsburgh façades and window detail   102–03

Homes in Mount Adams, Cincinnati   105

San Francisco wood gingerbread Victorian   118

The Lowreys' French Quarter house in New Orleans:
    before and after   122–23

Amazing variety of architecture in downtown
    Savannah   132–33

Houses in Church Hill, Richmond   139

The Stamms' living room   151

The Stanforths' foyer and stairway   160

The Stanforths' garden apartment: before
    and after   162–63

The Stanforths' garden: before and after   168–69

Circular iron stairway in Park Slope house in
    Brooklyn   177

The Stanforths' dining room and kitchen   182

A brick colonial house in Society Hill, Philadelphia:
    before and after   186–87

The façade of the Lowreys' French Quarter house:
    before and after   190–91

Renovated bathroom: before and after   298–99

Detail of the Stanforths' kitchen   302

Renovated kitchen: before and after   303

Maps

Boston   31

Providence   38

Brooklyn   56

Philadelphia   71

Baltimore   83

Washington   92

Pittsburgh   100

Chicago   107

San Francisco   113

Richmond   138

Diagrams and Floor Plans

Plans showing division of space in 2-story house   175

Cross section of typical high-stooped house   176

Original and two alternative plans for dividing
        space   179–81

Plumbing diagram   269

Alternative plans for bathroom   273

Acknowledgments

WE ARE GRATEFUL for James Stanforth's many contributions and good advice. Thanks also for the knowledge gained from working with Michael Caiafa and David Schwab, and for the encouragement and editorial assistance of Evelyn Gendel.

There are many people whose help was invaluable in collecting the material needed for this book. To all those whose names are mentioned in the text, our heartfelt thanks, and sincere appreciation also to all those whose names are not mentioned, who opened their homes and revealed their trials and tribulations to two inquisitive strangers.

Very special thanks to Mrs. William Gardner, Bette Austin of the Redevelopment Authority of the City of Philadelphia, Mrs. Don F. Cathcart, Mrs. Alex M. Hitz, Jr., and Reid Williamson of Historic Savannah Foundation.

We are also obliged to: Florence Adams, Nedda Allbray, Mrs. William Slater Allen, Sylvia Barkan, Haughton Bell, Susan Bragstad of the San Francisco Redevelopment Agency, Mrs. Frank P. Brannen, Frederic L. Chase, Jr., of the Providence Preservation Society, Margaret Constantine of the Chicago *Sun Times,* Mrs. Harry T. Cottman, Barbara Snow Delaney of *Antiques* magazine, Jerry Dilts, Mrs. John R. Fordyce III, Dorothy Kahn of the Brownstone Revival Committee, Jeannette Lerner, Yura Mohr, Marion Morra of the

New Haven Redevelopment Agency, Arthur Myrhum, John Pearce of the National Trust for Historic Preservation, Mrs. Peter G. Platt, Roy Russinof, Carol Salguero, Bill Sikes, Carole Smith, Romaine Somerville of the Baltimore Commission for Historical and Architectural Preservation, and Margot Wellington and Donald Moore of the Downtown Brooklyn Development Committee.

The purpose of this book is not to be construed as an end in itself on the various topics discussed herein. Neither of us is an attorney, architect, contractor, or real estate broker, and the advice we offer in this book is not meant as a substitute for consulting a professional. We hope that our considerable experience and research will prove helpful and useful to anyone interested in buying and renovating an old house. If we do nothing more than point out the danger signs in this area to direct you to an expert, we feel we have fulfilled our mission.

Deirdre Stanforth and Martha Stamm

Buying and
Renovating a House
in the City

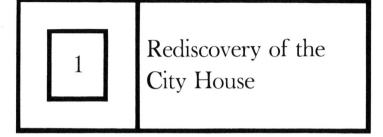

1 Rediscovery of the City House

Is IT TRUE that only the wealthy can afford town houses? Far from it! It *is* true that a private house in Manhattan's Sutton Place or Turtle Bay or Washington's Georgetown is a privilege reserved for the rich. But—and few realize this—those chic addresses were once far from fashionable. They were down-at-the-heels, decaying neighborhoods where you could have bought a house for next to nothing.

In cities all over America young families are discovering that they can create their own Georgetowns, achieving spacious, luxurious homes with private gardens on incredibly modest budgets. They are able to live in a style that is generally thought to be impossible today, in a casual, country atmosphere with convenient access to all the vitality and variety the city has to offer.

Many couples are finding that they can buy more space than they can afford to rent, discovering they can even live rent-free in houses that were built with twelve-foot ceilings, wood paneling, and half a dozen marble-manteled fireplaces instead of boxy little plasterboard rooms. Some are enchanted to own homes with elaborate old parquet floors and intricate brass hardware. Others who prefer a contemporary setting buy "shells," and gut them. Dramatic new spatial environments are created by stripping to the bare walls and redesigning the interiors.

The raw material is readily available. Every city has houses as good as those in Georgetown or Turtle Bay, as

A. Only simple, inexpensive refinishing—painting and floor scraping—was needed to restore this living room in the Stanforths' 1881 Manhattan brownstone from the rooming-house quarters it had become.

B. Most city houses have delightful hidden gardens, large enough for flowers, shrubs, and trees, but small enough for minimum maintenance.

C. Dramatic contemporary interior created by architect Gerard Cugini in his old house in Boston's North End.

A

B

C

structurally sound, as potentially beautiful, often with greater historic value. The astonishing fact is that most of our architectural heritage has been left to die in our slums. How did it happen?

Cities originally grew around a center—town hall, churches, stores—with the homes of citizens erected nearby, clustered close together for convenience and safety. As cities prospered, the business sections spread outward, and the more affluent began to move. The first residential neighborhoods were abandoned for more fashionable ones. With the advent of the automobile, people were tempted to move even farther away to the new suburbs. In larger cities the creation of the apartment house lured others from private homes. Meanwhile, the early residential neighborhoods, deserted in this phased withdrawal and now considered totally undesirable, became housing for the desperately poor. Because of their poverty and the greed of absentee landlords, they were inevitably packed like the proverbial sardines into houses that had been built for one family. Result: slums.

Ironically, the automobile, which made possible the creation of the suburbs, has contributed to their undoing. By its very proliferation, the automobile began to strangle its own mobility, forcing commuters to spend hours on traffic-clogged expressways, traveling from suburban homes to city jobs. Urban sprawl has made suburbs almost indistinguishable from cities; some have even spawned their own slums. The rural atmosphere that once lured city dwellers has been gradually vanishing in a pall of pollution.

The cycle was complete. People began to rediscover the center of the city as a place to live . . . in those lovely old houses that had been built as homes by their forefathers. Not only did these houses have charm and history; they were built to last, and despite the ravages of time and frightful abuse, were still more solid and substantial than anything built in the past several decades. Best of all, to the first who discovered them, they were cheap—because nobody wanted them. The larger ones were even adaptable to provide home-plus-income.

Georgetown was the first notable example of an entire community reborn in this manner. Today Georgetown is the top address in the nation's capital, the home of society and statesmen. However, in 1930, when the first young couple scraped together all their savings for the down payment on a run-down house in the midst of Georgetown's blight and deterioration, their family and friends thought they were insane to want to live there, to invest their hard-earned money in such a ramshackle, squalid neighborhood.

Two centuries ago, in 1751, Georgetown was born as a tiny village on the Potomac. Initially a tobacco port, it became one of the important shipping centers of the colonial period. By the time Washington was made America's capital in 1800, Georgetown, well established on its hill four miles away, was the thriving home of prosperous merchants and landowners. The streets of Washington were still mudholes when Pierre L'Enfant took up residence in a Georgetown tavern while creating his famous plan for the layout of the city. But the growth of Washington swallowed Georgetown, robbing it of its identity. Congress revoked its right to a separate government and finally even the use of its name. A hodgepodge of new construction went up, and many federal-style buildings were defaced by remodeling.

The decline of Georgetown began with the Civil War, and by the 1920's all but a few families had moved away to newly fashionable neighborhoods. In the early thirties, when the first stirrings of the historic-preservation movement were beginning in Williamsburg, Charleston, and New Orleans, a few houses were bought and saved as museum pieces. The prices were low, and word spread to some of the bright young men who had been brought in to

A

B

A.-B. *The C. Jared Ingersolls' eighteenth-century house in Philadelphia's Society Hill, showing one room before and another after restoration.*

C.-D. *A house in Savannah's Marshall Row before and after restoration.*

C

D

staff Franklin Roosevelt's New Deal. In those Depression days, the small-scaled bargain houses in Georgetown tempted young couples who could not afford new houses.

The new frontier of city blight demanded a pioneer spirit akin to that of the first American settlers. Fortunately for Georgetown and all the city neighborhoods that have followed its example, these latter-day homesteaders had the courage to tackle the urban wilderness. Financing was hard to come by, as banks and the FHA * showed total lack of interest. In the opinion of financiers, Georgetown property was being "overimproved" in relation to its value: Their theory was that you should only upgrade to the level of the neighborhood. On this basis, Georgetown would have barely risen above slum level. But the new pioneers wanted quality equal to the best the suburbs had to offer. They made the most of the Georgian simplicity of architecture, enhancing it with bright new paint and carriage lamps, restoring the charming village atmosphere of tree-lined streets and brick sidewalks. Their instinct for quality was well rewarded, for their "overimprovement" played a large part in attracting newcomers and beginning a chain reaction. Their confidence was infectious, their enthusiasm created enthusiasm. Prices doubled and redoubled many times, proving that a rising neighborhood is the best investment of all.

The lesson of Georgetown showed that the transformation of a neighborhood can begin with one house, one block. Its influence has been enormous in beckoning millions back to the cities.

The same story is being repeated nationwide—in Baltimore, Philadelphia, Pittsburgh, Richmond, Columbus, San Francisco, New York, and many other cities. The types of houses may vary, but the motivation and spirit are universal; and the problems are the same. Any member of the "renovation generation" from Manhattan would

* Federal Housing Administration.

find himself equally at home with his opposite number in Washington's Capitol Hill or the Fan District of Richmond. As a front page story in the *National Observer* (December 15, 1969) put it, "For a growing number of young, educated, child-bearing middle class Americans, happiness is a home in a slum. . . . The trend is national and unmistakable."

The trend began in the 1960's, a largely unnoticed countermovement to the flight to suburbia that had characterized the forties and fifties. National attention in the sixties was focused on urban renewal, as massive government programs and billions of dollars were poured into an effort to resurrect our dying cities. Emphasis was on demolition and rebuilding until at last there came a reaction against wanton destruction, as many Americans began to realize that most of our architectural heritage was being wiped out along with the slums. A country that made the worship of the new and the waste of the old a way of life suddenly became conservation- and preservation-minded. While millions traveled to Europe to admire old buildings, we began discovering some of our own were worth saving.

In 1960 the Washington *Star* wrote, "Pioneering restoration activity is almost always carried forward by private families of average means. . . . Optimism is a characteristic of the restorationist." Areas of many cities where no government programs exist are being privately renewed by these optimistic families, who crave economic living space; and as a result, decaying neighborhoods are undergoing dramatic changes. The emerging new communities have a sense of identity, pride, and purpose that no amount of government planning could have created.

One does not have to be a pioneer, but the pioneers get the real bargains. A pioneer is a trend setter, not a status seeker. He has to have abundant self-confidence and the courage of his convictions. Often he is not a native of the city where he buys his home; thus he is more objective and less prejudiced about the potential of neighborhoods where

A

B

C

Variety of doorways found in old city houses: A. *Brooklyn Heights,* B. *Savannah,* C. *West Seventy-sixth Street, Manhattan,* D. *Park Slope, Brooklyn,* E. *Newport,* F. *Stamm house, Manhattan's Upper West Side,* G. *West Eighty-fifth Street, Manhattan.*

D

E

F

G

it is generally believed "one simply doesn't live." Pioneers all over America in places such as Brooklyn's Boerum Hill, Chicago's Old Town, and Boston's South End have seen the value of their houses skyrocket in a few years.

In this computerized age the effectiveness of the individual dominates the movement to reclaim old houses in the urban environment, to make cities come alive again. People are rebelling against the conformity and sterility of city apartments, developments, and suburbia in favor of creating their own life styles in houses from a more gracious era —in spite of all obstacles.

2 | The Infinite Possibilities of Old Houses

PEOPLE OFTEN DO NOT THINK of homes in connection with cities at all. Countless New Yorkers and visitors to the city never dream that people actually live in houses there.

Many city houses look surprisingly un-urban, particularly those that were built in America's early years, when even the hearts of cities were more rural than today's suburbs. Among the oldest houses that remain standing are the city dwellings of New England, the clapboards of Providence and Newport, and the lovely brick colonials of Philadelphia and Alexandria. It is remarkable that so many have survived the ravages of time, deterioration, and the bulldozer. These houses were usually built free-standing, on narrow lots, two stories with five rooms on each floor, laid out around a central chimney. Most were homes for well-to-do merchants and artisans, and are ideally designed for family living (they are, in fact, the prototype for many a suburban home) without any need for structural change. Usually the objects of loving authentic restoration, their interiors need only the addition of modern conveniences in the form of plumbing, heating, wiring, bathrooms, and kitchens in order to convert them from charm-

Village atmosphere in downtown Philadelphia.

ing eighteenth-century fossils to equally charming but useful twentieth-century life.

However, the Victorian is the type of house most abun-
dantly available. The exterior may vary from New Orleans
Greek revival to San Francisco wood gingerbread to New
York brownstone—but whether it is built free-standing or
as a row house with party walls, whether it is in Chicago,
Baltimore, Washington, or Pittsburgh, the interior design
is essentially the same. These houses come in a number of
sizes (from two stories up to five) and in a variety of widths
and depths, but they generally tend to be long and narrow,
with major rooms front and rear, and a stairway running
up one side through the center.

Mid-nineteenth-century houses had simple wide plank
pine flooring (intended to be covered), classic marble mantels, and wide curved moldings for door and window
frames, with the Greek ear motif at the corners. A decade

or so later the decoration increased, with plaster moldings and ceiling medallions, and parquet floors. In the 1890's the style we associate with Victorian began to flourish. Plaster and marble were replaced by dark woodwork, which was paneled, inlaid, carved, turned; and the more involved, the better.

After having been disdained for half a century, the intricate late Victorian spooled woodwork and curlicues have become popular again. Since this vogue's turn-of-the-century heyday coincided with a period of building boom, treasure troves of exuberant Victoriana are often easiest to come by. Almost all these houses have louvered shutters that fold back into recesses on either side of the windows. Many have etched or stained glass, marble washbasins or marble flooring in foyers, elegant pier mirrors, and filigree-patterned brass or bronze hardware. And most of those built between the 1870's and 1890's have exquisite parquet floors. Often they can be discovered under countless layers of linoleum in rooming houses, and with a minimum of refinishing they can be restored to their original beauty.

These houses can be full of surprises, not only because of the treasures they may contain, but in terms of imaginative treatment by renovators. Although the exteriors are rarely altered drastically, you never know what to expect inside. It is quite possible to find two, side by side, with identical façades and unbelievably different worlds (even different centuries) behind the front doors.

There are three approaches to renovation:

1. Authentic restoration
2. Gutting and redesigning the interior
3. Partial restoration

For those whose taste runs to the traditional, there are still many houses to be found with all the original detail intact. Though these architectural features make a house visually attractive, their origins were often purely practical. It is interesting to learn that more than a few fashions in

A

A. *Wide moldings used in typical inner front door of Brooklyn house. Doors are two inches thick with beveled glass panels.*

B. *Mid-nineteenth-century marble mantel found in Brooklyn's Boerum Hill. (Similar mantels are found in houses of the period in Savannah, New Orleans, Boston, San Francisco, though they may be covered with paint and have to be stripped.)*

C. *Late-nineteenth-century carved wood mantel in Manhattan house—stripped of many layers of paint by the owner.*

building were devised as means to avoid paying taxes. The characteristic colonial multiple-paned window evolved because large panes of glass were more heavily taxed. Both the mansard roof (named for the noted French architect) and the top floor half-story commonly seen in Europe and New England allowed additional floor space while avoiding tax because they did not count as a story.

Many Brooklyn houses have a large arched alcove for the master's bed, as well as small curved niches for marble washbasins. Also common is the coffin niche (an architectural detail popular from 1850 to 1870), placed at the curve of the stairway between the parlor floor and the next to make it possible to maneuver the coffin down the stairs from the master bedroom. A somewhat differently designed variation is seen in Boston, where it is called a coffin corner. Many homeowners are unaware of the original purpose of the charming niches they use for decorative placement of statuary or vases.

B   C

When architectural detail is well preserved, it can be restored to make a lovely home. However, some houses either have no architectural detail left to save or had none to begin with. These provide the perfect opportunity for imaginative architectural design, where totally new spatial arrangements are created within the shell of exterior walls. Some striking examples are to be found in New Haven, Connecticut, where a number of architects have done particularly spectacular work in redesigning the space within the period façades of nineteenth-century houses, creating contemporary environments for their own living.

Three of them have made their family homes plus rental units in brownstones facing Wooster Square. They gutted their deteriorated rooming houses and rearranged the interiors to make dramatic two-story living rooms, each strikingly and unforgettably different from the other. Caswell Cooke has a fantastic cityscape view of the Sound from the glass-walled, cut-back, terraced rear of his top floor duplex.

Behind this typical nineteenth-century brownstone façade in New Haven, Connecticut, is architect Caswell Cooke's spectacular contemporary home. Bought from the New Haven Redevelopment Agency, it had an interior in bad condition and nothing worth saving.

And on the upper balcony, jutting out high over his living room, a shaft of light from a cutout in the roof illuminates his drafting table. From this spot he can see the statue of Columbus in the square through a strategically placed small window in the façade—which he designed for that purpose only.

Charles Moore, dean of the Yale School of Architecture, has made his home in a charming frame house with columned portico, its period exterior unchanged except for an interesting paint color. One is therefore unprepared for

A

A. *Late-nineteenth-century parquet.*

B. *Mid-nineteenth-century wide plank flooring (both found in former rooming houses).*

B

the interior, which is a shocker: a never-ending adventure in spatial relationships created with two vertical wells cut through the house from top to bottom, and further varied with painted plywood cutouts in kaleidoscopic shapes, changing at every level.

Moore's house was not stripped bare. He actually retained a certain amount of the original house, imposing a new character upon it by devising new environments within the old. Without entirely erasing the original structure, he achieved a complete metamorphosis in mood.

The Moore house is a larger-than-life example of the unlimited potential for combining the old with the new —a really far-out eclecticism. Nancy and Rik Pierce's house in Boerum Hill, Brooklyn, is a much less extreme case of partial restoration. They ripped out the front half of the parlor floor of their four-story brownstone to make a stunning two-story living room, with bookcases on either side of the fireplace running all the way up the full two-story height. Their dining room, on the remaining rear half of the parlor floor, is a balcony overlooking the living room. Even though the window frames are now elongated to double their length, the Pierces have retained the original Greek ear moldings and made effective use of the elaborate openwork plaster ceiling decorations, boldly emphasizing them with gilt, set off by white and rich red.

Combining old and new is probably the most common method of exploiting the potential of nineteenth-century houses. Often a few pieces of carved woodwork or molded plaster can be more effectively set off by a starkly simple background or a natural brick wall than they were in their original setting. There is, after all, no reason to assume that the design of these houses is sacred just because they are old. Ironically, some of them were the equivalent of today's development houses, built by the score from pattern books without benefit of architect. Many renovators prefer to play up whatever remaining detail they find,

A B

A.-B. *Typical nineteenth-century hardware, usually found covered with paint or black with neglect.*

C. *Ornate gilded pier mirror and valance in painter Stamos' nineteenth-century West Side Manhattan house.*

spending hours lovingly stripping layers of paint from a newel post and surrounding it with a contemporary setting rather than going the route of authentic restoration or gutting to the bone.

There is another alternative for filling in the gaps where pieces are missing, or even for providing decoration where none exists. What does a renovator do when he needs a paneled door or some brass hardware? He goes in search of someone else's discards—becomes a scavenger. This is a common avocation of the renovation generation. It is not unusual to find the back seat of the renovator's automobile crammed with shutters, balustrades, or paneling, or to see him suddenly slam on the brakes as he spots a carved door on the curb awaiting the rubbish removal truck. With

C

some, scavenging becomes habit or passion. Unable to bear the waste of a handsome object, they are overcome by a compulsion to salvage, even if they have no idea what to do with the prize. Martha Stamm has a cellar full of such found objects—hardware of all sorts and sizes, paneling and assorted shutters that maddeningly refuse to fit anyone's windows.

Original details were intact in the front parlor of the Stanforth house. Plaster frieze, marble mantel, and parquet floor were easy and inexpensive to restore. Note typically wide baseboard.

Martha visited every renovation site within twenty blocks over a period of several years, searching for discards, always prepared with screwdriver in handbag. Due to this diligence, and hours spent with paint remover, the Stamm's house boasts woodwork and hardware handsomer than many a million-dollar custom job. By careful advance planning, they were able to use four pairs of matching

paneled doors she acquired for the pantry wall opposite the kitchen appliances. Charlie Stamm cleverly made matching drawers and cabinets with other found bits of paneling.

James Plauché spent twelve years collecting old marble flooring and fluted cypress columns from the façades of ante-bellum mansions* to grace the exotic atrium and pool of his elegant home in New Orleans's French Quarter. This was perhaps the ultimate Cinderella transformation from drudge to princess through the cast-off finery of deceased royalty—because Plauché's residence began life as a fish cannery!

Though the Plauché house was done lavishly, other renovators have used the same method modestly. As will be seen in the tour of renovation neighborhoods throughout the country, all kinds of people have used their imagination and ingenuity to create exciting homes to suit their personal tastes.

---

* Those who haven't the time or inclination for treasure hunting can find house-wrecking sources in many cities, where the fruits of someone else's efforts can be purchased at relatively low cost.

3

A Tour of Renovation Neighborhoods

A COMPLETE GUIDE to all renovation neighborhoods in America would become dated as rapidly as the telephone book, for old houses are being discovered and rescued every day. A Trenton attorney and his wife have recently bought the first center-city house to be renovated as a residence in the New Jersey capital. There is renovation activity in Annapolis, Little Rock, Mobile; and citizens of Portsmouth, New Hampshire, are fighting to save an area of old houses from urban-renewal demolition. On the other hand, in Santa Barbara, California, the renovation movement began as long ago as 1922, when Mr. and Mrs. Bernhard Hoffmann purchased the Lugo adobe for adaptation to offices. Since that time Santa Barbara has become very much aware of the charm of its early-nineteenth-century Spanish tile-roofed adobes, with their flower-filled courtyards and deeply recessed windows. Nantucket, Massachusetts, and Cape May, New Jersey, both have a great many marvelous old houses renovated as vacation homes.

Here is a brief survey of cities where there is significant renovation activity, moving regionally from Northeast to West to South.

- THE EAST
- BOSTON

Boston has undergone greater changes in topography at the hands of man than any other city, ancient or modern. After choosing the hilly peninsula for their city in 1630, the Puritans and their successors set about leveling hills, filling in marshes, bays, and coves, until it bore little resemblance to the land they had found and was more than doubled in size. Back Bay was originally a body of water, and Beacon Hill was a small triple-peaked mountain, whose top was removed to fill more land for the growing city.

While Bostonians have always revered Beacon Hill's distinguished buildings and long ago protected them with historic designation, other neighborhoods with many lovely old houses have only recently been rescued from oblivion by renovators. Among these is the South End, with its spendid Victorian mansions; historic Charlestown, scene of the Battle of Bunker Hill; the North End, site of Paul Revere's house and the Old North Church, from whose steeple the signal was given that the British were coming. While renovation is completed in Bay Village, it has only just begun in Roxbury's Highland Park.

The sprawling South End is the largest and most active of the neighborhoods undergoing renaissance. The South End was planned in 1801, but Chester and Worcester squares and Union Park were not laid out until 1850. The five-story brick bow-front houses around oval parks were magnificently ornamented inside and out. But within two decades after they were built, the panic of 1873 sent the area into a decline, and the newly fashionable Back Bay took its place as the distinguished place to live.

The man most responsible for the revival of the South End is Royal Cloyd, who happened to go on a tour of Boston neighborhoods in 1959. That tour was to change the future of a 616-acre section of the city. For when the bus

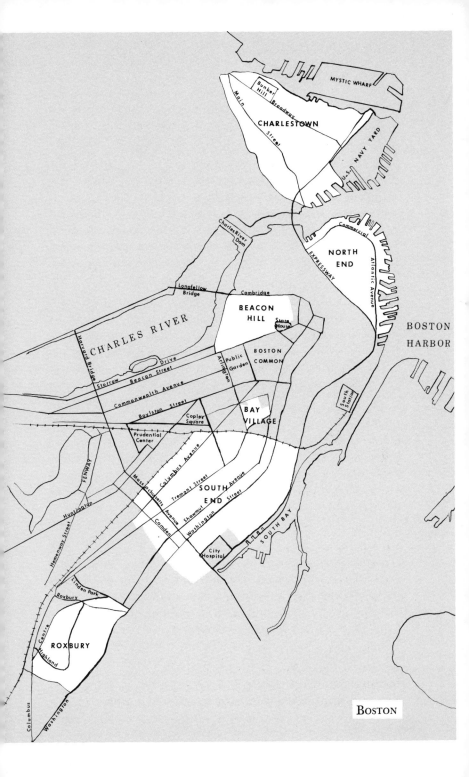

MYSTIC WHARF

CHARLESTOWN

Main Street
Bunker Hill
Broadway

U.S. NAVY YARD

Charles River Dam

Commercial

NORTH END

EXPRESSWAY

Atlantic Avenue

Longfellow Bridge

Cambridge

BEACON HILL

State House

BOSTON HARBOR

Harvard Bridge

CHARLES RIVER

Drive

Storrow

Beacon Street

Arlington

Public Garden

BOSTON COMMON

Commonwealth Avenue

Boylston Street

South Station

Copley Square

BAY VILLAGE

Prudential Center

FENWAY

Massachusetts Avenue

Columbus Avenue

Tremont Street

SOUTH END

Shawmut Avenue

Washington Street

SOUTH BAY

Huntington

Hemenway Street

Camden

City Hospital

Linden Park

Roxbury

Centre

ROXBURY

Highland

Columbus

Washington

BOSTON

stopped in the oval of Victorian houses called Union Park, Cloyd got out, and as the tour went on, he remained there, intrigued with the inherent grandeur of the mansions neglected and falling to ruin around the park. Unlike most renovators, Royal Cloyd was not motivated by a need for more economic living space or a location nearer the center of the city; perhaps in an unconscious urge to live up to his first name, he wanted to own a mansion.

There was an ancient "For Sale" sign on one house, and he decided to buy it, despite the South End's reputation as Boston's Skid Row. He phoned the owner, who named a price that seemed absurdly low to him and, he now realizes, must have seemed just as absurdly high to the owner. But when he went to his bank for a mortgage, he was greeted with utter disbelief. His bank would be delighted to give him a mortgage elsewhere, but *not* in the South End.

Undaunted, Cloyd found someone with influence to ask the bank's president to give him a mortgage. The bank did their best to dissuade him. It was against their policy to invest in the South End because they had lost large sums of money there. Cloyd assumed they referred to the Depression of the 1930's, but he later learned that they meant the panic of 1873! In the conservative manner of banks everywhere, they had not put a penny into the South End in this century.

When they realized that he was determined to live on Union Park, they revealed that they were trustees for another property on the same block and asked him to consider that house instead. He did, and found it even more to his liking than the first. A date was set for a public auction, and he was told what to bid—an even lower price than he had agreed to pay for the other house.

So at ten o'clock one morning he and two officials from the bank appeared on the sidewalk at Union Park. In a curious charade a bank employee unrolled an auction notice and hung it on the fence. Another man bid a prearranged figure, and Cloyd, as instructed, raised the bid by a hundred dollars. The house was his.

He and his wife moved in and began cleaning up and decorating. Several months later there was a newspaper story about the couple who had dared to move into the South End to live in a splendid old five-story mansion with a magnificent 29 x 54 foot double parlor, two Italian marble mantels, and ornate plaster moldings on the soaring ceiling. There was an immediate response. People began calling the Cloyds, including a woman from Maine who owned two South End houses she wanted to sell. Royal found a buyer, who made a considerable profit in reselling one after making his home in the other. Many other families bought and moved into the area as a result of this publicity.

The next milestone in overcoming the area's terrible reputation was a television program on which Cloyd told his story. This brought in another flood of homeowners. As renovators came in, they began to organize and join block associations to improve the neighborhood, sponsoring clean-up campaigns, street fairs, house tours. They conquered the problem of garbage in the streets by inventing a contest, ridiculously easy to win, in which the prizes were new garbage cans. Block associations were further organized into a parent body called SEFCO (the South End Federation of Citizens' Organizations). With their strong organization, they decided to make an effort to bring Urban Renewal into the area. (Royal Cloyd points out that this step can be a disaster unless there is strong citizen organization, because without community control, more harm than good can result from large government-run projects.) Urban Renewal was needed, for even though the area sounds like the phoenix rising from the ashes, the South End is too big for total self-renewal. It has been called the largest area of Victorian houses remaining anywhere in the United States.

At the time, houses were being systematically razed at

the rate of two a day. When Cloyd tried to stop this wanton destruction, his most difficult adversary was the contractor who had been awarded the demolition job. But it *was* stopped and there is an Urban Renewal plan for the South End, based on rehabilitation of 80% of the existing buildings.

As could be expected, the price of houses has since doubled, tripled, and even quadrupled. Nevertheless, new homeowners continue to come in because of the size, space, and variety of the houses, all with rear gardens, and easy parking (which Beacon Hill does not have), and proximity to the new Prudential Center in the heart of Boston. Many houses need no more work than the Cloyds': replumbing, rewiring, and redecorating to restore them to the brief glory they enjoyed in the mid-nineteenth century. These huge old houses lend themselves to division into several large apartments for people who do not need such an abundance of space. There are also smaller houses suited for one or two families, originally built for servants and coachmen behind the mansions. The David Myers gutted one of these, a house with no architectural detail, to create a handsome two-story living room, with the brick floor extending into the stone-walled bathroom.

The bad reputation of a neighborhood dies hard, however. In spite of the influx of so many people from all walks of life, in spite of news and magazine stories, the taxi driver who took us to Union Park told us that it used to be a fine neighborhood, and could not be convinced that it was anything but terrible today.

From the top of Bunker Hill in Charlestown one can see new signs of life in the houses standing around Monument Square, as renovators move in to reclaim them as homes. Charlestown is extremely hilly, which gives it a special charm and spectacular views across the Charles River to downtown Boston. A few blocks downhill from Bunker Hill Monument is Harvard Hill and the original

Harvard Square, site of the first Massachusetts colony laid out by the English (who later burned it down during the Battle of Bunker Hill). Therefore most of the houses in Charlestown are postrevolutionary—though the Larkin house, where Paul Revere borrowed the horse for his famous ride, still stands, as does a tavern he used to frequent.

At the turn of the century Charlestown was one of the most elegant sections of Boston, with a population of 60,000. When Main Street's fine trees were replaced by an elevated train, the wealthier families moved out, and the population dropped to 12,000. The working-class families who took over the neighborhood formed a solid, nontransient community (90% homeowners), with the lowest crime rate in the city. It became John F. Kennedy's first political stronghold.

These proud families have kept their houses in good condition, but it takes a keen eye to detect their actual vintage and architectural origins, for so many of them have been totally disguised like masqueraders at a costume ball. Though layered over with asbestos siding, aluminum windows, and every other conceivable form of modern improvement, the original houses are still there, well preserved beneath, waiting to be released like the Frog Prince in the fairy tale. However, most of the owners are elderly people who hold onto their houses tenaciously, so the market is scarcely flooded with them.

J. Rivers Adams, a young industrial salesman, and his interior-decorator wife were among the first renovators to come into Charlestown, in 1965, from an apartment in Back Bay. They found their lovely 1860 house through an advertisement. Adams financed his house through a G.I. loan and succeeded in getting the first 312 loan (see page 247) granted in Boston to pay for his renovation: a duplex apartment for himself and two floor-through rental apartments. Adams has since bought more property in Charlestown, often through advertisements for government sales. He has renovated and rented houses he has acquired, some as homes and some as apartments, while he carries on his full-time job. He sees a great future for Charlestown, with Urban Renewal coming in to remove the blight of the el and build a shopping center, schools, parks, and playgrounds.

Renovators have recently discovered the charming old houses in the narrow streets of the North End, long the territory of Boston's tightly-knit Italian community. The site of Paul Revere's house and the Old North Church, it also boasts picturesque Copp's Hill, the only one of Boston's three original hills spared alteration in the rearrangement of the city's topography. Today the whole area is being transformed by the Waterfront Urban Renewal, and Copp's Hill will be enhanced by an adjacent, large waterside recreational park that is planned. New apartment towers rise along the harbor near old wharf buildings, where attractive housing units have already been created by imaginative builders. Abandoned commercial structures will be cleared but worthwhile buildings of historical or architectural value will be rehabilitated. The area has become a mecca for young architects, who have found its convenience to the new City Hall complex and downtown Boston ideal for location of their homes and offices.

Bay Village, a small area of delightful Philadelphia-style brick houses, built in the 1820's by French Huguenots, was privately renovated by individuals. It began in the early 1960's and is now completely finished, including gas lamps. The area was previously surrounded by sleazy hotels and night clubs, but the tragic Cocoanut Grove fire provided the opening wedge toward their removal, clearing the way for the emergence of this charming little enclave of homes.

Always synonymous with elegance, the section of Beacon Hill nearest Beacon Street and the Common has never lost its prestige or its price as *the* place to live in Boston. However, the back side of the Hill has some houses that are certainly candidates for rescue. Parking is a serious problem, and many houses lack gardens, so whether the price and address compare to value received in the South End, Charlestown, and the North End is a decision to be made by the individual.

Highland Park in Roxbury has inexpensive houses with great potential and hilly terrain with a view. Though a handful of pioneers has begun to move there, they have encountered difficulties, which may or may not affect its future prospects.

· PROVIDENCE, RHODE ISLAND

Providence, one of America's oldest cities, was founded in 1636 by Roger Williams. The town was settled around the harbor; and as the city grew, it radiated outward to the north, south, and west. Its quaint street names attest to the influence of Williams and the city's maritime era. Capital of Rhode Island, with a third of the state's population, it boasts an extraordinary number of colleges for a city of its size. Several are located in the oldest section of the city, and hence it is called College Hill. This area roughly coincides with the original home lots laid out by Williams in the years following the settlement of Providence Plantations. Benefit Street came into being in 1753 as a thoroughfare "for the benefit of all," running from the waterfront level on the west to the brow of the hill on the east. Thanks to the Providence River and the steep hillside that now contributes to its unique charm, the area was saved from major business encroachments, but was not spared urban blight as people moved to newly fashionable residential neighborhoods farther from the center city. There followed the usual sad cycle of deterioration, as many of the dignified colonial clapboard homes of silversmiths,

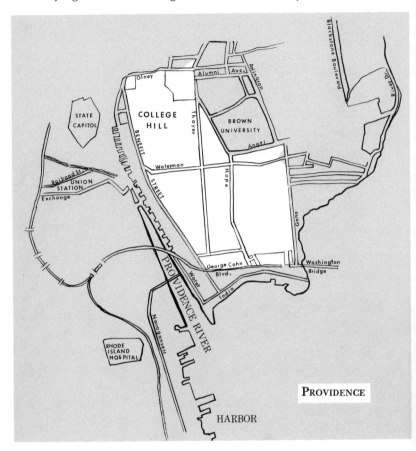

teachers, judges, and merchants were first rented out by absentee owners and then sold to slum landlords. In fifteen years the number of inhabitants doubled with the increase of laborers brought in to work in prospering mills. The result was tenant-jammed houses, junk-filled yards, sagging roof lines, and rotting clapboards concealed under asbestos siding.

In 1956, when Brown University razed two blocks, a group of concerned citizens formed the Providence Preservation Society to prevent the loss of their historical heritage. The society and the City Plan Commission worked

Transformation of Providence's Benefit Street, accomplished with removal of artificial siding and cobbled-on additions, and application of bright new paint.

Neglected, ruined eighteenth-century Providence clapboard rescued and restored to its simple beauty and original function as a home.

together to obtain an Urban Renewal Administration grant for a pilot study to save the College Hill area and its notable examples of Federal, Georgian, Greek revival, and Victorian architecture. An award-winning study was made, with imaginative, well-thought-out plans for urban renewal, incorporating the restoration of the many historic and architecturally varied houses surrounding Brown University and the Rhode Island School of Design. Meanwhile, through the enterprising and exemplary efforts of one woman, Mrs. Malcolm G. Chace, Jr., the rescue of some seventeen of the early houses was started, initiating the snowballing effect that invariably takes place when there is visible evidence of the transformation of a neighborhood.

Over a period of two years Mrs. Chace bought thirty of these decaying houses on the open market, and through

the cheaper-by-the-dozen method put a contractor to work at once in order to make them sound, weatherproof "shells." They were stripped of cobbled-on additions, asbestos siding, and obsolete utilities, made structurally sound, and restored on the exterior with new roofs, pointed-up brickwork, and paint. They were then put up for sale at low prices, so that families who wanted to live in them could renovate the interiors to suit their own needs and tastes. This exterior restoration made such a dramatic change in North Benefit Street that the renewed potential of its eighteenth-century charm was easily apparent.

Mr. and Mrs. Robert Goff were the first to move into the area, while the house they rescued was still surrounded by its derelict neighbors, overcrowded with poor families, and subject to frequent fires. From the enormous eighteenth-century stone fireplace in the Goffs' rustic family room at the rear of their house on Benefit Street, the view at night downhill across their delightful garden culminates in a startling sight: the sparkling white marble dome of the state capitol building in downtown Providence. Looking out the front window at the neighboring clapboard houses through the branches of old trees, it is easy to imagine you are in an Early American village at the time these houses were built. The house across the street dates from 1774!

Today these charming, brightly painted clapboard houses march proudly along the rim of steep College Hill just above the central business district of Providence, each wearing a historically dated plaque to identify the role it plays in "A Mile of History."

These houses and many more have been beautifully restored as family residences by owners of all types and ages, representing many levels on the economic scale, and they all know each other. In one area a group of rear yards have been thrown together and landscaped as a community garden (like New York's Turtle Bay), with participating property owners contributing toward its upkeep.

As is commonly found in renovation neighborhoods, the renovators are generally anxious to maintain diversity in the population. Remaining homeowners have taken new pride in their homes, and as those around them have been upgraded, they have also made improvements. In the southern Fox Point section of College Hill, an effort is being made to urge improvement of property by owners who want to stay as newcomers move in.

The Providence Preservation Society works to further continuing restoration by acting as a clearinghouse between real estate agents and individuals who want to buy houses. They have a Consultant Bureau, to furnish homeowners with historic and architectural information and free advice on restoration problems. They also continue to work toward the improvement of the entire area in terms of parks, playgrounds, landscaping, traffic, and university problems.

· NEWPORT, RHODE ISLAND

Few cities can equal Newport's combination of rich, colorful history and scenic splendor. Founded in 1639 by followers of Roger Williams who were fleeing religious intolerance, it became the home of America's first Quakers and a colony of Jewish families from Holland. A prosperous port dealing in molasses, rum, and sperm oil brought in by New England whalers, it was also the center of African slave trade in the 1700's. Deeply involved in the American Revolution, it was occupied by the British for two years.

Newport's fame as a summer resort began in the eighteenth century. Though it has passed its peak period of outlandish opulence, its spectacular rocky coast is still studded with palatial estates and mammoth mansions silhouetted against the ocean. The old town's narrow streets funnel down to the waterfront, for Newport is almost entirely at sea, connected only on its northern side to the mainland.

In the July 1963 *Antiques* magazine Mr. J. A. Lloyd Hyde wrote, "18th century houses are as common in Newport as Victorian brownstones used to be in New York. In fact they are all over the old part of town, mostly forlorn and neglected and to be had for very little money." Mr. Hyde had the foresight to buy one of these forlorn houses, and the elegant photographs of the swan that had emerged from his ugly duckling illustrate his article.

Also in 1963 Mrs. Charles Pepys became aware of the plight of these charming clapboards and created an organization called Operation Clapboard, Inc., to save them. She acquired options and contracts to buy some $60,000 worth of real estate (houses were then selling for $2,000 to $7,000) on the assumption that she would find enough interested buyers before it was necessary to take title. In two years thirty houses were placed in the hands of renovators.

Operation Clapboard was created on the revolving-fund basis inaugurated in Charleston—with a new twist, the sale of stock at $25 a share to provide capital for the purchase and resale of houses to individuals. Through the exceptional farsightedness of the Newport National Bank (which may have been sympathetic because its headquarters are in an eighteenth-century house) mortgages were made available to them. The program was also assisted by

A double house in Newport lends itself to two-family contemporary living.

a broad-minded and intelligent tax assessor, who has not discouraged restoration with high tax assessments.

Operation Clapboard (recently combined with Oldport Association) provides research information and dated façade plaques for appropriate restorations, and its director, Stephen Snell, also offers advice to homeowners on contractors and how to deal with them. He is working toward co-ordination of groups all over Rhode Island in order to save buildings that give a community its character, quality, and scale—and put them to practical use.

· SCHENECTADY, NEW YORK

Schenectady has an area of restored homes that comes as a surprise to the visitor. Tucked behind the business district at the foot of a hill, its narrow tree-shaded streets are lined with painted brick three- and four-story houses.

After an Indian massacre wiped out the original New York settlement in 1690, the Stockade area was rebuilt behind renewed fortifications. Dutch, English, and colonial architecture are represented in houses built close to the street on narrow lots in the traditional Dutch manner, with lovely gardens behind them.

Somehow, most of the early buildings of the Stockade survived the development of the business district, though many fell into disrepair and some were torn down. In 1932 several were rescued by individuals and transformed into fine homes, leading the way for the restoration of the entire area. In 1950 homeowners formed the Stockade Association, which with the help of the Schenectady Historical Society won passage of a city ordinance that allows them to control architectural changes.

For ten years the Stockade Association and the Friends of the Stockade have been sponsoring an annual Walkabout, in which a number of restored homes are open to the public. Houses built before 1825 wear descriptive markers and fly flags from the period in which they were built: 'Dutch, English, and various flags of the American colonial period.

· New Haven, Connecticut

When Richard Lee took office as mayor in 1954, New Haven was described as a big slum surrounding a big school (Yale). Under Lee's administration, a dynamic Urban Renewal program has raised the city from the dead with massive rebuilding and rehabilitation. A pioneer project in terms of stressing rehabilitation as opposed to demolition, particularly in the nineteenth-century houses of the Wooster Square area, its chief impact, however, was in making the city as a whole an attractive and desirable place to live again. Urban renewal used in this total, sweeping manner in Philadelphia and New Haven, wiping out depressing, grimy slums, bringing in new businesses, providing new services and facilities, making the city alive and beautiful again, gives a much-needed impetus to bring families back to urban living.

Though the main emphasis in New Haven's program has been on imaginative, forceful, and effective inducement of existing owners to rehabilitate architecturally worthwhile buildings, there have been houses made available at minimum cost to individuals for private renovation. A number of Yale architects have taken advantage of the opportunity to design spectacular contemporary homes for themselves in these nineteenth-century buildings (see photographs, pages 20–21).

· New York City

Many people don't realize that Manhattan is only one, and by far the smallest in size, of the five boroughs of New York City. New York leads the nation in most things, and renovation is no exception, for it began in Manhattan in the 1920's. But it has also begun in the other four boroughs: Queens, the Bronx, Staten Island, and Brooklyn, where the recent surge of private renewal is perhaps the most dramatic anywhere in the United States. Manhattan and Brooklyn will be treated separately.

· *Manhattan.* It is a common misconception that Manhattan has no houses. New Yorkers aware of the large number of houses remaining on the east-west streets above Fifty-ninth Street often think of these "brownstones" (many are not literally brownstones, but the term has become a generic one) as representative of the elegance of a bygone era—a nice idea, but alas, another misconception. Many New York brownstones were the "development" houses of the late nineteenth century; most were built in the area above Fifty-ninth Street in the ten years between 1880 and 1890, without benefit of architect. The row house was not originally conceived to conserve space, but to imitate British "terrace houses"; and the earliest stood in groups of four or more in the middle of open fields. The high stoop (from the Dutch *stoep*) was a New York innovation, designed as the entrance to the parlor floor, with a servant's entrance beneath to the ground floor kitchen.

The development of Manhattan began at its southern tip and marched northward up the island. During each period of building boom another area of open fields was divided into lots and covered with houses. Once all the land was used up, New Yorkers could not continue to abandon neighborhoods and move farther out to create new ones as citizens of other cities have done, because they had reached the limits of their island. Therefore, deteriorated neighborhoods have been rediscovered and revived far sooner and more intensively than elsewhere.

Greenwich Village was the earliest area to be settled, some three hundred years ago. As the grid street-plan was not imposed on the city until 1811, the Village's short, narrow, crazily curving and crisscrossing streets and lanes

A

B

C

D

Variety of Manhattan houses: A. *St. Luke's Place,* B. *West Fourth Street,* C. *Washington Mews,* D. *Henderson Place (East Eighty-sixth Street),* E. *Grove Street.*

E

remain to confuse and charm visitors to this day. However, the hills crowned by mansions of estate owners were flattened so that the newly laid-out streets could be divided into building lots.

By 1822 the Village estates had been broken up, and the area became densely settled. The Chelsea estate was broken up in 1830—the town houses there were adversely affected by the steam locomotives of New York's first elevated railway on Ninth Avenue. Turtle Bay brownstones (building began there in the mid-eighteenth century and boomed after the Civil War) went into a decline with the opening of the Third Avenue el in 1878. Ironically, while the railway provides the transportation that makes building possible, elevated railways always doom fashionable residential neighborhoods.

The Turtle Bay area began its comeback after World War I, when its brownstones were rediscovered and renovated. In 1920 Mrs. Walton Martin created the incomparable Turtle Bay gardens, the entire block from Forty-eighth to Forty-ninth between Second and Third avenues, with a community garden in the center made by subtracting six feet from the rear garden of each house. At the same time, a run-down section of Avenue A just to the north (Fifty-seventh Street) was being renovated and rechristened Sutton Place by Mrs. William K. Vanderbilt and Anne Morgan (daughter of J. P.). Not until the els were removed did the entire Upper East Side become the chic and expensive neighborhood it is today. The Second Avenue el came down in 1942. In 1944 a group of tenements on an L-shaped courtyard in Turtle Bay was remodeled imaginatively into a delightful enclave of garden homes and offices by interior designer James Amster. The Third Avenue el came down in 1956, and the ensuing renovation and redevelopment made the East Side almost the exclusive property of the well-to-do.

The seesaw of fashion has constantly affected New York neighborhoods, and Chelsea has had more ups and downs than most. It was influenced by a succession of circumstances, first with the opening of the Ninth Avenue el, then by the temporary blossoming of the theater district on Twenty-third Street. It became New York's bohemia when the theater moved uptown, and also enjoyed a brief boom as a pre-Hollywood motion picture center. It was not until the fifties that Chelsea town houses began to be restored to their original glory.

Early in the twentieth century artists and writers deserted Chelsea's bohemia (with a few notable exceptions such as Thomas Wolfe, who continued to live in the Chelsea Hotel) for Greenwich Village, where they found cheap quarters and contributed to the area's character and atmosphere. Most of them were later pushed out by climbing prices as the charming houses were seized upon by renovators and the Village became a fashionable, expensive place to live.

Artists and writers moved on to find cheaper housing on the Upper West Side, in Brooklyn, and in the East Village, all of which became the next targets of New Yorkers seeking inexpensive living space to make over.

The houses on Manhattan's Upper West Side were built during the boom period of the 1880's and 1890's as the homes of prosperous New Yorkers. Downtown was then Fourteenth Street, and this northern territory was still farmland, considered so distant from the city that when the first luxury apartment house went up on Seventy-second Street in 1884, citizens joked about it being in the Dakota Territory—so it is called the Dakota to this day. The West Side became fashionable as the East Side declined (later the West Side went down as the East Side came up). The top floors of the four- and five-story buildings housed servants, who scurried down all those stairs in the gray light of dawn to fire the furnace in the cellar, then cook breakfast in the ground floor kitchen and send it up on the dumbwaiter. The parlor floor was lavished with all the elegance the family could afford—high ceilings, par-

*Fanciful details of
Upper West Side
brownstone façades.*

quiet floors, elaborate brass hardware, mahogany woodwork and paneling, and carved mantels. (However, it is ironic that much of this detail work that we revere today was ordered out of catalogues at the turn of the century.)*

The decline of the West Side began with the coming of apartment houses and the going of servants. Family fortunes fell with the Depression of the thirties, and remaining resident owners took in roomers to make ends meet. Most of the formerly elegant town houses passed into the hands of absentee landlords, who hastily erected partitions to divide the spacious rooms into as many rental units as possible. The West Side became the province of SRO—single room occupancy—which meant large families living in a single room with a hot plate and a shared bathroom down the hall. People moved from this sick neighborhood as soon as they could afford to, making an unstable neighborhood even more unstable. It became the home of the transient, the unemployed, the prostitute, pimp, and dope addict—and crime, their constant companion, was the inevitable accompaniment.

This was the gloomy picture until in 1956 New York City obtained a federal grant to study the area and explore various ways to renew it. A twenty-block area was designated for Urban Renewal: from Eighty-seventh to Ninety-seventh streets and from Central Park West to Amsterdam Avenue. It was decided that SRO must go. Other more adequate housing had to be provided. The city took possession of some houses and then sold them to individuals for renovation, with owner-occupancy a top priority. The first houses were incredibly cheap for Manhattan, and when the word got out, many young families who wanted a city home were ready to meet the challenge. It *was* a challenge, even though Urban Renewal made possible what was virtually impossible on an individual basis alone.

---

* Including canvas-backed plaster friezes and ceiling medallions, which were glued on where ornamentation was desired. There is a new synthetic version available today called anaglypta.

Urban Renewal helped people meet the challenge in many ways: by the wholesale cleaning out of blocks of festering rooming houses, by demolishing groups of tenements, by clearing sites for low, middle-income, and luxury high-rise apartment buildings. In the district field office the homesteader was encouraged by being shown committed plans for the future. He was offered advice and assistance in financing and tax abatement, architectural sketches and suggestions, and the estimated worth of each specific property, plus an example of rehabilitation and carrying costs on a hypothetical house.

The pioneers in the West Side Urban Renewal area reaped the same financial rewards as all pioneer homesteaders, but they paid the same price for the advantage; living in a depressed, dirty, sometimes dangerous neighborhood in a state of upheaval. However, the people who buy the first houses invariably became leaders, more involved in making things happen in their communities. They always do their best to encourage others to buy houses; then, watching the snowballing effect that invariably follows, they have the indescribable satisfaction of seeing people scramble to buy at prices double, triple, and quadruple what they acquired with a great deal less money and a great deal more courage, nerve, and foresight.

Peggy Houlton, the first of the West Side renovators, started the Little Old New York Citizens' Committee to foster interest in her new neighborhood. The committee keeps a list of houses available for sale, puts out a newsletter, acts as a pressure group for homeowners, and sponsors house tours to encourage newcomers.

The Urban Renewal area does not have the architectural controls that are enforced in a historic district, with a resulting aesthetic loss. And compared with the lightning change that takes place in areas renewed through private initiative, the pace in the government-run project would lose a race with a tortoise.

However, the West Side Urban Renewal area has unquestionably had an enormous influence on the New York renovation scene. The Stamms and the Stanforths, for instance, were both encouraged to buy houses because of it, and yet neither bought in the Urban Renewal area. They became part of a whole new renovation frontier to the south. Others have gone north into the West One-Hundreds, and latecomers who found prices too high surged over into the East Village and Brooklyn.

Renovators are still buying houses on the Upper West Side and in Chelsea and Greenwich Village, but prices have accelerated to the point where purchase is only practical with sufficient rental income to help cover costs or with co-operative house-sharing, a trend that is becoming more and more popular.

Everything is always intensified in New York: When renovation begins in any neighborhood, it moves faster than in any other city. Once a new area is staked out by the pioneers, within two or three years investors and speculators move in and the neighborhood is priced out of the range of ordinary mortals. However, there is no telling where the caprice of fashion will strike; as a *New York Times Magazine* article said in 1929, "mansions of one age became the slums of another. . . . If one waits long enough neighborhoods may return to their original destinies." *

• *Brooklyn.*   Renovation fever has caught on and spread in Brooklyn like an epidemic. Although by itself Brooklyn is the fourth largest city in the United States, it has suffered from its proximity to the tiny island of Manhattan. Just as Georgetown slid into a decline when it was swallowed by the city of Washington, so Brooklyn withered and dried up after its annexation as a borough of the city

* From "New York's Turtle Bay," by Edmund T. Delaney.

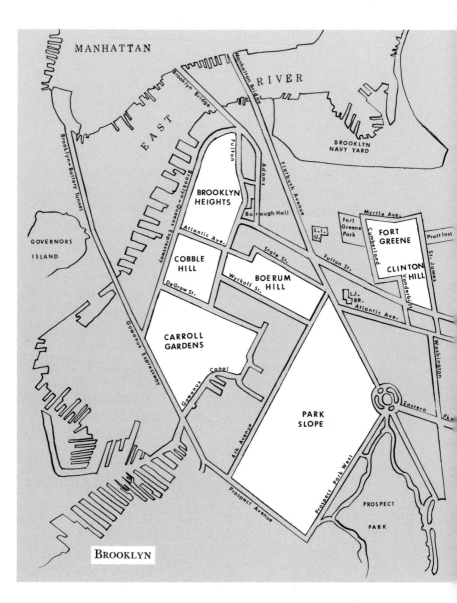

of New York. Pete Hamill called it the 1898 Mistake in his sensitive and perceptive article in an issue of *New York* magazine devoted entirely to Brooklyn.

Before the 1898 Mistake, Brooklyn was the favored suburb of Manhattan magnates. With the business section of the city just a short boat trip across the East River and Greenwich Village a long, dusty carriage ride uptown, the bluff of Brooklyn Heights was the natural site for the homes of wealthy businessmen. They lived in rows of magnificent town houses along the Heights, and later some of the wealthiest built palatial mansions in two other elevated areas, Clinton Hill and Park Slope. The Hill was the purlieu of Charles Pratt, kerosene tycoon and Rockefeller partner. He not only built grand houses for himself and each of his children, but he also founded, endowed, and ran Pratt Institute, within easy access of his front door. The Pratt family mansions were surrounded by many others, and people who didn't build on the Heights or the Hill chose the Slope, whose western border along Prospect Park was known as the Gold Coast because of its lavish homes. In the 1890's Park Slope had the highest per capita income in the United States.

When Brooklyn became part of New York City, it began to lose its status and its millionaires. It became more fashionable to live in Manhattan. The turning point came when Charles Pratt's last son chose to build his home on Park Avenue instead of on the Hill.

By the 1950's Brooklyn was dying from a monstrous inferiority complex, with most of its people who could afford to do so having left for the suburbs, its downtown totally dead on Saturday night, its fine museums, parks, and theaters ignored for those in Manhattan.

Brooklyn Heights followed the familiar pattern of city decline, along with the rest of Brooklyn. According to a real estate broker, in the early 1930's nearly one third of its houses were boarded up due to bank foreclosures following the Depression. These houses were taken over as rooming houses by rapacious absentee landlords. The tide of decay spread through some of the finest houses, the best blocks.

Still, there were a number of residents who refused to flee. There were even some who bought and moved into the gorgeous homes with spectacular views in spite of the influx of prostitutes and addicts. This stalwart group continued to work through the Brooklyn Heights Association for the improvement of the neighborhood, even at a time when it seemed past hope. Founded in 1910, it is the oldest such organization in the country, and through its valiant efforts a potential tragedy was converted to one of Brooklyn Heights' greatest assets. Few people realize that thirty years ago Brooklyn Heights narrowly escaped destruction. If Robert Moses had had his way, it would have been wiped off the map, and perhaps other renovation neighborhoods that followed its example would never have happened.

The strong-willed Moses, formidable czar of parks, bridges, and highways, seemed to have fallen in love with the idea of embalming everything in concrete. He planned to bisect Brooklyn Heights with the Brooklyn–Queens Expressway. If he had, it would have spelled death for the enchanting fifty-block enclave of distinguished nineteenth-century houses that became New York City's first historic district.

Thanks to vigorous opposition from the Brooklyn Heights Association, the city revised its plan: The six-lane expressway was to run around the Heights seventy feet above the waterfront through the rear gardens of homes on Columbia Heights. While this was nowhere near so destructive as the first plan, nevertheless it would have ruined the finest houses along the shore line and destroyed the fabulous view of the harbor for everyone.

Ferdinand Nitardy, one of the affected homeowners on Columbia Heights, proposed a third alternative: building two three-lane highways into the embankment, one above the other, with the upper roadway covered over. In a last-ditch effort at a City Hall hearing, Mr. Nitardy rose to speak for the double-deck covered highway. Addressing himself directly to Robert Moses, he made his plea, offering the city right-of-way through his property and that of his neighbors on condition that the existing gardens be replaced on top of the cover. Moses agreed to study the proposal, but said he would prefer to see the area used for a public promenade rather than having it revert to private gardens.

The result was the Esplanade, "one of the few brilliant solutions for the relationship of automobile, pedestrian and city" in the words of the American Institute of Architects' *Guide to New York.* A delightful wide expanse of hexagonal paving blocks, with benches, shrubs, and trees, the Esplanade makes the most of Brooklyn Heights' most spectacular asset, the view of New York harbor and Manhattan's skyline. It is an oasis in the city—of the kind that is usually found only in Europe.

In 1950, sculptor Neil Estern and his wife rented two floors of a Brooklyn Heights house. Compared to Manhattan the rent was ridiculously low. Artists and writers always find the least expensive places to live and work: At this time they had surrendered Greenwich Village to the more affluent and were moving to Brooklyn.

The Esterns soon outgrew their apartment and decided to buy a house that would give them rental income as well as increased living space. No one they knew was buying houses in Brooklyn at that time—people thought they were crazy to consider it. Finding a house was easy, but no Brooklyn bank would give them a mortgage, so they made do with the financing that remained on the house (arranged some years earlier through a Manhattan savings bank). Doing their own contracting, the Esterns made a larger apartment for themselves, plus one for rental, and were able to live rent-free.

That was in 1953. By 1957, they had decided to buy a larger house, an exceptionally wide and handsome one with a two-story coach house at the rear of the garden. They put their first house on the market for their original purchase price plus renovation costs. For eight months nobody wanted it. Then almost overnight there was a fantastic surge of enthusiasm for Brooklyn Heights, and in one week they had three people begging to buy. Prices skyrocketed. Their artist friends who failed to buy when the Esterns did had to go to Park Slope to find houses they could afford.

A whole new wave of young homeowners came in, and it was this group that fought Robert Moses' next and last assault on Brooklyn Heights. This time, in 1958, it was a slum clearance plan for Cadman Plaza at the northeast corner of the Heights, which included building a huge high-rental apartment house made up primarily of small studio and one-bedroom units totally inappropriate to the character of a residential community. This time the new, younger crowd took up the gauntlet and went into battle. They did exhaustive surveys of every structure in the fifty-block area, documenting the architectural importance of its 640 pre-Civil War brownstones, counting owner-occupants, making maps showing the use of each plot of land. As a part of the campaign Martin Schneider and Richard Margolis wrote a document entitled "The 60's Belong to the City," in which they quoted the president of the National Association of Real Estate Boards as saying, "the flight back to the city is the urban wave of the future. . . . We must realize that the central city is on the verge of a tremendous comeback."

Brooklyn Heights won the battle of Cadman Plaza, illustrating the point made by Royal Cloyd in Boston—that it takes strong citizen organization to make Urban Renewal work *for* the community. In 1965, as an outgrowth of the work done by Brooklyn Heights' citizens in fighting the

Cadman Plaza project, New York got a Landmarks Preservation Commission, which named Brooklyn Heights as its first historic district.

So a corner of Brooklyn regained its pride, and its influence began to spread more rapidly than the decay that had eaten it away. It took Brooklyn Heights ten to fifteen years to make its comeback, but the revival of each of the nearby neighborhoods accelerated the pace, so that the most recent one achieved complete reversal within five years. This is chain reaction on an area basis, as well as on an individual one.

The first spillover was into neighboring Cobble Hill. The Heights had become too expensive, but only a few blocks away there were more streets lined with brownstones, and people began buying there, usually finding houses by renting first. In long-established homeowning areas like Cobble Hill there is much less turnover in houses than in absentee-landlord rooming-house neighborhoods.

Usually the old-time residents of such neighborhoods move away as quickly as they can afford to, particularly the second generation. In a few cases in Cobble Hill this tendency is being reversed. Seeing the value placed upon their houses by others, some are now returning. One couple who grew up in Cobble Hill moved away to Flatbush when they married, but when they heard what was happening to their old neighborhood, they came back and bought a house. It had suffered a recent renovation during which all the interesting details had been removed in the name of modernization. In a paradoxical situation, they are carefully collecting and replacing mantels, doors, woodwork, while the husband's mother, who just bought in Park Slope, is stripping her house bare.

Cobble Hill has been a safe, stable neighborhood because of its large homeowning family base, but nearby

Boerum Hill, which in turn benefited from the overflow of house hunters from Cobble Hill, is an entirely different story.

It is interesting to note the apparent appeal of "Hill" as a name for renovation communities, because Boerum Hill is not a hill by any stretch of the imagination. There are three "Hills" in Brooklyn alone, Cobble, Boerum, and Clinton. Added to these, consider Capitol Hill in Washington, Society Hill in Philadelphia, College Hill in Providence, Church Hill in Richmond, Bolton, Federal, and Seton Hills in Baltimore, and Piety Hill in Detroit. Most of these are recent, made-up names, not designated on maps and unknown even to natives who are uninformed about renovation transformation. So if you were to ask the man in the street the whereabouts of Boerum Hill, he would surely give you a blank stare.

Unlike Brooklyn Heights and Cobble Hill, Boerum Hill was entirely a slum rooming-house neighborhood—bums, winos, addicts, prostitutes, broken glass in the street. While it is a few convenient blocks from downtown Brooklyn, it would seem to have been the least likely prospect for recovery.

The temptation, as usual, lay in space and economics. Ironically, as L. J. Davis points out in a *New York* magazine article, "none of the young families who have moved into Boerum Hill could have afforded to rent as much space as they were able to buy."

While most of them *were* young, the initial pioneer who bought and moved into a house in Boerum Hill was sixty-seven-year-old writer Helen Buckler. She was not followed by an eager rush of homeowners. From 1962 through 1965 there was a total of seven renovations scattered over the three-year period. No real estate broker in nearby respectable neighborhoods would touch a Boerum Hill property. So the courageous and enterprising Miss Buckler started the Boerum Hill Association to do

Behind almost austere exteriors is found extravagantly handsome plaster work, floor-length windows, wide moldings, and marble mantels—here lovingly restored by writer L. J. Davis in Brooklyn's Boerum Hill.

something about the situation. The small group came to the conclusion that they needed their own real estate agency, so one was started by a resident. That, plus house tours, made the difference.

By 1966 Boerum Hill had attracted thirty new people; in 1967 there were ninety more, and in 1968 over two hundred new settlers moved into the area. Since there are only 675 houses, there was a tremendous change in two or three years.

Due to the spectacular rise in prices as these areas undergo their metamorphoses, pioneers can make disastrous mistakes and yet emerge unscathed. The David Wilsons bought a house in Boerum Hill, and after struggling for about a year to make it work, found that they were broke—in over their heads financially, and to make matters direr still, they discovered that the house had a serious structural defect. If they had had the house checked out by an engineer, they undoubtedly would have been warned not to buy it, but they have no regrets. Because the value of property had begun its climb, they were able to sell for twice what they paid and buy another house for much less in Clinton Hill, where they are very happy.

The brick houses of Boerum Hill must have looked very grim indeed when they were at their worst, but cleaned up and painted they have an elegant simplicity. Inside they are even better, with their long, tall windows to the floor, beautiful plaster ornamentation, and exquisitely carved Italian marble mantels.

Writer L. J. Davis came house-hunting from the East Village, merely looking for cheap space for his family. He became intrigued after he moved into his house on Dean Street, and spent many hours scraping and sanding old paint from the walls and handsome ceiling of his lovely parlor floor. Now it is bright and smooth, flooded with light. He removed four layers of draperies that shrouded the floor-length windows, determined to have no curtains at all.

Boerum Hill pioneers suffered through a few rough years, because the area was quite rugged before it became fashionable. Now the trend is impossible to halt because of stories like this: A man who had paid $8,000 for his house was approached by a real estate broker who asked if he would sell it. The man thought of the largest amount he could imagine, and said yes, for $17,500. She brought him the money next morning, and he went off happily to buy a house in the suburbs, bragging to his friends that he had fooled the agent. She immediately sold it to a real estate speculator for $45,000, who shortly sold it again for $55,000.

Carroll Gárdens, bordering both Boerum Hill and Cobble Hill, is vastly different. Its pioneers have never had anything more serious to worry about than the usual scarcity of financing. Along several blocks brownstones are set back thirty feet from the sidewalk, with large tree-shaded front gardens. There is a quiet villagey atmosphere about these city houses twenty minutes from Manhattan. You might even wonder if you were in the twentieth century when you behold the vegetable peddler in his horse-drawn wagon. And on special saints' days there are colorful street festivals and parades, because this is solid Italian territory, even more so than adjacent Cobble Hill.

Changing fashions and tastes were never more evident than in Carroll Gardens. The last generation of homeowners tended to modernize the nineteenth-century houses with aluminum awnings, shiny new flush doors with wedge-shaped windows, and Permastone (artificial facing) applied over the original stone. Long-time homeowners are puzzled when they see renovators removing the new front doors to replace them with the old-fashioned elaborately carved ones that have been retrieved from cellars. However, sometimes the newcomer's taste seems to rub off. For a while it was possible to keep track of new families moving in as shutters, long folded back and nailed

A. *Many Carroll Gardens brownstones have gardens in front as well as rear.*

B. *A living museum of Victoriana, Park Slope brownstones like these continue in uninterrupted rows for blocks and blocks.*

A

into recesses, reappeared in the windows. Then it became apparent that the older residents were imitating the renovators, releasing the shutters from their long imprisonment.

Park Slope, which attracted many people who were forced out of the Heights, including most of the artists, has incredible uninterrupted rows of brownstones on tree-lined streets and many handsome central-entry limestones that need only minor modernization. These houses seem untouched by time, with stoops and ornamentation intact, unpainted, un-Permastoned, unchanged. Inside, many are equally well preserved, with all their fantastic Victorian spoolwork, curlicues, parquet patterns, and built-in glass-doored china cabinets just as they were some eighty years ago—an art-nouveau paradise. Park Slope, never so abused

B

as some of the other renovation areas, caught on very quickly, no doubt due to its pleasant quiet and cleanliness, definite neighborhood feeling, and friendly, casual atmosphere. Though other Brooklyn renovation areas promote their proximity to Manhattan, Park Slope, slightly farther away, is chauvinistic about its own advantages and largely unconcerned about that city across the river. Park Slopers take more interest in Prospect Park, Brooklyn Museum, the Botanic Gardens, and the Brooklyn Public Library and

Academy of Music. They are also well organized for improvement, with a Civic Council, a Betterment Council, and four annual house tours, including one similar to the Capitol Hill House-in-Process tour, with houses in all stages of renovation and owners on hand to answer questions. They have an annual party for bankers, which has succeeded so well that in one case a bank completely reversed its mortgage policy the day after its representative attended.

The mansions of Clinton Hill are an impressive and astonishing sight—unlike anything in the New York City area—set back on wide boulevards with unaccustomed open space around them. In neighboring blocks there are also the more conventional brownstone row houses and a rich variety of other architectural styles. It is a calm, heterogeneous family neighborhood.

Robert Moses disrupted the calm in 1954 with a slum clearance plan for Clinton Hill. There was no community organization to object, so he demolished a five-block area of private homes, apartment houses, and Pratt student boardinghouses. The only justification was that most of the buildings were erected prior to 1902 (which seems a better argument for preservation than condemnation). Some factories that might have deserved demolition were left standing. The result of this ill-advised project was to create a slum where none had previously existed. The doomed buildings were used as flophouses, bringing a new, undesirable element to the quiet streets of Clinton Hill, causing long-time residents to panic and flee. The resulting crime problem finally forced the residents to organize in order to take effective action.

Clinton Hill has caught on with the renovation generation. Due to the mortgage pool of the Bedford-Stuyvesant Restoration Corporation, which has extended its boundaries to include Clinton Hill, it is currently easier to buy a house there than anywhere else. There is no flood of houses on the market, but they are often such gems that they are worth waiting for.

Fort Greene, next door to Clinton Hill, is almost in the heart of downtown Brooklyn, just the other side of the business district from Boerum Hill. It also has a very urban feeling, and has had slum blocks as tough as those in Boerum Hill or the Upper West Side. But like all of these contiguous neighborhoods, it has its own character and some handsome houses, particularly among the long block of mansions facing Fort Greene Park. The popularity of Fort Greene has grown quickly, but at least in the early stages, houses were so absurdly cheap that in one case we found a single young man living alone, by choice, in five stories. Fort Greene renovators, like many of the Brooklyn breed, usually move in at once and do their renovations little by little, hiring plumbers and electricians rather than general contractors—and rarely ever using an architect.

Two more recently discovered areas are Prospect Heights and Lefferts Gardens. There are new neighborhoods being discovered every day—the list seems endless.

Perhaps the magnitude of the Brooklyn renovation boom can best be illustrated by the interest it has inspired in business circles. The Downtown Brooklyn Committee, a nonprofit organization formed by business leaders, has exciting plans for the rejuvenation of the business center, which go hand-in-hand with the renaissance of neighboring residential districts, each influencing the other. In 1966 the Brooklyn Union Gas Company bought, renovated, decorated, and furnished a demonstration house, making a color film of the entire project, entitled *Cinderella of Berkely Place*. In 1969 Con Edison published and advertised extensively a brochure called "The Brownstone Hunter's Guide," which they give away on request. The Chemical Bank also came out with a folder on five Landmark tours of Brooklyn.

Most interesting and useful of all, the Brooklyn YWCA began offering a course in "Brownstoning," which led to the sponsoring by Abraham and Straus (a major Brooklyn department store) of a "Brownstone Grapevine," including weekly evening sessions for free exchange of advice and ideas, with numerous valuable courses, lectures, and printed information.

In Brooklyn the surge of renovation has been recognized as a whole new way of life.

· PHILADELPHIA

Twenty years ago Philadelphia was a grim, ugly, dying city surrounded by beautiful suburbs and lovely hilly country. One could easily see why its residents were abandoning it. As part of his campaign for election as mayor in 1956, reform Democrat Richardson Dilworth promised to use urban planning and massive government assistance to transform Philadelphia into a model city. The need was for drastic surgery complete with transfusion. Though Philadelphia had one of America's largest, loveliest parks, and handsome Benjamin Franklin Parkway, its northwest end crowned with the spectacular Grecian temple of the art museum, downtown was bisected by hideous raised railroad tracks known as the Chinese wall, which spawned ugliness all around it.

Perhaps because Philadelphia came closer to dying than any other city, it is now experiencing the most dynamic rebirth. Today the statue of William Penn gazes down from its tower atop the once-more beautiful French Renaissance city hall with renewed pride in the sparkling new buildings surrounding the junction of Broad and Market Streets that cross beneath.

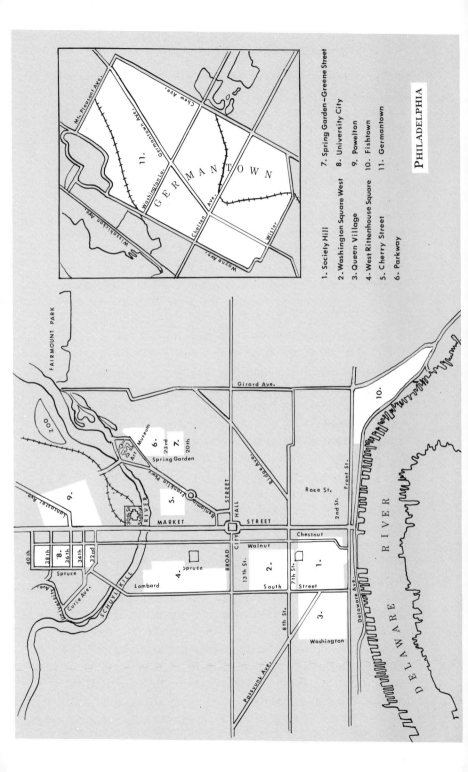

PHILADELPHIA

1. Society Hill
2. Washington Square West
3. Queen Village
4. West Rittenhouse Square
5. Cherry Street
6. Parkway
7. Spring Garden–Greene Street
8. University City
9. Powelton
10. Fishtown
11. Germantown

GERMANTOWN

Mt. Pleasant Ave.
Wissahickon Ave.
Washington Lo. Germantown Ave.
Chew Ave.
Chelten Ave.
Wister
Wayne Ave.

FAIRMOUNT PARK
ZOO
Lancaster Ave.
Girard Ave.
Art Museum
Spring Garden
23rd
20th
Ridge Ave.
Benjamin Franklin Pkwy.
30th St. Station
SCHUYLKILL RIVER
MARKET STREET
Race St.
Front St.
2nd St.
Chestnut
Walnut
South
Washington
Street
Spruce
Lombard
Curie Ave.
Baltimore Ave.
40th
38th
36th
34th
32nd
BROAD STREET
CITY HALL
13th St.
8th St.
Passyunk Ave.
7th St.
Delaware Ave.
DELAWARE RIVER

The streets and alleys of the center city have become totally captivating; block after block of uninterruptedly charming houses with the unique character of mellowed brick and stone, they are enhanced and dramatized by their proximity to the contemporary glass towers nearby.

A few blocks of houses in these streets have always been maintained as expensive private homes. Others had become commercial, such as the carriage house on Chancellor Street that the Sol Mednicks transformed from a paint contractor's warehouse to a home with exciting skylighted open spaces and a soaring spiral stairway to the roof garden, which has the same spooky combination of spectacular past-present views found on Benefit Street in Providence. In one glance you are looking down on a quaint lamplit alley, while over your shoulder you can almost touch a towering skyscraper.

While the Chinese wall was being removed and the business district undergoing metamorphosis, Society Hill was Mayor Dilworth's primary target for neighborhood rescue. Scattered and sporadic attempts to save individual historic buildings in the 1940's had culminated in the drawing up of plans by Edmund Bacon and Roy Larsen of the Philadelphia City Planning Commission for the entire Society Hill area, but nothing was done until Dilworth was elected. In 1959 the Redevelopment Authority of the City of Philadelphia began condemnation proceedings.

Named for the Free Society of Traders, founded by William Penn on the banks of the Delaware to develop his American colony, Society Hill has been called the most historic square mile in the nation. On its twenty-five square blocks and 120 acres remain more eighteenth- and nineteenth-century houses than anywhere else in America. However, in spite of their proximity to Independence Hall, they were allowed to deteriorate to the point where the bulldozer might reasonably have been considered the only solution. The area had gone heavily commercial, with

Center city Philadelphia has many alleys like this one, lined with small houses imaginatively renovated.

fine period homes becoming flophouses. The 150-year-old wholesale food market, which served the entire city, generated dirt, noise, and congestion in the "Bloody Fifth" ward, where votes were bought and sold as freely as produce, and murder, rape, and muggings were taken for granted.

The first step was removal of the Dock Street market, clearance of the fifteen waterfront acres it occupied, and erection on the site of three thirty-one-story apartment towers designed by I. M. Pei. Not until four years after

The Ingersolls' elegant eighteenth-century dining room emerged from this grimy ruin, typical of the Society Hill area before renovation.

their completion had prejudice against city living been overcome to the point where all the apartments were rented. Meanwhile, the Redevelopment Authority acquired all the remaining houses in the area and made them available for purchase through the Old Philadelphia Corporation, with the proviso that the owners conform to appropriate exterior restoration.

Mayor Dilworth led the way (followed by such eminent Philadelphians as the Jared Ingersolls), moving into his own restored home on Washington Square. The Ingersolls fell in love with a derelict house at 217 Spruce Street, which had been a candidate for demolition. When they first saw it, the Redevelopment Authority was in the process of evacuating the squatters who occupied every room

despite lack of heat, water, and electricity. Mrs. Ingersoll writes, "as soon as one left, two others would appear to flop in the filthy rooms. We stumbled about with flashlights, picking our way among indescribable rubbish ankle deep, scattering as we walked roaches and mice and, yes, even rats. . . . In one room a coffin-shaped carton half-full of ladies' handbags indicated the headquarters of a snatcher. A dead cat lay in the only bathtub. The stench everywhere was suffocating."

This "nightmare of a flophouse" became their "dream house," and they resolved to restore its beautifully proportioned rooms to their eighteenth-century condition, adding modern necessities as unobtrusively as possible. They went so far as to have the paint painstakingly scraped off with a scalpel and microscopically examined to determine the original colors. They are thrilled to be walking on the same random-width pine floors that were laid in 1759 and trod upon by the second owner, a major in Washington's army at Valley Forge.

The Ingersolls could afford one of the expensive custom restorations, of which there are a number in Society Hill. However, because the Redevelopment Authority bought up so many of the houses and continued to resell them at

Before and after: two houses in Philadelphia's Society Hill.

minimum prices, modest restoration has also been possible. Albert Zaid, a young bachelor, bought and restored a charming small 1766 house for less than he would have paid for an assembly-line product in a development. With all borrowed money and a 3% federal loan (312 loan) he managed to cut unheard-of corners and effect architectural feats that "couldn't be done." Zaid got his architectural plans drawn by a draftsman girl friend, who, never having done it before, did so well that she got a letter of commen-

dation from the Historical Society. Working nights and weekends with engineer and carpenter friends, Zaid managed to do the work on the proverbial shoestring. And yet he became just as interested in historical accuracy as the Ingersolls. Finding that his house had originally been roofed with wood shingles, he determined to use them; but because of the fire hazard, he had a long fight to be allowed his wood-shingled roof. Virtually the only other Philadelphia building that is wood-shingled is Independence Hall, whose head carpenter gave him a book to study and lessons in laying the shingles.

Zaid discovered that it was a mistake to remove any of the old plaster lining from the fireplaces. Everything he put on to replace it fell off—the original having been made from a lost recipe of pigs' bristles, chicken droppings, and other ingredients reminiscent of the witches' brew in *Macbeth*. When he had to rebuild a section of the façade, he scavenged for the eight hundred black header bricks he needed. (Black header bricks were originally thought of as "seconds" when their ends, closest to the hickory smoke from the fires that baked them, became glazed a shiny bluish-black. They later gained popularity to accentuate the pattern in Flemish bond bricklaying—a colonial fashion.)

Not all houses in Society Hill are restorations. Carol and Bud Skelly, both landscape architects, gutted their house on Delancey Street when they converted it back to a home from kosher restaurant and rooming house. They created a simple contemporary setting for their exceptional print collection, with quarry-tile floor and two-story glass-walled living room overlooking the garden on the long expanse of their double lot. Today their house is worth twice what they invested in it four years ago.

In spite of the variety of tastes hidden inside their eighteenth-century façades, the blocks of houses behind Independence Hall are like a delightful walk through history. "Philadelphia brick" has become a descriptive term for a good reason: William Penn decreed that there should be no wooden houses, as he founded the city just after the Great Fire of London. There are brick sidewalks, too, and many of the houses wear "busybodies," angled mirrors affixed near upstairs windows to give a view of callers at the front door. Houses often have two metal plaques on their façades; one is the Historical Society's certification of authentic restoration; the other, proof that the eighteenth-century owner had paid his dues to the fire department, which would not put out his fire unless the plaque was displayed.*

Society Hill is a success. It reversed urban blight, saved historic houses, restored architectural unity, and influenced people to return to the city. It became fashionable to live in town again. Small opportunity remains for renovation in Society Hill, but there are many other areas of Philadelphia to choose from.

Washington Square West, adjacent to Society Hill, recently became an Urban Renewal area, although private renewal began there early in the 1960's. Typical streets where renovation has been done are Quince, Iseminger, Camac, and Hutchinson. Individuals began the renovation; then the commercial developers came in to buy rows of houses, renovate them, and resell them. There has also been substantial new building in the area. It differs from Society Hill in that it is now, and probably will be, more heterogeneous. An Urban Renewal plan for the rehabilitation of rooming houses and hotels involves moving the present tenants to nearby quarters during renovation and giving them first priority on the rehabilitated apartments. At this time a few houses remain for renovation by individuals.

* A custom imported from England.

Queen Village, a newly developing pioneer neighborhood, is a very old working-class section of South Philadelphia on the river just below Society Hill. There Emily and Will Brown are involved in the do-it-yourself renovation of their own house—plus a second that they bought for rental income at a sheriff's sale, for a price that would hardly buy a good used car. This tiny building, on the quaint little alley behind their house, is a Philadelphia phenomenon called a Father, Son, and Holy Ghost house —three rooms stacked vertically, one above the other, connected by a corner winding stairway. The Browns are another case in point for those who think that city houses are the exclusive privilege of the wealthy—both of them work, and they have invested under $10,000 in the purchase of their two houses.

Private renewal began in West Rittenhouse Square in the late fifties on Panama and Van Pelt Streets in an area of tiny row houses, some of the most attractive smaller houses of the center city. Houses in this area are now becoming scarce and expensive, but renovation is spreading south of Lombard Street, where the prices are lower. Young architect Benjamin Kitchen cleverly and economically designed a house for his family (with many innovative ideas, such as recessed, dust-free baseboards) in the 2300 block of Naudain Street. Though this is still a mixed neighborhood where street brawls can erupt on weekends, the Kitchens have not felt endangered. They have a number of renovation companions with whom they have a close relationship. As is often done in similar situations, they keep each other's keys, watch each other's houses, and drop in to visit when they crave company.

The Cherry Street area is a small community of two- and three-story red brick row houses where renovation has occurred spontaneously and independently, though it probably received some impetus from an Urban Renewal project to the north and west of it along the Parkway—the building of three high-rise apartment buildings on what was a city dump. Though essentially residential, the Cherry Street community is surrounded by some building and light industry, as well as the Franklin Institute and the Moore School of Art. A new development proposal to the south involving motels, offices, and shops has included plans for high-rise apartments, but so far the community has been successful in preventing this, and the Cherry Street area remains a residential pocket—small, perhaps struggling, but intact.

The Parkway area, just north of the art museum, has also been renovated independently. It has the advantage of being almost a part of beautiful Fairmount Park, with the East River Drive just to the south and the art museum practically in its front yard. Aside from the renovated town houses, the community is generally a low-income neighborhood.

The Spring Garden–Greene Street area probably has more to offer in terms of actual houses than the Parkway area, because this was a section of the city once populated by Philadelphia's wealthy, who left behind fine old Victorian houses, some with lawns surrounded by iron fences. However, although a few houses have been bought and renovated, most have been converted to wretched, overcrowded apartment houses, and others, such as a residence for nuns, are used by institutions.

University City is undergoing a major face-lifting under the guidance of the West Philadelphia Corporation. In this sprawling university complex many blocks of large Victorian houses set on big yards are being renovated by young couples, most of them faculty and hospital staff. Still very much in the city, these houses have a totally different feeling and character than those in Society Hill and the Rittenhouse Square area. They are far more typical of early suburban or small-town houses.

Nearby Powelton also attracts teachers from the University of Pennsylvania and Drexel, with the university helping to obtain mortgages for its professors. The first West Philadelphia section settled by wealthy merchants, Powelton suffered a slump after World War II. It began its comeback in the fifties, and is struggling to surmount the detrimental effect of its many fraternity houses.

The Harold Powers, a university family, bought a spacious 1865 house in Powelton, surrounded by a large yard and huge trees—a country atmosphere in the city. The Powers have created a handsome contemporary interior inside their mansard-roofed Victorian, overcoming in the process typical problems with a contractor whom they failed to check because their architect assured them that they need not bother.

Germantown has a great mixture of historical sites and handsome Victorian houses. Germantown and Morton are both Urban Renewal areas, but there has been quite a bit of private renovation, with houses generally less expensive than in other sections of the city.

Fishtown (Lower Kensington), along the river north of Society Hill, has many small eighteenth-century and Georgian houses like those in Society Hill. Though commercial developers have been renovating for resale, the area is still considered pioneer territory.

· BALTIMORE

Baltimore has an extraordinary number of houses—mile after mile in unbroken rows, with simple red brick façades and low white marble steps. It was a residential city until

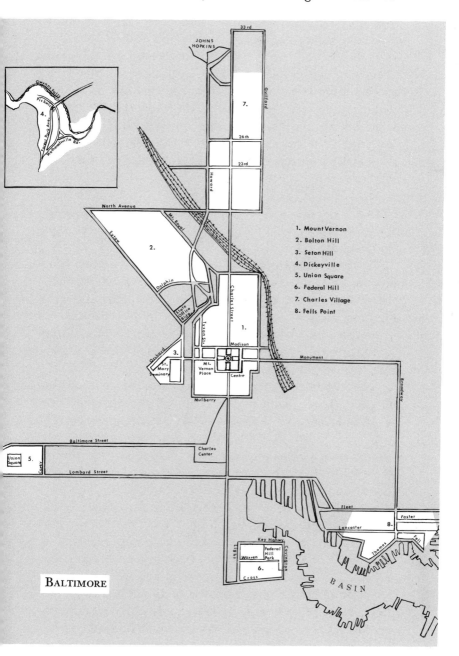

1. Mount Vernon
2. Bolton Hill
3. Seton Hill
4. Dickeyville
5. Union Square
6. Federal Hill
7. Charles Village
8. Fells Point

BALTIMORE

the 1930's, when most old families moved out to the suburbs; today their children are coming back to take advantage of the city's tremendous potential for in-town living.

Baltimore grew up around the harbor, with its fortune based on shipping and shipbuilding, but after a fire in 1904 the city was rebuilt further inland, and until recently formulated plans for Waterfront Renewal, this natural asset has been neglected. The return to the city has been encouraged by the highly successful new Charles Center downtown, but the still unresolved threat of an expressway through Fells Point and Federal Hill has delayed development, though some renovation in these areas has flourished in spite of it.

Baltimore has an advantage that most cities sorely lack: Several of its renovation neighborhoods have exceptionally fine public schools. Although one or two of its many renovation areas are well developed, the others are only in the early stages of their renaissance, and the possibilities are not only highly promising, but almost endless.

The renovation movement was initiated in the two-block area of Tyson Street, when an artist bought the first house in the 1930's for about $1,500, or approximately one tenth what it would cost today. All of these tiny, charming houses have long since been finished, painted in bright colors with contrasting shutters, setting a tempting example for others to follow.

Tyson Street houses are too small for family living; the city's most popular family renovation community is Bolton Hill. Built as a fine residential neighborhood between the 1860's and the turn of the century, it became a depressed area during World War II. Houses were referred to as "hot beds," because defense plant workers slept in shifts under appalling conditions.

In 1949, in the totally inexplicable and spontaneous

manner in which pioneering has started in so many cities, five or six families who wanted to live in the city bought houses in a four-block area in the center of Bolton Hill, with financing from private sources or purchase-money

Bolton Hill. Note brick sidewalks and typical Baltimore steps.

mortgages from sellers. These families found life there very rugged for a while—in fact, their area was called a "tight little island," an oasis surrounded by slums. However, Bolton Hill had never descended so low as Tyson Street, and like Brooklyn Heights it kept a nucleus of old families who had refused to leave.

The new group was warmly welcomed by the old, and they joined forces in the Mount Royal Improvement Association to fight further encroachment by Urban Renewal after a large section of Bolton Hill was torn down in 1960 for a state office building, apartments, and new town houses.

Bolton Hill's real estate brokers, like those in Washington and Brooklyn, have lived in the area and played an important part in its development. Though there are still houses to be renovated in the outer blocks of Bolton Hill, today one rarely finds any available in the heart of the area. Prices have risen, of course, as the neighborhood has become popular with young professional families. However, it is still possible to own twice as much space in Bolton Hill as can be bought in the suburbs for the same money.

Bolton Hill has particularly strong community spirit and a multitude of neighborhood activities: street fairs and community suppers all summer long, blocks closed off for roller skating, and Christmas caroling, decoration of streets, lampposts, and houses, and a children's tour of decorated trees.

Residents can walk to the Lyric Theatre for symphony concerts, and are looking forward to a new cultural center that will be built in their community. The Maryland Institute, encouraged by the Bolton Hill renaissance, decided to remain in the area and expand, following the example of renovators by rehabilitating the old abandoned B. & O. Railroad station as library, auditorium, gallery, and art studios—an outstanding new use for an old building.

While Bolton Hill may lack some commercial conveniences, Mount Vernon has everything anyone could possibly want in a downtown neighborhood. Situated in the heart of the city around a beautiful cruciform of parks, where the men who made Baltimore built their palatial homes, it has an atmosphere reminiscent of Beacon Hill—and the only brownstone façades in a city of brick houses. A city ordinance limits any building in the area to the height of the monument that dominates the open green of parks—a soaring column topped with a statue of George Washington. Where the parks cross stand the famous Walters Art Gallery and the Peabody Conservatory of Music, and facing them are a number of private dining clubs housed in nineteenth-century mansions.

Residents enjoy the convenience of abundant antique shops, restaurants, gourmet grocery stores, and proximity to the city's commercial district. In addition to the Peabody and the Walters Gallery, Mount Vernon has the Pratt Library and one of the first purposely integrated private schools in the country.

The area has been undergoing a renaissance in the past five years, and currently shelters a combination of wealthy people, roomers, and hippies. Facing the main streets there are many houses of exceptionally fine quality, patches of carriage houses and small houses, and a few of medium size. Houses are generally available, but not surprisingly, they are more expensive than those in other Baltimore neighborhoods.

Pioneers who want to live in the heart of the city have three areas to choose from: Seton Hill, Federal Hill, and Fells Point. Seton Hill, built around St. Mary's Seminary, is named after Mother Seton, founder of the Sisters of Charity, whose home has been completely restored. All around the seminary the very old and badly neglected brick houses are being rediscovered by enthusiastic young renovators, who are bringing them back to life with imaginative interiors and colorful exteriors. Seton Hill is very urban, and has a feeling much like Brooklyn's Boerum Hill in its early stages. At this time approximately 50 of the 130 early and mid-nineteenth-century houses have been restored. Though these small houses are not individually important historically or architecturally, as a group they are an excellent illustration of the small residential structure of the period, and for this reason the Baltimore Commission for Historical and Architectural Preservation is seeking Historic District designation for the area.

Fells Point and Federal Hill, on either side of Baltimore's harbor, have both been under threat of destruction by a proposed expressway. Because the city was built around the harbor, most of the oldest remaining houses are in these two areas. Many brave and indomitable renovators have continued to pour their efforts and resources into these houses as they battle to save them from demolition.

Today a Waterfront Renewal project is planned to take advantage of the long-neglected natural asset of the harbor. There will be walks, stores, recreational facilities, marinas and yacht clubs, hotels, and a trade center. Both Federal Hill and Fells Point should benefit enormously from this project, if the latter is spared to enjoy it.

Federal Hill has been reprieved, not because the government gave preference to preservation over automobiles, but because building a bridge across the harbor high enough to permit passage of boats proved impossible. The city bought up many houses to be razed in the path of the expressway, and presumably they may now be made available to renovators, for Federal Hill has great potential as a delightful residential district. Set just behind a large park on a hill overlooking the harbor, with a fantastic view of the city, are rows and rows of Baltimore's earliest houses. Unfortunately many (here and elsewhere in the city) have been defaced by Baltimore's version of Permastone, called Formstone, but apparently it can be removed from brick façades without damaging the surface as it does brownstone.

With Federal Hill's ideal setting and location, and the advantages it will have from the new commercial and recreational facilities of Waterfront Renewal, it is an outstanding prospect for development. On the National Register for ten years, it is now being studied for Historic District designation. Since Federal Hill has been a proud German community, its houses have never descended to slum status and can be bought in livable condition. Three-story houses, some as early as the eighteenth century, are constantly coming on the market, and though prices are rising, they are still moderate.

Union Square, recently made a Historic District, is another new renovation area with great potential. Its houses are also in excellent condition, well maintained by the Lithuanian families living there. Within walking distance of downtown and the University of Maryland complex, it has one of the few surviving nineteenth-century city squares, with an 1850 circular Greek temple, built to shelter a spring that supplied water for early residents, now a fountain. Union Square has an excellent playground and community center, but most important, and exceptional in today's cities, it has one of the country's finest public schools, using revolutionary teaching techniques.

Two- and three-story houses of various sizes, built in the 1880's, are being bought by young families as they become available. Generally they are in fairly good condition, needing only modernization and decorating, and are moderately priced.

Charles Village has been attracting some of the renovators unable to afford the rising prices of Bolton Hill. The area has recently had an upsurge of big expansion, though renovation had begun there earlier. Its turn-of-the-century Edwardian houses are extremely well built, with large gardens, and many are available in move-in condition, so that they can be renovated by families in residence and do-it-yourselfers. Charles Village has numerous assets for family living. It is near Johns Hopkins University, the Baltimore Museum of Art, Wyman Park, and Union Memorial Hospital. It has movies, restaurants, and a branch of the public library nearby, and excellent public transportation.

The residents of this integrated neighborhood raised private funds to upgrade their public school. There is a great deal of community activity, with a monthly outdoor art show in summer, Saturday morning breakfast lectures and discussion group, and a neighborhood newsletter. Charles Village never really declined, it just went out of style. Today it is coming back into fashion along with Tiffany lamps. As of now about 250 of its 1,000 houses have been renovated. Its potential for expansion could make it one of Baltimore's largest new residential neighborhoods.

Dickeyville, completely restored, is a rare example of a nineteenth-century mill village surviving intact into the twentieth century. Abandoned and totally shut down, the entire town was sold at auction in 1934 for $42,000: sixty acres, eighty-one dwellings, three factories, and a three-story mansion. Within the Baltimore city limits, it is an incredible rural enclave, almost like the mythical village of Brigadoon, suspended in time. Surrounded by woods and streams, its white brick and stone houses are set on rolling hills with the sound of waterfalls nearby. Dickeyville seems the perfect solution for those who love country life but do not want to leave the city.

Two other Baltimore areas that are not exactly urban but are nevertheless renovation neighborhoods are Windsor Hill and Catonsville. Windsor Hill, an evenly integrated community, has rambling, shingle-style houses on

These houses are exceptionally urban-looking in the rural atmosphere of Dickeyville in Baltimore.

big lots. Catonsville, just outside the city limits, was once an area of summer homes for the wealthy. Enormous old houses are now being bought there for bargain prices by perceptive renovators, who have been rescuing them from the brink of demolition.

· WASHINGTON, D. C.

Georgetown, which set the precedent for neighborhood rehabilitation nation-wide, has naturally influenced the renaissance of other areas in Washington (and across the Potomac in Alexandria's Old Town as well). Though houses are still being renovated in Georgetown today, just as they are on Manhattan's East Side, their prices have risen so that they are beyond the reach of most of us.

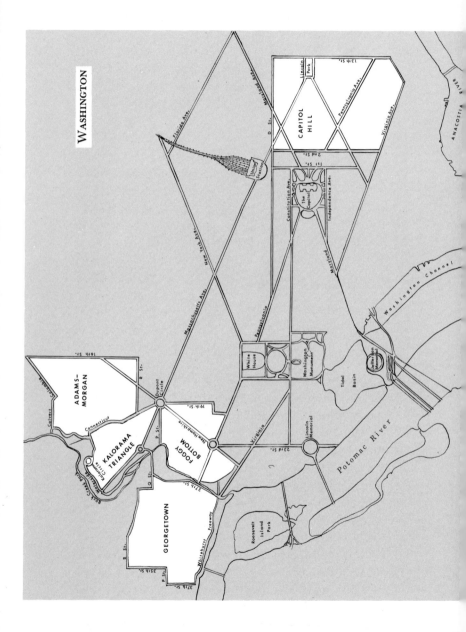

As Georgetown prices skyrocketed, Washingtonians anxious to live in the city began looking elsewhere for houses to renovate. They have found them all over the city: adjacent to Georgetown in Foggy Bottom, Kalorama Triangle, Dupont Circle, and across town, just behind the Capitol and Library of Congress, biggest and most active of all, Capitol Hill.

Capitol Hill had its beginning in 1791, when L'Enfant selected Jenkins Hill as the site of Congress House, which later became the Capitol building. Many early statesmen lodged in the boardinghouses around it. The earliest remaining houses were built around 1795. The building of homes for justices and major public officials continued after the Civil War until about 1910.

The Hill began losing some of its prestigious citizens to the Northwest with the advent of the automobile. Exodus to the suburbs accelerated when the government took over some of the housing for Depression victims. During the mid-1930's alley dwellings with outside plumbing, some of the most decayed and squalid housing in Washington, provoked the Alley Dwelling Act for the elimination of such substandard housing.

Flight to the suburbs continued after World War II until the first restoration began in the 1940's, starting with a few houses in the midst of the blight and deterioration immediately surrounding the Capitol. (It is amazing that the areas adjacent to our country's most important buildings—the Capitol of the United States as well as Independence Hall in Philadelphia—were allowed to degenerate into miserable slums.)

Scarcely more than eight to ten houses were restored in the next eight years, until the Washington *Star* published an article in September 1949 announcing, "The reclamation of housing in the Capitol Hill area is under way." The *Star* noted that there was nothing particularly organized about it—it was primarily by individuals who wanted to live in the area. By May of 1951 St. Peter's Catholic Church sponsored the first house tour, and by 1955 the Capitol Hill Restoration Society was formed.

Some Washingtonians still think of Capitol Hill as a slum. But it is not. It is an exciting community bursting with activity, vitality, and neighborhood spirit. On its wide, tree-lined boulevards, such as East Capitol Street with its dramatic view of the Capitol dome, and on its enchanting little alleys, its brightly painted houses of all sizes are full of charm. Almost all architectural styles are represented, Federal through Victorian, row house and free-standing, and the diverse types of people who live there have done delightful work on them.

There is a great deal of do-it-yourself enthusiasm in Capitol Hill. For example, a young couple, in the course

A small sample of the wide variety of architectural styles found in Capitol Hill.

of helping friends work on the house they had bought in Capitol Hill, were bitten themselves by the renovation bug. Through their friends they met Bill Creager, who had abandoned a graphic arts career to sell real estate; so carried away had he become with the renaissance of Capitol Hill that he had designed and renovated several houses himself. Creager showed them a house they wanted to buy and lent them his commission to make it possible. In order

to raise the cash for the down payment, they had to sell almost all their possessions.

The couple moved in and went to work. Except for the plumbing and wiring, they did all the work themselves evenings and weekends after their full-time jobs—knowing that in the end they would resell the finished house so that they could afford to buy one they could afford to keep.

Younger people with limited capital generally do the renovation work themselves, whereas older ones moving back from the suburbs hire contractors and architects. Representing the opposite of the do-it-yourself method are C. Dudley Brown and H. Curley Boswell. Both are award-winning restoration experts, living and working in the Capitol Hill area. They will design a carefully planned restoration and carry it out down to the placement of the last ashtray. Dudley Brown's clients hire him to assume all of their renovation headaches. He has found that the best way to achieve the perfection he's after is to become a general contractor himself, with his own crew of men to execute his plans. Though this approach is unquestionably more expensive, for those who can afford it there is a great advantage in employing the knowledge of experts who are able to get the best work from men who are not simply doing a one-shot job and have little to lose by doing it badly.

Many people have proved their faith in Capitol Hill by buying more than one house—Barbara Held, of the Barbara Held Real Estate Agency, has owned several dozen houses herself, renovated as charming homes by her husband, Bob Reich. Barbara and Bob challenge all stereotypes of real estate brokers and developers. Reich is an imaginative and creative builder. He has an enormous collection of material salvaged from razed buildings, which he incorporates to great effect in the houses (sometimes whole blocks) he buys to do over and resell.

Barbara Held has become involved by living in the area

where she sells and by employing people such as Arline Roback and Bill Creager, who care about and have a stake in the community. Perhaps the best illustration of the kind of business she operates is her Houses-in-Process tour. This concept is not only astute business, but shows an understanding of the kind of encouragement that helps convince prospective homeowners. Free and open to the public, the tour begins at a punch party in the Held office, in the groovy, gaudy-colored boutique row on Eastern Market Row. There Barbara and Bob Reich greet their guests and launch them onto buses, often with drink in hand, to make the rounds of half a dozen houses in the vicinity. Unlike the conventional tour of expensively designed and decorated houses, this one is deliberately made up of houses in varying stages of completion, with owners in attendance ready to answer questions.

Capitol Hill has gotten where it is today through sheer individual momentum. Though Washington is the source of FHA and Urban Renewal, no federal programs have helped the city's renovators. Washington's zoning laws often hamper renovation through their capricious rules limiting the number of flats (as apartments are called in Washington) allowed in a building, usually depending on past use rather than current need. Renovation has also been impeded by demolition of restored homes that were in the path of federal expansion. The distinguished block of mid-eighteenth-century houses known as Philadelphia Row (slated to be replaced by a highway) had a hairsbreadth rescue through the efforts of Helen Duprey Bullock of the National Trust for Historic Preservation.

The houses situated closest to the Capitol and the Library of Congress are considered most desirable, but they were also most vulnerable to the whim of the late Architect of the Capitol, a powerful political appointee who was not an architect at all, but who could wipe out houses more or less as he pleased. The houses in the Northeast, nearer the Capitol, tend to be sounder structurally and need less renovation; Southeast houses are likely to be older, more interesting, and also cheaper because of their ramshackle condition.

Another section of Washington in a state of renaissance is Adams-Morgan. Bigger houses can be bought there for less than half the price of equivalent property in Capitol Hill, according to Tedson Meyers, an attorney who has lived there in his sixteen-room house since 1966, about three years after the first redevelopment started. These houses were built as expensive homes around 1909, when Florida Avenue was the boundary line of the city and the area was called Washington Heights. Like Capitol Hill enthusiasts, Meyers has branched out, acquiring two properties adjoining his. In the empty lot next door he has built a garden-playground with garage underneath. In the large house on the other side of the garden he has created a number of attractive apartments, which were rented even before completion.

Meyers describes the neighborhood as a mixture of well-to-do and poor, black and white, young and old, drunk and sober, hooked and unhooked, culture and counter-culture.

The worst flotsam and jetsam of the 1968 riots was washed up on the doorsteps of Adams-Morgan; the dope center, accompanied by prostitutes and horrible crap games, moved to Eighteenth Street and Florida Avenue. The resulting crime wave had Meyers and his neighbors out trimming sidewalk hedges to remove protective covering for muggers, and forming a community pool to put bars on ground floor windows (which led Meyers to make an interesting sociological observation: there must have been a peaceful lull in America for a number of decades, because the last houses well equipped with barred windows were those of the Victorian era).

However, this kind of community organization, born of

necessity, is the hope of salvation for our cities. And it appears in abundance wherever there are renovators. As their pioneer forbears banded together against the dangers of the wilderness, these latter-day homesteaders, determined to reclaim their cities for their own use, have rediscovered that in unity there is strength. Through this unity they are accomplishing great things, from cleaning up sidewalks and streets to revitalizing their public schools.

· THE MIDWEST AND WEST

· PITTSBURGH

At the end of the nineteenth century Pittsburgh's North Side was the city's major residential district. Ridge Avenue, just north of the junction of three rivers that forms Pittsburgh's Golden Triangle, was the most fashionable place to live. Many mansions and block after block of row houses filled the area, surrounded by parks on three sides.

The neighborhood was abandoned as residents moved out to the East End and country estates north of the city in Sewickley. Today part of it is being revived, and houses are being reclaimed for contemporary living through the efforts of the Pittsburgh History and Landmarks Foundation, an organization formed by citizens concerned about the widespread decay and deterioration of so much of the city's architecture. PHLF hopes to change the image of the city in the eyes of the nation, beginning at home with its own citizens' inferiority complex. As a beginning, they did an architectural survey, resulting in a book called *Landmark Architecture of Allegheny County.*

PHLF has been experimenting with community renewal through restoration in a way that has not been tried before, achieving integrated neighborhoods as they save old buildings. They "began at the outset to utilize historic architecture as a means to community renewal," to quote

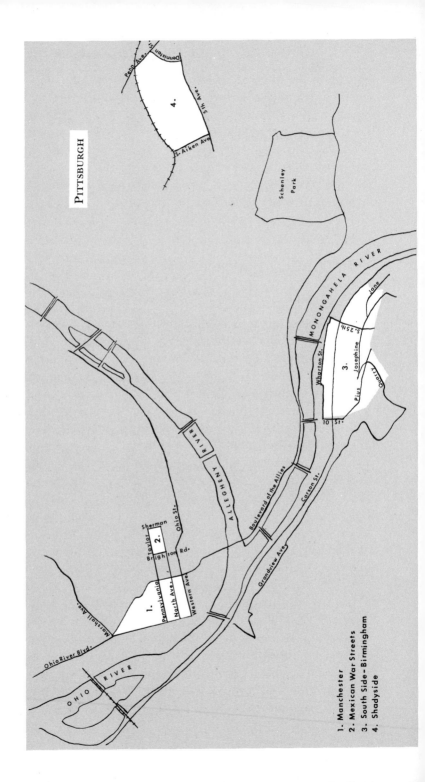

PITTSBURGH

1. Manchester
2. Mexican War Streets
3. South Side – Birmingham
4. Shadyside

director Arthur Ziegler. "The slums of our cities contain most of the valuable architecture of America. . . . To raze all these districts, areas that could provide delightful residential living—is to raze our architectural heritage."

The majority of their work to date has been in the North Side Mexican War Streets, a sixteen-block area laid out in 1848 and built up from that time until the 1890's in Greek revival, Italianate, French Second Empire, and Victorian architecture. PHLF's purpose is to restore buildings in bad condition, attract sympathetic investors, and induce owners to restore their homes. With a revolving fund based on a $100,000 grant from the Sarah Mellon Scaife Foundation, they rescued fifteen buildings from indifferent landlords. Using their own permanent team of workmen, they began renovation on three levels: complete restoration for new middle- and upper-middle-income tenants; moderate restoration for current residents; and minimum for low-income tenants. In order to retain the original neighborhood people who want to remain, as well as to attract new more affluent residents, they worked out a rent subsidy program with the Pittsburgh Housing Authority so that neighborhood people could live in the newly renovated apartments. The tangible evidence of rehabilitation has inspired property owners to spruce up their own homes; new people have come in to buy and restore; and the rentals and sales from restoration work have enabled the revolving fund to buy more houses. Through the efforts of PHLF, trolley tracks have been removed, streets paved, and trees planted.

New owners are pleased with the alive, integrated community, relatively low-cost houses, and convenient location. A fifteen-minute walk from downtown, the area borders a portion of the Allegheny Commons, with its new lake and ice-skating rink, aviary, and flower gardens. It is also within walking distance of the Community College, Buhl Planetarium, the shopping mall of the Allegheny Center, and the proposed Museum of Pittsburgh. Many houses remain to be restored, and the Pittsburgh History and Land-marks Foundation encourages inquiries from anyone interested.

PHLF has begun another North Side project in Man-chester, a severely blighted area containing some important residential architecture—particularly in the 1300 block of Liverpool Street, which is the finest surviving block of homogeneous Victorian housing in the city. PHLF has bought and gone to work on three houses in the area, and

Pittsburgh façades and window detail.

meanwhile has been working with the Urban Redevelopment Authority to get Model Cities to help with further restoration in Manchester. They have also encouraged considerable activity in house painting, street cleaning, and window-box gardening by community residents and landlords.

On the South Side, in the old Birmingham section, PHLF has been working to encourage businesses to renovate their storefronts in keeping with the buildings'

Victorian architecture, and has succeeded in promoting the total renovation of a large derelict commercial building into professional offices and apartments.

PHLF also has an artifacts-retrieval program, which salvages whatever it can from demolition: "When we cannot save a building, we try to save a piece of it."

Other areas of Pittsburgh that have seen old houses renovated for contemporary living are Shadyside, Point Breeze, and Mount Washington. Since 1958 there has been extensive renovation of late-nineteenth- and early-twentieth-century houses in Shadyside. There is enormous individual enthusiasm among property owners and residents, but prices have climbed, and renovation has largely been done by developers and investors rather than by individuals for their own use. The same is true of Point Breeze and Mount Washington, whose Grandview Avenue on the edge of a cliff overlooking the Monongahela enjoys the most fantastic views in Pittsburgh.

· COLUMBUS

Two cities in Ohio have had very interesting and extremely different manifestations of renovation. In 1947 in Columbus, tool engineer Frank Fetch, inspired by Georgetown, decided he must do something to rescue the small Dutch (*Deutsch*) houses built by German immigrants. Inhabited by families of hillbillies from West Virginia, Kentucky, and Tennessee, these neat little cottages set off by glazed brick sidewalks and handsome trees were going to ruin. Fetch bought several and rehabilitated them himself, and just as in Georgetown, the idea caught on. By 1959 there was enough of a community to form the German Village Society and wage a victorious battle against the threat of an expressway. By the early 1960's German Village was a proven success, with historic district designation, renovation spreading, and prices rising throughout its forty-block area.

- CINCINNATI

In Cincinnati three young men saw the potential of a slum called Mount Adams, perched high on a cliff with a spectacular view of downtown Cincinnati and Kentucky cities across the Ohio River. In 1961, just after he graduated from Harvard, Neil Bortz formed Towne Properties, Inc., with Marvin Rosenberg and Lambert Agin. Their first buy was a big risk, but the price was low, and within

Mount Adams homes are high on a hill overlooking downtown Cincinnati.

a few days they accepted an offer for more than twice as much as they had paid. They immediately reinvested the profit in Mount Adams, where eight years later they were spending a million dollars (in one year) on renovation and construction. By 1969 they had renovated fifty houses and sold a dozen others to renovators with clauses in each sales contract requiring that the new owner complete within a twelve-month period substantial renovation according to plans approved by Towne Properties. This condition prevented property speculation and quickly broadened the base of investor-owner interest on the Hill.

Towne Properties also started the first new business on Mount Adams in many years, a little basement bistro with an outside patio, which quickly became one of the most popular cocktail spots in the Cincinnati area. Its success inspired other new business ventures, including quaint restaurants and galleries like those in Chicago's Old Town. This former slum has become so attractive that one man sold his home in an exclusive suburb to move there and is spending a quarter of a million dollars on his renovation.

· CHICAGO

Chicago has probably done more to encourage private renewal than any other city. Compared to New York's cumbersome bureaucracy, Chicago's co-ordinated city departments allow the citizen easy access to the appropriate agency. Though Chicago has all the typical problems of a large industrial city, its system of ward politics encourages community cohesiveness.

From its birth as a port on Lake Michigan, Chicago's growth spread north and south along the lakefront, with its business district centered around the Loop and residential areas forming an arc around the hub. Though Chicago was the home of the first skyscraper and has seen constant commercial growth since the Great Fire of 1871, it has a

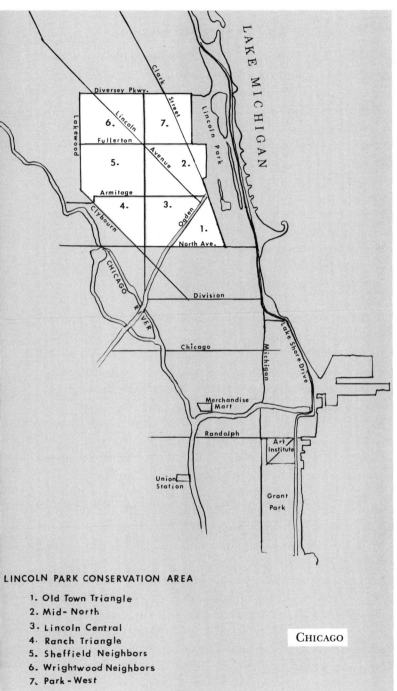

LINCOLN PARK CONSERVATION AREA

1. Old Town Triangle
2. Mid-North
3. Lincoln Central
4. Ranch Triangle
5. Sheffield Neighbors
6. Wrightwood Neighbors
7. Park-West

CHICAGO

large number of late-nineteenth- and early-twentieth-century houses remaining in its old residential neighborhoods.

Its three main renovation areas are the Near North Side, a posh neighborhood of majestic buildings, handsome stone mansions, and stately town houses; Lincoln Park, a large residential area of early postfire houses; and Hyde Park–Kenwood, the home of the University of Chicago and Chicago's pioneer project in Urban Renewal conservation.

The Near North Side might be equated with New York's East Side and Washington's Georgetown, while Lincoln Park might be compared to New York's West Side or Washington's Capitol Hill. Both are prime residential areas, and each has a distinct character of its own.

Chicago's renovation movement began in the 1940's with the discovery by artists and writers of a shabby, deteriorating area just north of the Loop. Dubbed Old Town, it contained a conglomeration of postfire architecture ranging from duplications of earlier high-stooped cottages to baroque homes embellished with gingerbread inside and out, Swiss chalet-type houses, and the early modern row houses of Louis Sullivan. There is a grand and glorious mixture of styles known as Victorian, combining adaptations from the French (mansard roofs), Italian Renaissance (arched windows, pilasters, and loggias), and Gothic (pointed windows and stained glass), with American immigrant buildings in brick, masonry, and white pine.

The Old Town Triangle Association, formed in 1949, embarked on a program to reverse deterioration and attract other renovators by changing the image of the neighborhood. In 1950 they inaugurated an annual Arts and Crafts Street Fair, called Old Town Holiday, drawing thousands of people to the neighborhood each year. Included are garden tours to show off the city flowers and greenery in which Old Town renovators take special pride.

Early renovators in Old Town had the same problems

as renovators everywhere: decaying houses, trash-littered streets, and a bad reputation. Says Paul Angle, former director of the Chicago Historical Society, of his purchase of a house in 1947: "We were certainly not the first to buy here, and yet it was still a real speculation at the time. We couldn't get banks to finance houses in the neighborhood."

Efforts to revitalize Old Town were strengthened when the area was designated a conservation district and word of the community renaissance spread. Through all the remodeling, the area's original architectural character was kept intact. In spite of the hodgepodge of styles, the blend creates a charming whole, possibly because of a common scale, quality of material, and detail. These wood and brick buildings, constructed at a time when carpenters and masons took pride in their skill and versatility, have mellowed with age and become an integral part of the cityscape.

Old Town's success awakened residents to the problems of the surrounding area, called Lincoln Park, which in 1948 was characterized as "predominantly in a state of deterioration." In 1954 the Old Town Triangle Association joined forces with the Mid-North Association to create the Lincoln Park Conservation Association, and an attack was launched on all the problems confronting Lincoln Park in its efforts to renew itself.

Lincoln Park covers an area of two square miles, bordering the large city park from which it gets its name. It has seventy-two thousand inhabitants and is made up of seven distinct neighborhoods, each with its own organization. The LPCA serves the needs of all of them as well as of businesses and institutions in Lincoln Park.

In the 1850's and 1860's the area was called the Cabbage Patch because of its many truck farms and cow pastures—all wiped out in the Great Fire of 1871. Lincoln Park was developed as a prime residential neighborhood in the twenty-five years following the fire. Its development can be traced by driving north from Old Town: more modest homes give way to very large and elaborate houses in the northern sections. All phases of postfire architecture are represented in Lincoln Park. During its years of growth it became the home of De Paul University, McCormick Theological Seminary, numerous hospitals, churches, and schools, and the Chicago Historical Society—as well as the garage that was the scene of the St. Valentine's Day Massacre.

Real estate values have soared as renovators have moved in. Just as in Brooklyn, when prices in Old Town became too high, renovators moved into adjoining areas, so the renovation movement has snowballed.

When LPCA approached the municipal government for help, the city declared all of Lincoln Park a Conservation Area in 1956. To quote Commissioner Lewis W. Hill: "My belief is that the kind of effort the city makes in conservation areas like Lincoln Park will set in motion economic and social forces with the power to renew the face of the city."

Chicago has shown unusual responsiveness to the need for furthering the renovation movement, encouraging private citizens to revitalize their neighborhoods. The city recognized what had made Old Town renovation work so well, and incorporated these objectives into a General Neighborhood Renewal Plan formulated for the whole area, to be implemented in stages over a period of ten to fifteen years. This plan stipulates that rehabilitation of existing structures is the prime goal of renewal; the distinctiveness of the community and its attraction as a family residential area are to be maintained; and the population density of the neighborhood is to remain the same. Project I, encompassing all of Old Town and parts of adjoining Mid-North, is almost complete, and Project II is being implemented. By the end of 1968, $11.3 million had been invested in renovation work requiring building permits, and this does not include money spent for modernization, exterior repairs, and painting or other beautification projects such as tree planting.

The LPCA has been a great help to the renovator. A nonprofit organization with a paid executive and staff, it publishes a newsletter to inform its membership of problems and projects. It is involved in planning code enforcement, area cleanup, youth activities, school improvements, and anything else of vital interest to the residents.

The LPCA works very closely with the various city departments and provides information on renovation: financing, zoning laws, building-department regulations affecting renovators, and so on. Much of this information is in printed form, available from the city and distributed to residents through the LPCA. Two such booklets are "Your 'Where-to-Call' Guide" (similar to one put out by the San Francisco Planning and Urban Renewal Association) and "Your Building Department," a brief explanation of the building code and how it affects renovation. Would that every city made such information available to its citizens!

The State of Illinois was a year ahead of the United States government in passing a law in 1953 designed for the conservation and improvement of older communities through rehabilitation of property by owners and limited clearance of blight with public funds. In 1954 Congress passed legislation for federal renewal through conservation as well as slum clearance. Chicago's faith in the private sector is shown by the fact that in 1966 the city had designated fourteen different conservation areas, only six of which were in federally approved projects.

As helpful as the city might be, any government project is full of red tape and delays. It took ten years of planning to initiate Project I in Lincoln Park, and the individual renovator was at work long before the government entered the picture. The Lincoln Park Conservation Association is by no means unique in Chicago. In nearly every older section of the city that has been well maintained, preserved, and upgraded, there is a strong over-all community organization.

It may be that Chicago has had so much successful renovation because the city is aware of its importance and has a policy of encouraging private development of all kinds.

· SAN FRANCISCO

San Francisco is a sophisticated urban city whose small buildings nestled among steep hills and magnificent views of the cityscape give it a Mediterranean quality. Its unusually temperate climate makes it a year-round oasis of greenery and flowers. Few visitors who marvel at geraniums and begonias in full bloom at Christmas time realize that lush foliage was not native to the area. It was not until the 1870's that residents began replacing the thinly scattered brush with the groves of trees so prevalent today.

San Franciscans have lived in fear of earthquake and fire since the disaster of 1906 destroyed large portions of the city. The earthquake problem may have been a blessing in disguise, because until very recently a strict building code severely limited the construction of tall buildings. During the first fifty years of this century there was no rush to tear down low buildings to build taller ones, and the character of the city was not obliterated in the rapid business growth that destroyed early architecture in most urban centers. The skyscraper, which has caused the eradication of the character of so many American cities, is a relative newcomer to San Francisco. Modern construction techniques and materials, along with a revised building code, has made the skyscraper not only possible but economically feasible as well. The threat of a changed cityscape looms on the horizon, and San Franciscans may have to fight to preserve the unique character and quality of their city.

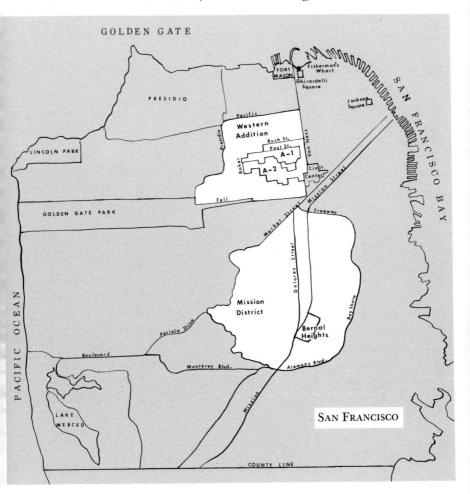

The Gold Rush transformed San Francisco from an obscure settlement to a famous city. In the early days of rapid growth, when the area was flooded with people seeking their fortunes, the city had to be laid out rapidly so that property lines could be quickly and easily determined. There was no time for planning, and the grid pattern of streets, totally unsuited to San Francisco's terrain, was imposed arbitrarily upon the steep barren hills, resulting in a staggering amount of cutting, leveling, and filling to make the street plan work.

San Francisco experienced a residential building boom typical of most American cities in the last quarter of the nineteenth century. This period saw the emergence of San Francisco Victorian. Because stone and brick were not readily available, the Victorian, based on the common floor plan of the era, was built of wood and lavishly embellished with ornate cornices, bays, and woodwork. Unlike its Eastern counterpart, the San Francisco Victorian is almost exclusively two stories tall, but is generally both wider and longer than its Eastern cousin. The Victorian was sometimes built in rows, but is most often found unattached or paired on narrow lots with windows along one or both sides. Because of the added width and depth, plus the presence of windows on all four sides, these houses are more flexible, and it is often possible to accommodate on one floor an apartment that would require two floors of an East Coast house. In addition, cellars often open onto street level at either front or rear, making it possible to use this space for an apartment. Since San Francisco's zoning law groups one- to four-family houses in the same category, a renovator is limited only by the building code if he plans to create no more than four apartments.

These nineteenth-century two-story houses were often built to house two families, one above the other, each floor containing a separate large apartment adorned with the architectural detail of the period. Each apartment was provided with its own front door and street number (worked into the stained-glass transom), the two entrances side by side in the house façade. This tradition has been carried over into twentieth-century building, and even apartment houses have separate exterior entrances for each apartment. This type of house is ideal for the renovator because no structural changes are necessary. New plumbing and wiring and the refurbishing of existing rooms is usually all that is required. Few San Francisco neighborhoods do not contain this type of house.

San Francisco is not typical of modern American cities. A lack of industry to pollute the environment and encroach upon residential neighborhoods, a mild climate that is kind to building exteriors, a multitude of small houses, and a large homeowning population tend to make San Francisco a residential city, even though many people have left for the bay-area suburbs. Blight and decay have not run rampant in San Francisco. Although there are many houses that do not comply with the building code, and although slumlord, rooming house, and overcrowding are not unknown, San Francisco's deteriorated neighborhoods do not resemble the depressing slums of industrialized cities, where soot and pollution have fouled exteriors and skyscrapers have obscured sunlight from tightly packed row houses.

San Francisco does have areas of decaying real estate that are prime targets for renovation. Two will be discussed in some detail. Private renovation began in the Mission District a decade ago, and parts of the area are now receiving assistance from the city and federal governments. The Western Addition was the city's first project in community rehabilitation. However, houses for renovation are not limited to these areas. San Francisco is a conglomerate of residential neighborhoods, many of which contain old houses awaiting the loving care of the renovator.

The Mission District is a large area that from 1850 until the 1880's was a resort with race track and pleasure gardens. Its resort days were numbered, however, because it was needed to house the expanding population of the fast-growing city. The most self-contained of San Francisco's districts, it still seems like a city within a city, and its residents are particularly community-conscious. The Mission District contains the city's oldest building, the Mission Delores, a number of elegant mansions, and many stately Victorians. Nondescript houses nestled among the curving, short streets of the hillsides are reminiscent of an old.Spanish village.

Renovators were first attracted to the deteriorated Victorians, with their elaborate woodwork and marble mantels. However, in a city where real estate prices are high, it did not take the renovators long to discover the low prices and magnificent views of the undistinguished hillside dwellings. Bernal Heights is one of the hillside neighborhoods undergoing transformation. One early pioneer found that the twentieth century had by-passed the street on which his house stood—it took five years of petitioning the city to get the street paved.

Many of the houses in Bernal Heights were built as one-room dwellings and added onto piecemeal over the years, with the parts often bearing little relationship to each other or the whole. Many of them have serious structural problems and should be inspected by a competent professional before purchase. In spite of their chopped-up nature, they offer an opportunity for the imaginative renovator to create exciting living space when interior partitions are removed and kitchens and baths designed to function in an over-all layout. Marvin Mayeux, attracted by this challenge, moved into his Bernal Heights house immediately after taking title and gradually renovated it himself. Ripping out all unnecessary partitions and leaving the varying ceiling heights intact, he transformed the tiny unco-ordinated rooms into a spacious, airy house. The lean-to addition that housed the bath was converted to a solarium, opening onto a lovely secluded garden with a magnificent view of San Francisco and the rooftops on the hill below.

Bernal Heights has an active neighborhood association, formed originally to fight the impending demolition of the area when it was designated by the city for urban renewal. The residents have convinced the city that the community is a viable one and worthy of preservation. Now that its destiny has been assured by its recent designation as one of seven rehabilitation areas, the residents can get on with the job of improving their community. Bernal Heights, as well as the rest of the Mission District, has many houses crying out for renovation. Hopefully, city rehabilitation will encourage others to join the renovation movement there.

The Western Addition is a term originally used to designate an area between the city's surveyed boundaries and the western limit set by the legislative charter of 1851. The area was opened for development in 1855, but most of its development into a prime residential area did not occur until the 1870's and 1880's. The area abounds in Victorians of various sizes and architectural styles. Fully developed by the turn of the century, the area's earlier residential quality was modified as the larger homes were cut into increasingly smaller apartments and others were converted to rooming houses. The Western Addition slid steadily downhill as the wealthier moved and the poorer owners were unable to maintain their property. It had become a slum in the eyes of most San Franciscans when the Redevelopment Agency chose part of the area for urban renewal (Project A-1) in the early days of San Francisco's program.

When the bulldozer leveled the whole project area, there was a loud outcry against the wanton destruction of so many handsome, though deteriorated, Victorians and the uprooting of a large portion of the old neighborhood. San Franciscans, intensely proud of their city, became preservation-minded as they realized that the bulldozer could strike anywhere and that their city could end up looking exactly like New York, Chicago, or any other metropolis.

Due to the objections of an aroused public, urban renewal for San Francisco's residential areas now takes the form of Federally Assisted Code Enforcement (FACE), a program designed to halt the spread of decay through rehabilitation, with only spot clearance of blighting influ-

San Francisco wood gingerbread Victorian.

ences. The remainder of the Western Addition (A-2), with most of its Victorians still intact, was declared an Urban Renewal Project under the FACE program in 1964. There was much community opposition to the project until residents realized that the Redevelopment Agency really intended to clear only those buildings that were eyesores, leaving the rest of the community intact. The plan for the area called for rehabilitation by the owners themselves with assistance in planning and financing supplied by a local project office. The city has not taken property through its right of eminent domain for resale to renovators as New Haven did in Wooster Square and other urban renewal projects. Although the San Francisco Redevelopment Agency has the authority to take property when an owner refuses to meet building-code requirements, James E. Vann, chief of rehabilitation for the San Francisco Redevelopment Agency, does not believe it will be necessary. As a result of the sensitivity, diligence, and enthusiasm of Vann and the staff of the A-2 project office, houses in the Western Addition, long neglected and forlorn, are beginning to blossom, proudly wearing new coats of paint and restored façades. The project office is equipped with a showroom where appropriate paint colors, along with inexpensive products of good design, are on display; and members of the staff spend long hours with each renovator to insure that all work will be in harmony with the character of the neighborhood. Although the Redevelopment Agency is not actively seeking new owners, the services of the project office are available to any property owner, longtime resident, or newcomer.

The renovation of the Western Addition is in its early stages and therefore offers many opportunities for the renovator. He can renovate in a conventional manner or take advantage of the help offered by the Redevelopment Agency and the 3% federal loans available under the 312 program. The Redevelopment Agency publishes two booklets, both of which are helpful in acquainting renovators with pertinent building code regulations and as guidelines for renovation specifications: "General Rehabilitation Specifications" and "Area 2 Rehabilitation Standards."

The FACE program has recently been expanded to include seven new project areas, of which Bernal Heights in the Mission District is one. The programs for these areas will follow the pattern set by A-2, with local project offices providing assistance to renovators and residents of each area. The desire to arrest and remove blight while maintaining the city's character seems to have permeated the government as well as the citizens of San Francisco.

As a result of the uproar caused by the razing of A-1 in the Western Addition, the Junior League undertook a block-by-block survey of all San Francisco buildings to learn as much as possible about those worthy of preservation. The result is a lavishly illustrated book entitled *Here Today, San Francisco's Architectural Heritage.* A Landmarks Commission has been established, and a citizens' organization called SPUR (San Francisco Planning and Urban Renewal Association) was founded to further sound planning and development, conservation and rebuilding, and to preserve and enhance the environment. SPUR works with the many community organizations active in neighborhood interests, and renovators interested in a specific neighborhood can contact SPUR for names of pertinent local organizations. In addition, SPUR publishes two booklets that may be helpful: "Your Neighborhood Troubleshooter, or where you can get help for neighborhood problems" and "SPUR Bright Spots," which describes plazas, parks, and exceptional places created by the people of San Francisco, a guide for residents as well as tourists.

In addition to the assistance given to renovators in FACE areas, the city offers further help to any prospective purchaser. San Francisco law requires the seller to supply on request a report (called a 3-R report) documenting the legal occupancy of the property and giving other pertinent information about permits issued, zoning requirements, records on file at the building department, and so on. The building department, for a fee of thirty-five dollars per floor, will inspect any building for a prospective purchaser, noting code violations and structural problems that must be remedied.

There are many old houses in need of loving attention in all parts of the city. That renovation is generally accepted as a sound investment can be seen by the number of successful commercial renovations: Jackson Square, a complex of early warehouses in the business district that have been tastefully remodeled as headquarters for the city's fabric, wallpaper, and furniture dealers; Ghirardelli Square, an imaginative renovation of the Ghirardelli chocolate factory and other factories into a shopping and entertainment center; and the Cannery, a recently completed delightful maze of boutiques and shops on three levels made from an old brick fish cannery.

· THE SOUTH

· NEW ORLEANS

New Orleans was born in the Vieux Carré around the military parade ground at Jackson Square, where the flags of Spain, France, and the United States were raised and lowered in turn as the city changed hands. Laid out in a grid around the "old square" are the first streets of New Orleans, lined with the homes of its earliest residents, in an architectural style that, like New Orleans food, is a unique blend of French and Spanish, reflecting the changing status of the city's nationality.

In the 1930's, shortly after Charleston passed the first Historic District zoning legislation, the Vieux Carré Commission was created to ensure the preservation of the French Quarter's architectural heritage* because the city realized it was a priceless asset. But it was not always so. These delightful buildings, now considered invaluable historically and financially, were the homes of chickens and pigs belonging to the Italian immigrant residents, who strung clotheslines between the fanlights to dry long strands of homemade spaghetti amongst the laundry for their large families.

As usual, it took the artists and writers to discover the area. Lyle Saxon, author of the classic *Fabulous New Or-*

---

* All plans for demolition, renovation, or restoration must be approved by this board.

Courtyard view of the Lowreys' French Quarter house, before and after restoration.

leans, was the first to flaunt convention and buy a house in the Quarter, followed by Roark Bradford and a series of more transitory residents, such as William Faulkner, Sherwood Anderson, and Tennessee Williams. Even today the proper New Orleanian doesn't consider the Quarter an appropriate address, but so many others enjoy living in its colorful atmosphere that there are few, if any, bargains left to be found.

Some, however, armed with determination and imagination, have continued to seek out forlorn derelicts to rescue and restore as homes. The Lowrey brothers, Mark and Walter, an architect and a writer, were so in love with the Vieux Carré that when Walter returned from a sojourn in Europe with his Scandinavian wife, they resolved to join forces and make their home there. The typical layout of a French Quarter house, with separate slave quarters at the rear of the courtyard behind the house, makes it ideal for a home-plus-rental unit or, in the Lowreys' case, family plus bachelor quarters.

It took them nearly a year, with the help of a hardworking real estate agent, to hunt down the bargain their finances required. During that time they considered all of the varieties that the Quarter has to offer: shotgun cottages (New Orleans nomenclature for the one-room-behind-another layout called a railroad flat in New York), Victorian doubles, town houses ranging from modest to mansion.

The house the Lowreys settled upon was the smelly, filthy, trash-strewn wreck so familiar to renovators everywhere. Theirs was inhabited by a pack of mongrel dogs and fleas—so many fleas that their pants were black with them from their initial exploration. In fact, they were forced to fumigate before the demolition crew would go in to begin the cleanup.

The Lowreys did their renovation on a cost-plus basis, and the work dragged on and on while the cost went up and up. Finally, their cash and patience exhausted, the

Lowreys moved in and finished up themselves. They accomplished the magic metamorphosis from miserable wreck to clean-lined classic beauty—an excellent restoration that proudly wears a plaque from the Vieux Carré Commission.*

The Walter Lowreys, who have two daughters, are convinced that the French Quarter is a fine place to raise children, though this is scarcely a popular opinion in New Orleans. The girls are getting a liberal education about the real world from its sidewalks—and when the mother of an uptown schoolmate wonders if it is safe to send her child there to play, Mrs. Lowrey points out that the Quarter courtyards are enclosed from the dangers of traffic, unlike the yards and streets where children play in other parts of the city.

The French Quarter comes to an end at Esplanade Avenue, but a few pioneers have ventured across to the other side (raffishly known as the Fringe Quarter) away from the honky-tonk midway atmosphere of the night clubs and strip joints in its center, where there are houses equally old and charming—and less expensive. Terry and Leonard Flettrich bought a house that appears to be perched squarely in the middle of the street as the road curves abruptly around it. Built in 1810 on farmland that was part of the Marigny plantation and once owned by Governor Claiborne's brother, it stands opposite the house where the game of craps was introduced to the gambling city of New Orleans. Its quaint stuccoed brick façade conceals an astonishingly spacious interior; central hall dividing double rooms on either side, a long room across the rear (overlooking a delightful garden) with a stairway leading up to second-floor bedrooms under the steeply slanting roof.

* Documented in detail, including costs, in a book the Lowreys wrote called *912 Orleans Street—The Story of a Rescue.*

There are other houses of the same style and vintage in various stages of neglect in the vicinity of the Municipal Auditorium, an area bound to appreciate in value when the projected cultural center is built there. One can only hope that these charming old houses will be rescued and restored as homes before the value of the land under them tempts real estate developers to replace them with hamburger palaces and motels.

And what of Esplanade Avenue itself? How ironic that a city so in love with its past seems to have forgotten the glorious oak- and magnolia-shaded double boulevard that was its very first "good address," home of the early Creole aristocracy!

Centrally convenient as well as lovely, Esplanade runs all the way from the edge of the French Quarter and downtown New Orleans to the Fairgrounds Race Track and City Park. Grand Route St. John at the end of Esplanade was the road that brought Bienville into the city. The first encampment was at Bayou St. John, the city's commercial outlet before the settlers could navigate the Mississippi River. A few wealthy residents have lived for many years in houses overlooking Bayou St. John, yet early houses in this historic area can be bought for prices much lower than in other parts of New Orleans.

The gorgeous old Creole houses along Esplanade Avenue are neglected as the French Quarter once was. Many have already been destroyed to make way for vile brick excrescences, instant slums into which too many poor families are being packed and which the government encourages by granting large sums of money to their builders.

But it is still not too late to save many of the beautiful, spacious old houses, to reconvert them from rooming houses and brothels into delightful homes. There are some thirty blocks of houses suitable for restoration, and a handful of perceptive New Orleanians has discovered them and made a beginning.

Chris Friedrichs, a young landscape architect, has made

his home, office, and three apartments in a handsome 120-year-old two-story house in the 1800 block of Esplanade Avenue. Inside its Southern façade with two-story columns and wrought-iron-railed upper gallery there is an enormous high-ceilinged double parlor, with sliding doors separating it from a dining room across the rear. The front entrance hall and stairway, the Italian marble mantels and windows to the floor, the elegant parlor with its central plaster arch and chandelier rosettes, are surprisingly similar to details in Manhattan, Brooklyn, and Boston houses of the same era.

Chris discovered the plaster arch while he was knocking down the partition that had been erected to divide the parlor into separate rooms to house some of the fourteen tenants it had been forced to accommodate. Unaware that the arch existed at all, he was on the verge of destroying it with his hammer when he realized that he was striking something other than the partition. But he stopped in time, and made one of the exciting discoveries known only to archeologists and owners of old houses—unexpected hidden treasure.

Chris Friedrichs bought his house in 1964, after having his rent tripled on the office he had renovated in the French Quarter. He was interested in buying in the Quarter, but found it too expensive. Driving up Esplanade Avenue one day, he passed the house he had long admired just as a "For Sale" sign was being nailed to the door. Going back to look inside, he almost cried when he saw the sad condition of the handsome parlor. Still, he thought he could simply move in, clean it up, and live there while he gradually repaired and redecorated. It is hard to understand how he could have believed this, because he had the house checked by two architects and a structural engineer, and was warned that it would have to be shored up and the foundations completely rebuilt due to termite damage and the sperading and sinking of the original underpinnings in New Orleans's watery ground. Before he was finished, he had to rip off and repair the roof and façade as well.

The purchase price was about half the cost of a much smaller property in the French Quarter and probably one third of an equivalent house in the Garden District. Friedrichs encountered the same financing difficulties faced by Royal Cloyd in Boston and pioneer renovators everywhere. He was able to get a mortgage only because his father mortgaged his own house to get it for him. (In New Orleans all mortgages are made through the Homestead, a counterpart of savings and loan associations.)

Friedrichs' architect had to be restrained from gutting the old house. Friedrichs wanted to retain its character, even to the extent of reusing the original bathroom fixtures. (This latter idiosyncracy provoked the ire of the plumber, who deliberately broke some of them to avoid reinstalling them.)

He created two apartments in the rambling two-story extension of the main house, each with its own small garden and entrance through the driveway. The garage houses still another apartment, the income from all three making the house self-supporting. And what a lovely house he has for himself, with tropical foliage providing privacy from the street for his veranda complete with porch swing, expansive parlor and dining room, two bedrooms opening out onto the upper gallery, and office at the top of the stairs.

Coliseum Square and Magazine Street also offer exciting possibilities on the fringe of the chic, expensive Garden District. Louis Sporl has set up his home, shop, and budding real estate empire there. He began by converting a large old house from a rooming house into apartments, with spacious bachelor's quarters for himself. Before he even finished the apartments, he built a swimming pool in the rear and began buying houses to renovate all around it. His tenants pay handsome rents to live in the attractive air-conditioned apartments, swim in his pool, and attend the annual art shows he assembles in the central community garden of his enclave. He is branching out into surrounding blocks, backed by a group of New Orleanians anxious to upgrade the neighborhood adjoining their Garden District homes.

A few others have been brave enough to pioneer on Magazine Street, but most of the handsome houses around Coliseum Square still wear cardboard signs advertising "Rooms" on their elegant Greek revival façades. However, prices in the area have already begun to rise as owners realize what handsome homes and apartments their old houses can become. Another neighborhood renaissance is on its way.

· Savannah

Savannah, like its neighbor Charleston, was a bustling port and growing city in the heyday of King Cotton. Savannah grew slowly at first, with simple one-story wooden houses, but after the Revolution and until the Civil War it blossomed into a sophisticated city of glorious homes where such personages as Washington and Lafayette were lavishly entertained. During this period of prosperity Oglethorpe's 1733 city plan of grid streets laid out around squares was expanded, with eighteen new squares added to the original six, forming the thirteen acres now known as Historic Savannah. This area, containing over eleven hundred buildings of architectural merit, was designated a Registered Historic Landmark by the National Park Service of the Department of the Interior in 1966. Savannah became the proud possessor of the largest central-city historic district in the United States.

Savannah's architecture was influenced by Northerners and Europeans who helped rebuild after a fire in 1796 destroyed two thirds of the city. The influence of New York builders is evident in stoops and dormer windows, while gambrel roofs characteristic of Rhode Island and light porticos derived from Bulfinch attest to the presence of New Englanders. The high stoop so typical of Savannah was necessitated by the sandy, unpaved streets, as local carpenters designed tall row houses suited to the narrow lots of Oglethorpe's plan. Savannah gray bricks were a popular building material, and ornate ironwork like that found in New Orleans and Charleston came into fashion.

The twentieth century has seen Atlanta develop as the state's center of commerce and industry, while Savannah slipped quietly into the backwater, becoming a sleepy port as Atlanta blossomed and flourished. Time stood still for the city, and the decay found in Society Hill and Benefit Street in Providence visited Historic Savannah. By the end of World War II many of the lovely homes and stately mansions had been divided up to house numerous families where one family had lived so lavishly. Three of the lovely squares had been cut through for traffic and houses were being razed for the salvage value of the old Savannah gray brick; gas stations were built on some of the empty sites, while others became parking lots. Occasionally a building was saved by a few history buffs dabbling in restoration, but not until the 1950's did Savannah become aware of its wealth of great architecture.

Savannah's recognition of its architectural heritage stems directly from the vision and effort of one woman. In 1945 Mrs. Hansell Hillyer perceived the historic value of thirty slum buildings surrounding the gas works high on a bluff over the Savannah River. With enormous imagination and care she created the Trustees' Garden Village, a restoration that converted these derelicts into fifty-five delightful apartments and twelve offices. This, in turn, led to renovation in the adjacent areas.

One of the pioneers in nearby Washington Ward was Mills B. Lane, president of the Citizens & Southern Bank. He invested in the future of Savannah's Historic District himself, and also made Citizens & Southern Bank money available to renovators. Other banks followed suit, and it is probably the availability of financing that has made Savannah restoration so successful.

But residents did not take real action until they became alarmed by the increasing demolition of old buildings in the downtown area. Rudely awakened when their old city market became a parking garage, a group of citizens formed the Historic Savannah Foundation to halt destruction. The foundation was patterned on the earlier Historic Charleston Foundation and made use of their innovative revolving-fund example. However, with only about a third of the seed money used in Charleston, Savannah has accomplished miracles, transforming 130 houses in the amazingly short time of three years.

With a revolving fund of two hundred thousand dollars Historic Savannah launched two area-restoration projects. The first was a pilot project in the business district, where two commercial structures were threatened with demolition. The second, a residential project, was begun in 1965 in an area called Pulaski Square–West Jones Street. As a result, eighty-five per cent of the houses rated as valuable have been reclaimed. In just four and a half years more than $1.7 million has been invested in the renovation of fifty-eight houses, and the neighborhood has moved from slum status to the favorite of young renovators.

Reid Williamson, executive director of Historic Savannah Foundation, and his wife purchased two houses on the trust lot opposite Pulaski Square. They razed one and walled in the lot to create a spacious side garden for the remaining house, whose Federal façade had been disguised by a series of porches, removed to reveal a handsome high-stooped 1842 clapboard complete with dormer windows. The house required total renovation and loving restoration, including the replacing of Victorian marble mantels with period ones salvaged from other houses. The William-

A small sample of the amazing variety of architecture in downtown Savannah.

sons, like many Savannah renovators, made a ground floor rental apartment while retaining the rest of the house for themselves.

The renovators in the Pulaski Square–West Jones Street area are very budget-conscious, and most have contracted their jobs themselves. Some owners move in at once and do their restoration over a number of years. On the other hand, Caroline and Ed Hill, who needed the rental income from their ground floor apartment, had an architect draw plans for the rental unit, and finished it immediately. They then gradually finished their own quarters, which were in wretched condition. By trial and error and ingenuity they put the house back together almost as it had been originally, duplicating the old plaster moldings that adorned the living room ceiling. Seeing the renovated house, one would never guess that the Hills accomplished their miracle on a very modest budget.

The Historic Savannah Foundation has purchased and resold to renovators (with restrictive covenants) properties throughout the entire Historic area as well as encouraging purchase directly from owners. They did a survey of all buildings, culminating in the publication of a handsome book, *Historic Savannah*. They are pushing for local historic zoning (which is nearly a reality) and are working to make businessmen and bankers aware of the economic potential of preservation of the old city, as Savannah is rapidly becoming a tourist mecca.

The renovation movement in Savannah is in full swing. The variety of styles and sizes of houses is a bonanza for the renovator, whatever his taste or means. There are two-story brick workmen's cottages similar to those in Philadelphia, ideal for single-family homes. Two-story New England clapboards lend a suburban quality to the center city, while an abundance of high-stooped urban town houses are easily adapted for family plus income. Elegant row houses reminiscent of New York's Gramercy Park beckon the sophisticated. Fabulous mansions with ornate iron balconies and secluded side gardens are suggestive of New Orleans' French Quarter. And every house is within a few short blocks of a beautiful green square. Though paint may be peeling, shutters sagging, windows broken, stoops decaying, the grandeur of the houses is still easily apparent.

· ATLANTA

Because the city was left in ashes after Sherman's famous march to the sea, Atlanta has no pre-Civil War architecture. Most early postwar houses were torn down to make way for new building as Atlanta became a modern metropolis. One lone line of brick row houses called Baltimore Block remains sadly contemplating the fate of its neighbors that were removed to make way for a used-car lot across the street.

Renovators have had to be content with whatever early city houses remain. The only section that has seen much activity so far is Ansley Park, one of Atlanta's first suburbs, laid out about 1918, with winding streets around parks of gnarled old trees. The houses are described by one resident as "early ugly." However, architects like Henri Jova have turned them into gracious homes by face-lifting on the exterior and surgery on the interior. The initial attraction of Ansley Park was its in-town location and low prices. Prices are no longer low, but Ansley Park has led the way in making center-city neighborhoods fashionable again. Renovators are discovering other areas with potential: the newly named Uptown Neighborhood to the south of Ansley Park, and the Inman Park section just off Little Five Points.

Also recently discovered and undergoing a combination of restoration and renovation is Underground Atlanta. Like Ghirardelli Square in San Francisco and Larimer Square in Denver, this is a group of nineteenth-century buildings whose charm is being exploited for commercial use in shops, restaurants, and night clubs. These buildings were entombed under Atlanta's sidewalks when street levels were raised to that of the viaducts that had been built to carry traffic over railroad tracks. For this reason they had been spared, passed over and forgotten by the twentieth century until an Atlanta developer recognized the potential for their revival.

· Charleston, South Carolina

Charleston, now celebrating her three hundredth birthday, was the first city in the United States to enact historic-district legislation in 1931 to preserve her incomparable architectural heritage. Named Charles Towne in honor of King Charles II when it was settled in 1670 by 148 Englishmen, it became one of the three largest ports in the New World. As a colorful plantation life based on rice and indigo grew up in the surrounding country, life in the city thrived with balls, champagne suppers, musicales, theaters, duels, and romance.

Charleston was saved by poverty. For more than a century after the Civil War, while prosperous cities bristled with industry and tore down their old buildings to make way for expansion, Charleston was too poor to change. By the time Charlestonians became prosperous once more, they had begun to appreciate their architecture. With her church spires still her tallest structures, Charleston is one city where living in the center of town has never become unfashionable. Charleston is an antique that is alive, where citizens dwell in their museums, the homes of their families for centuries. It is a city of beautiful homes, luxuriant gardens behind stone walls and iron grillwork fences, narrow red-brick streets and cobblestone alleyways bordered by ancient oaks dripping with Spanish moss.

However, in spite of the prideful preservation of splendid homes, Charleston somehow overlooked a downtown section called Ansonborough, which had become a dismal slum. Named after Captain George Anson of the Royal Navy, who had won it in a card game in 1726, it had been the finest residential area in ante-bellum Charleston. Among its 125 pre-Civil War buildings, decayed almost beyond recognition, was the city's oldest house (1712).

In 1959 the Historic Charleston Foundation was formed to save the entire neighborhood of Ansonborough; and in order to carry out their ambitious undertaking, they inaugurated the use of a revolving fund, which has since been imitated successfully in Savannah, Newport, and Pittsburgh. The foundation planned to acquire a nucleus of buildings that would gradually be enlarged, creating enough improvement and stability to encourage individuals to join in an over-all restoration that no one could do alone. At the start the foundation bought seven buildings. As these were sold, the proceeds were immediately put back to work buying others. In the first seven years forty-seven properties were acquired, and twenty were sold to individuals, who restored them as homes under minimal supervision and a restrictive covenant regarding exterior alteration. Five large buildings unsuitable as private homes were converted to apartments, providing much-needed housing for young families. All proceeds from rental over mortgage payments go back into the revolving fund for further improvement of Ansonborough.

By 1970 about ninety homes had been restored, and more than 150 families had moved into the area, ideal for its proximity to Charleston's midtown shopping district. Ansonborough has been transformed from an eyesore to an antique showcase and fashionable place to live once more.

Another small pocket of restoration instigated by individual initiative is Rainbow Row on East Bay. Originally built as winter homes of plantation owners and wealthy merchants, these houses too had deteriorated into a slum. Justice and Mrs. Lionel K. Legge bought the first house in

1932. Their restoration inspired the usual chain reaction, and within six years the other houses were bought and restored to make a handsome, colorful row.

· RICHMOND, VIRGINIA

Richmond, capital of Virginia and erstwhile capital of the Confederacy, personifies the graciousness and historic feeling associated with a Southern city, combining the casual charm of a Savannah or Charleston with the vitality of a twentieth-century metropolis. There are visible reminders of Richmond's illustrious past in the neoclassic state capitol designed by Jefferson, the statues of Civil War

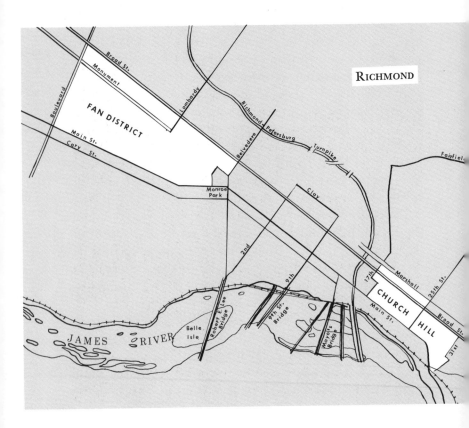

heroes along Monument Avenue, and the Revolutionary War landmark, St. John's Church, erected four years after the city was founded in 1737.

Richmond has two neighborhoods undergoing renovation: Church Hill, high on a bluff over the James River in the eastern sector of the city, and the Fan District, west of the downtown shopping and business district.

The lacy ironwork on these Church Hill, Richmond houses can also be found in New Orleans, Charleston, Savannah, and New York City.

Church Hill derives its name from St. John's Church, located in its center. There at the Virginia Convention of 1775 Patrick Henry spoke the famous words "Give me liberty or give me death." The city's tobacco barons and leading families built their handsome Greek revival homes around the church before the Civil War, and the area became Richmond's first suburb. Although business never climbed the hill, soot from factory smokestacks and coal-burning trains below blew black clouds upon its mansions, driving prosperous families away to other neighborhoods in the west and north. By the time the pollution situation began to be alleviated by the piping in of natural gas and the replacement of coal-burning locomotives with diesel engines, blight had already overtaken the area: It had become a slum. Even though tourists still visited Patrick Henry's historic shrine, they had to go through a dismal area to get there.

In 1950 the Association for the Preservation of Virginia Antiquities initiated the movement to revive Church Hill with the restoration of the Ann Adams Carrington house. In 1956 the Historic Richmond Foundation was organized, and the restoration of Church Hill began in earnest. In May 1957 an ordinance was passed designating the twenty-block area surrounding St. John's Church a historic zone and prohibiting demolition, exterior changes, and new construction without approval of the Commission of Architectural Review.

The foundation restored and established its headquarters in a historic house on East Grace Street. Concentrating their first efforts in the blocks immediately surrounding St. John's Church, they have completed restoration of a pilot block on the north side of East Grace Street and are now at work on the Broad Street side. Some of the thirty-three houses renovated are owned and rented out by the foundation; others have been bought by private individuals and are being restored under the guidance of the foundation. The foundation has a long waiting list for its apartments, which are rented mostly by young professional people—lawyers, doctors, artists, teachers, and architects.

The Church Hill Mews has been transformed from an unsightly alley to a beautiful mall bordered with Victorian ironwork; one aspect of the beautification and revitalizing of the area is a residential section convenient to downtown Richmond and the Medical College of Virginia.

There is a rich choice of houses waiting to be restored on Church Hill: The area contains examples of all periods of town-house architecture, including Federal, Greek revival, and Victorian. The restoration work done by the foundation was intended as a demonstration to encourage private initiative.

The Fan District derives its name from its fan shape: All its major east-west streets fan off Park Avenue. The area was largely rural until 1867, when the city limits were extended; and most of the building was done between 1870 and 1920. There are many charming Victorian town houses with high ceilings, double doors, spacious rooms, and fireplaces. The Fan District suffered a decline due to the typical exodus to suburbia, but in the late fifties people began to appreciate the convenience of in-town living and returned to renovate these delightful houses.

The Fan is approximately ten blocks wide by sixteen to eighteen blocks long, and contains about seven thousand dwelling units: single- and two-family town houses and apartment houses. It is bisected by Monument Avenue, the city's handsomest boulevard, lined with beautiful homes and statues of Civil War heroes.

The Fan District's residents are fighting to keep their neighborhood as a viable in-town living area and preserve its real worth, which lies not in individual masterpieces, but in its architectural feeling as a whole.

The Fan District Association was founded in 1962, not to do actual restoration like the Historic Richmond Foundation, but as a civic organization to upgrade the area by encouraging renovation and beautification. The association launched an attempt several years ago to commission a Neighborhood Master Plan for the solution to traffic, pollution, open space, parking, and other problems plaguing the area.

The association has fostered Spring Garden and Christmas house tours. During the Christmas season a charming custom has been inaugurated: Every home keeps a single white candle lighted in each front window.

Many of the Fan District's widely varied houses are still available. A great deal of the work done by middle-income families is the do-it-yourself variety without benefit of architect (as in Brooklyn and Capitol Hill) and tends more toward renovation than restoration.

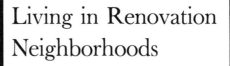

| 4 | Living in Renovation Neighborhoods |

In LIGHT OF the serious housing crisis the United States faces today, perhaps government will recognize the importance of the urban restoration movement, and help it to flourish and grow. Though planning cannot guarantee what spontaneous individual enthusiasm accomplishes, official action could encourage the pioneer spirit of the renovator to revive city neighborhoods. Some of the measures that could be taken toward this end are the improvement of schools, parks, and playgrounds as well as other public services such as police protection and sanitation. Building codes that are designed for skyscrapers and apartment houses should be modified to acknowledge the existence of rehabilitated one- and two-family housing. In some cities excessively liberal zoning allows houses to be chopped up into too many small apartments, whereas in others, restrictive zoning prevents the conversion of enormous mansions to homes for two or three families, leading to their uselessness, total loss, and demolition. Most needed of all is a change in tax assessment policy. Under our present system, owners are usually penalized with a higher assessment for improving their property, while those who allow their houses to deteriorate are rewarded with low taxation, clearly leading to the encouragement of slums and slumlords. This unfair and shortsighted policy is also responsible for forcing out poorer old-time owners whose property is reassessed at a higher rate than they can afford when a whole block is upgraded by renovation.

The most serious handicap is denial of financing to deteriorating neighborhoods, thereby preventing their rehabilitation. Government and financial institutions should encourage renovation by making funds available for revival of declining areas, rather than withholding assistance until it is too late for anything other than massive demolition and rebuilding—a far more costly solution.*

What kinds of problems have renovators faced as pioneers in deteriorated city neighborhoods? Surprisingly few, on the whole. We usually learn that although our neighbors may look forbidding, in truth, they are generally pretty nice people. Everyone, including the poor, would like to get rid of the undesirable element, such as pimps, prostitutes, addicts, and pushers. However, we come to learn that there is a real advantage to living in a diversified neighborhood rather than an entirely homogeneous (and basically sterile) one, where there is a real loss of what Jane Jacobs, in her classic book *The Death and Life of Great American Cities,* calls "eyes on the street." There have been many instances of such vigilance in Martha Stamm's block: a window-watching couple warning a widow that they saw a man get into her cellar; a building caretaker calling the police in time to catch a prowler who broke into a vacant building. The kind of people who go out to work every day and are busy with their own affairs simply do not watch the street or take an interest in other people's problems. And when too many buildings are converted to small apartments, you have a more or less tran-

* An excellent example of what can be done is the innovative mortgage pool set up by Brooklyn's Bedford-Stuyvesant Corporation for assistance to area residents.

sient population that does not care about or have a stake in the community.

There is a crime problem today in all American cities and in some suburbs as well. It is well known that our nation's capital has been hit particularly hard. After the riots following Martin Luther King's assassination, many of the worst element displaced from the burnt-out area moved over to the fringes of the Adams-Morgan renovation neighborhood, bringing a crime wave with them. Refusing to be driven out of their newly renovated homes, the people banded together (just as their pioneer forbears did in fighting the Indians) to fight back. Led by enterprising lawyer Tedson Meyers, they cut back sidewalk hedges that had acted as a screen for lurking muggers and installed floodlights so that their streets were daylight-bright at night. This solution was so effective that eighteen months later Meyers reports no further serious incidents occurring in the area. In Brooklyn's Park Slope a series of purse snatchings was halted by a community plan in which everyone carried police whistles to be blown loudly by victims or observers so that help could be summoned quickly. It worked and the crimes ended. Clinton Hill residents also launched an effective all-out attack on pushers and addicts on their streets.

Brooklyn homeowners in Fort Greene and Boerum Hill have reported remarkable success in converting "litterbugs" to cleanup patrol by enlisting their aid in sweeping the sidewalk and watering plants. Neighborhood pride can be infectious.

As for schools, they are unquestionably a problem worse in some cities than in others. However, not all city public schools are as bad as they are painted, and of course they will only be improved by parents who care. On the other hand, renovators often find that they can save enough of what they would normally pay in rent, commuting, or a second car to send their children to private schools if they so desire.

The motto of our country—In unity there is strength—is proved over and over again in countless renovation communities. There is no better way to accomplish neighborhood improvement than by the organized efforts of like-minded people. It seems to happen almost spontaneously in most cities. A few homeowners get together, and a block association is born. As a result block parties are given to promote community spirit and neighborliness or raise money for trees and window boxes, and house tours are organized to excite the interest of others in buying homes in the area.

Changing the image of the neighborhood is the basic root of the problem. Bad reputation and loss of pride lead to a lack of interest on the part of police, sanitation departments and city officials and a general defeatist attitude among residents. People who have lived in these neighborhoods for a long time have given up trying—and yet, encouraged by newcomers' successes, they usually participate. An interesting example was Martha Stamm's summoning police to end an outdoor crap game in her block. The first reaction was surprise, shock, and disapproval; however, the result was that other residents began to follow suit by taking action themselves.

Despair breeding discouragement accelerated the downfall of these neighborhoods; reversal of the trend is bringing them back to life. There is not the slightest doubt that improvement begets improvement, confidence instills confidence, and enthusiasm breeds enthusiasm.

In many cities grass-roots block associations have tended to mushroom into larger organizations: In Boston SEFCO (South End Federation of Citizens Organizations) co-ordinates efforts for the broader interests of the community, and almost every neighborhood in New York has an organization, from Chelsea and Greenwich Village in Manhattan, to Park Slope and Boerum Hill in Brooklyn. People have formed these organizations because they have found that together they can work miracles.

In New York City the Brownstone Revival Committee was created to co-ordinate the activities and further the interests of all the neighborhoods in the greater New York area. Beginning on a purely volunteer level, in a little more than two years it expanded its membership to reach the point where it now has a paid executive director and is making a concerted effort to reach other related organizations all over the country and the world. It has become an invaluable clearing house for the exchange of useful information and an instrument for promoting change in detrimental building codes, tax assessment policies, and zoning laws.

The National Trust for Historic Preservation in Washington, D.C., is another organization that has been enormously helpful and influential in the renovation movement. They publish a newsletter and magazine, literature on restoration, a national listing of related organizations, and a bibliography of useful books. They have spearheaded the battle to prevent destruction of valuable old buildings and neighborhoods: Their efforts helped prevent the demolition of Philadelphia Row in Capitol Hill for a highway, as well as the encroachment of an expressway on New Orleans' French Quarter.

Historic District Zoning has proved a useful tool to city communities fighting to retain their character (and their very existence) against defacement and demolition.

Though in some cities there has been valuable assistance from Urban Renewal programs and Historic Preservation groups, the most exciting aspect of this whole story is the reclamation and rebirth of large city areas through the initiative of individuals alone.

There are unlimited numbers of old houses all over America with marvelous potential, crying out to be reclaimed for contemporary living. We hope to encourage others to find them and take advantage of their exciting possibilities.

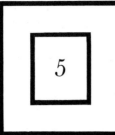

5 The Story of Two Renovations

SINCE MOST PEOPLE are amateurs when they tackle a renovation, it isn't until after they have finished that they realize the mistakes they have made and how they could have done better. There is a tremendous need for pooling the knowledge of those who have learned the hard way about the problems that lie in the path of a renovator, so that he need not stumble through them depending on luck —which can be bad as often as good. Few people really understand the very important financing of a house and the many different choices available. You might blunder into the right choice, but why take a chance? You could be stuck with the consequences of misinformed judgment for years to come. Did you know that a more expensive house could be a better buy than a comparable cheaper one, or did you think that purchase price was the only factor to consider?

You will probably need the help of at least some professionals, and you should know the entire scope of the services they provide in order to decide whether you need them or can do without them. Do you know what to expect of real estate brokers, architects, and contractors, how to choose them and use them? Would you really be saving money by eliminating an architect and doing your own contracting? And if you choose to do it that way, do you know the right order in which the work should be done and the consequences of doing the wrong things first?

Our objective is to inform you thoroughly about all of these and other elements that make up the successful renovation of a house. We propose to pass along the knowledge we have accumulated, exposing potential traps, pitfalls, and mistakes in the buying and renovation of an old house, so that you can avoid the problems, making your own decisions on an enlightened basis. We do not see why everyone should have to go through the experience in blind ignorance, as we did, in order to arrive at the goal.

We are average families who had no special training and no experience at all. Our stories, including the mistakes, will show you how as well as how *not* to do it, so that you may have the advantages we lacked.

· THE STAMMS' STORY

When Martha and Charlie Stamm decided to buy a house in Manhattan in 1964, they had only four thousand dollars in cash and ten thousand dollars a year income. They now live rent-free in an eight-room garden duplex in a four-story house of their own.

The Stamms had moved back to the city after two years of home ownership in suburban Long Island because Martha had begun to feel as though she lived with the children in Huntington while Charlie lived in Manhattan. They were much happier in a four-room city apartment, but two years later, with a third child on the way, they had to find something larger. They began house hunting in the city when they heard about the West Side Urban Renewal project.

In a twenty-block area the first buildings were being demolished in the planned rebuilding and rehabilitation of a mass of blighted tenements and rat-infested rooming houses. By law rooming houses had to be converted to apartments, and some were up for sale with forty-year FHA financing for ninety per cent of the cost of purchase and renovation. The Stamms had never dreamed that a city house was possible for them—but it seemed the answer to their housing problem. They could buy a four- or five-story house, take the two lower floors, garden, and cellar for themselves, and rent the rest. It was possible to buy and renovate for the same cash required for a very modest suburban development house, and the monthly carrying costs would be the same or even less.

During the next seven months they looked at every available house in the Urban Renewal area. Some had been boarded up for months and stripped of everything save the beams. Some were so overcrowded the Stamms could hardly see the house for the people and the broken-down furniture. They climbed hundreds of flights of stairs, sometimes guided only by a flashlight. They asked innumerable questions, gathered information, worked out various floor plans adaptable to most of the houses they saw, and became very realistic about what they could afford. They gave up the idea of ninety per cent financing when they found that the cash required for an FHA renovation was the same as that required for conventional financing and that the FHA job would be decidedly more expensive and take longer.

Finally, only a few weeks before their child was born, they saw an advertisement for a house, obviously written by someone who knew just what they were looking for: It was "close to Lincoln Center" and "ideal for owner-occupant," and best of all, "low cash."

With renewed hope, they went to see the house on West Seventy-eighth Street on a hot Sunday afternoon in August. Hot summer weekends bring out the worst in the city, but the Stamms did not notice the trash-littered street, the overcrowded and unsightly houses, or the noisy swarms of

The Stamms' ground-floor living room was originally the kitchen in their 1889 Manhattan brownstone. To maximize the eight-foot ceiling height, they removed the ceiling to expose the structural beams. Textured plaster was applied to the walls, and a new fireplace was created from the existing flue. Glass Dutch doors replaced windows to provide more light and give access to the enclosed garden.

people lining stoops and hanging from open windows. They saw only the unbroken line of row houses in an amazing variety of architectural styles, terminating in a park at the rear of the Museum of Natural History. Their vision of the potential beauty of the block blotted out the sordid reality.

The advertised house was painted a vile pinkish-beige, dirtied by soot over the years. The handsome two-inch-thick double entry doors at the top of the stoop were disguised with innumerable coats of peeling paint. The interior, however, was clean and freshly painted. The door to the owner's apartment, standing a full ten feet high, had been stripped to its natural mahogany splendor, set off with an expensive new doorknob.

The house was no castle. It still had the original 1889 plumbing and fixtures, with every shape and size of footed bathtub and an old wooden-tank pull-chain toilet. However, compared to the houses they had seen, it looked like a mansion.

The Stamms forgot that the house was in that "no-man's land" between Columbus and Amsterdam avenues, with no Urban Renewal plan for upgrading the neighborhood. It was perfect. The price was right. The cash was low. They could move in immediately and renovate whenever they were ready. There was even a new public school across the street for the children.

They knew they must work out costs to make sure their intuition was correct. And they must find a lawyer. Early Monday they called a corporate attorney friend, seeking his recommendations. He replied, "You must be crazy. That's the worst thing you could possibly do!" There followed a lecture on why they should not buy real estate in Manhattan, much less on the West Side, where they would never get a decent tenant for their rental apartment. They were undaunted. Reluctantly, their friend sent them to see a real estate attorney, hoping that he could "talk some sense into their heads."

And so the Stamms found an invaluable lawyer, bought a house, hired an architect, had a baby, and moved into their new-old house—all within two months. Two days before moving, there was a minor crisis when vandals broke into the house and ripped out a sink, causing a flood. To prevent further damage, Charlie packed a bag at ten o'clock in the evening and became the first Stamm resident of 117 West Seventy-eighth Street.

The rest of the Stamms followed two days later. When

they arrived with the movers, they found a house already full of furniture. Though Charlie was already in residence, they had failed to realize that the house had been sold furnished. Everything except their beds had to be stacked in one room, and by the end of the day it looked like a storage warehouse. The five Stamms now owned four double beds, six single beds, one set of bunk beds, and a crib, plus innumerable tables and chairs.

They had no idea of the frustrations that lay ahead of them, and they did not care. To them the house was beautiful, even with its half-dozen sinks and stoves, decrepit furniture, and old plumbing that sprang a new leak every day or two. They explored every inch, discovering beautiful doorknobs hidden under layers of paint, and stamped brass hinges on every door.

Looking back now with the knowledge they have since acquired, they realize they were very foolish in many ways, and frightfully ignorant. They purchased a house without adequate cash to pay for it. A personal loan from an out-of-state bank gave them enough money to buy and begin the conversion, but this loan was short-term and interest-bearing only, and had to be renewed three times in two years before they were able to pay it off. It could have been canceled at any time, leaving them up the proverbial creek.

They knew absolutely nothing about construction financing, which would have enabled them to renovate with far less financial strain. They were aware that the property could be refinanced when the renovation was complete, so they could repay the out-of-state loan, but they did not know how they would get from point A (purchase) to point B (completion and refinancing) with the little money they had.

The lack of money, though it caused them untold anxiety, was in some ways a blessing. It meant that they had to weigh every penny to be sure they got their money's worth. It also meant they had to live in the house while the work was being done, so they were aware of every nail that was driven and every stud erected. The knowledge of construction Martha absorbed while observing and asking questions, and the close relationship she developed with the workmen enabled her with no prior experience to see that all work was done properly. The importance of supervision became obvious, and the Stamms were thankful they were forced to be constantly present. Whenever a question arose (their plans and specifications gave only the barest essentials), the workmen could ask Martha.

The Stamms' financial situation also prevented them from letting their contractor get ahead of them. They could scarcely make regular payments, let alone make them before the work was done. They took out a personal loan, borrowed on insurance policies, got the existing second mortgage slightly increased, and cut their expenses to the minimum in order to save money for construction payments. When things began to look really desperate, they unexpectedly inherited a small sum of money sufficient to pay for the remaining construction.

The plans for renovation were completed and approved by the city about a month after the Stamms moved in. The construction budget had to be very low, but the first bids were more than double the amount they had planned. Despair over the high bids finally made them see the block as it actually was. They now understood why friends who came to visit were so strangely quiet when taken on a tour of the house as the Stamms proudly explained which walls would be removed, where the new kitchen would go, and how the mudhole in back would be transformed into an oasis of greenery. Depression was a mild word for their mood. It was at about this time that the doorbell rang and Martha was greeted by a menacing-looking stranger. Thoroughly scared, she wished she had followed advice about not opening the door unless she knew who was there. Then she realized what he was saying: He lived across the street and had seen her children sitting on the window ledge upstairs. He was afraid they would fall, and thought she ought to know. After thanking him profusely and soundly spanking the children, she decided that all was not wrong with the world. She realized she felt safer in her run-down, seedy block than anywhere else she had lived in Manhattan. She might not approve of the over-crowded rooming houses, but these people would not harm her or her family. It was a good block and there were good people living in it. She saw the same faces day after day, and they saw her. She was a human being who belonged there as much as they did. She and Charlie would renovate their house and do it well. And their block would look like the block they had visualized that Sunday afternoon in August. It would not be easy, but they could do it.

They did find a contractor they could afford, and accepted his bid without even thinking of checking his credentials. As it turned out, the Stamms were incredibly lucky. The contractor was a young man just starting in business for himself. He and the Stamms had a lot of learning to do together, but they were eager and willing.

There were many problems: a carpenter who did not know how to use a miter box, and consequently moldings that did not meet at the corners; tile men who walked off the job because they had not been paid; a plumber who let a gallon of filthy water drop in the middle of their bed when he removed a sprinkler pipe; hot and cold water lines reversed, so that Charlie froze when he took his first shower; and so forth. But the contractor was willing to rectify mistakes as soon as they were discovered.

The five Stamms lived in two rooms, cooking on a two-burner hot plate, washing dishes in the only bathtub. The situation was not what one could call ideal, but the work-men were pleasant and considerate. As the family moved about to allow work to be done around them, there were times when the only closet was on the top floor while the beds were on the ground floor. The telephone remained installed on the parlor floor, although they did not occupy that floor for nearly seven months. By the time the job was finished, Martha could reach the phone from any room in the four-story house in three rings.

They had originally planned to finish their own apartment on the lower two floors, leaving the remainder until a later date. After construction began, the contractor pointed out that it would be much cheaper to finish the entire house at once. So they revised their schedule to finish the rental unit first: The income would help pay for completion of their own apartment.

Renovation began December eighth, and by July they were ready to rent the duplex apartment on the third and fourth floors. It was a beautiful three-bedroom apartment, with mahogany and marble mantels, dishwasher and self-defrosting refrigerator, two handsome bathrooms, and a terrace. A long, descriptive advertisement in *The New York Times* brought no mad rush to take it off their hands; but the second Sunday they advertised, it was rented easily.

With rent coming in steadily, the Stamms could get on with the job of finishing their own apartment, which was far from complete. During the course of renovation they had taken on several other projects. A block association was formed and a campaign started to plant trees along the sidewalk. Long-time property owners at first resisted, certain that the children and bums would destroy the trees, but when those planted by newcomers in the spring were still thriving in the fall, everyone joined in, and thirty-five trees were planted.

The block association also worked with police and sanitation departments to rid the block of pushers, prostitutes, and garbage. People began taking an interest in their surroundings. When several newcomers painted the exteriors of their houses, other owners must have made the same observation as the Stamms' five-year-old: "But it makes the other houses look so dirty!" Seven other houses were painted the following month, and the whole atmosphere on the block began to change.

The Stamms bought two other houses on the block in

partnership with two neighbors who were also interested in improving the block. Both houses were available for low cash and only required minimal renovation of the existing apartments in order to rent to better tenants. When these projects were complete, the Stamms then bought a large rooming house with all the architectural details intact. After vacating it and getting approved plans and a contracting bid, they sold it to a couple who carried out the planned renovation.

When a twin house became available a few months later, the Stamms could not resist it, even though it looked more like a case for demolition than renovation. By a combination of gutting, salvaging, and scavenging, they made the most of the interior space, using all their accumulated knowledge to create an apartment that provided for the increased needs of the family. They were experienced enough to work out proper financing, and by the time they moved in, four years after buying their first house, they had sold off all four other properties. By making two floor-through apartments upstairs instead of one duplex, they could take advantage of the city's tax abatement program, enabling them to live rent-free in their larger home.

The Stamms' decision to buy a city house changed their lives. It gave them an opportunity to put down roots and gain a sense of identity with the city in which they live and work. It involved them in the upgrading of a neighborhood, giving them the satisfaction of accomplishing what others call a miracle. It enabled them to live in a style normally unattainable on their modest income.

· THE STANFORTHS' STORY

In 1965 Deirdre and Jim Stanforth faced eviction from their second home in eight years. Both had been large, rambling, high-ceilinged apartments in old rent-controlled buildings on Manhattan's Upper East Side, and both became victims of the wrecker's ball. The Stanforths were unwilling to go through endless street tramping and superintendent wooing to search out another such apartment in view of the fate of the previous two, and the prospect of living in the large, antiseptic new buildings did not appeal to them even if they had not been appalled by the exorbitant rents. Jim did not rule out the suburbs, but Deirdre would not consider it. She had come to New York twenty years before because she loved it, and she was determined to live right in the midst of it, where she could avail herself of the museums, theaters, and shops whenever she had the inclination without all the advance planning of a safari.

The Stanforths had flirted with the idea of buying a house twelve years earlier, but then they found their first large, cheap, rent-controlled apartment, and the moment passed. By 1965 East Side houses had tripled in price and were out of the question, even though the Stanforths had squirreled away considerable cash. It was at this time that they heard tempting stories about the brave new pioneers who were buying houses for fantastically low prices on the West Side. This area had a frightening image to many New Yorkers because of countless news reports of crime, poverty, filth, and addiction.

They started out by "casing" the area, driving skeptically back and forth from Seventieth through Ninety-sixth streets, taking notes on each block, rating its degree of acceptability. It was obvious that some blocks were struggling to make a comeback, with a few buildings visibly cleaned up, but others resembled bombed-out Berlin. They decided to look at some houses, though it was appalling to consider pouring their life's savings into a slum.

The turning point came when they visited a renovated house and met the owners, the Robert Caigans, whose handsome town house was on Eighty-eighth Street and Central Park West. They had been the first to move into the block and were anxious to encourage more home-owners to join them. When the Stanforths saw the splendor of the Caigans' house, they were convinced. After they walked down the block with Bob Caigan telling them the status of each house and exchanging greetings with the "natives" in Spanish, the neighborhood no longer seemed so frightening.

Soon after visiting the Caigans, they found a house; not in the Urban Renewal area, but four blocks below it. However, it had an enormous advantage: It was practically within spitting distance of Central Park. To the Stanforths' East Side minds, that meant a great deal, because unlike the Stamms, they had no vision of changing the block. It was a very narrow four-story house, one of a row of four with matching brownstone façades and columned porticoes. The small front parlor had a lovely herringbone-patterned parquet floor with a two-color inlaid ribbon border, and a foot-wide plaster frieze with wreaths and crossed torches above the picture molding. The living room had un-painted wood-paneled walls and a high beamed ceiling. Unlike most brownstones, where the stairs are straight ahead as you enter, the stairway, relatively light and grace-ful with a curve at the bottom, was built on the wall op-posite the door, providing a large open foyer. This kind of architectural detail was one of the attractions old houses had for the Stanforths.

Although they liked the house when they first saw it, they felt no sense of urgency until a few days later, when the broker said it was sold. Then (oh, the perversity of human nature) they knew they wanted it. It seemed exactly the right house, and the opportunity was lost. But within a week the broker called to say that the new owner was a rival speculator, and he offered to act as agent if they wanted to buy it from his competitor.

After another visit it was agreed that the house was indeed worth negotiating for. The price was almost the lowest they had ever heard of for a Manhattan house. Not long before, another real estate broker had called such a price "impossible."

The broker performed a real service in negotiating the sale. When the Stanforths would have given in to anxiety and agreed to a higher price, he made them wait over a weekend until it came down. Before they signed a contract and became irrevocably involved, they went through the

Unusual location of stairway provides an exceptionally large foyer, making the narrow fifteen-foot house seem much wider than it is. Needless to say, this picture was taken after renovation.

final throes of soul searching. Jim spent several evenings sitting in the car until after midnight, watching to see what happened in the block. A doorman around the corner said they were out of their minds even to consider it; the street was a hotbed of addicts and prostitutes. The owners of two of the respectable-looking houses in the block were more encouraging. In short, the Stanforths went through a great deal of agonizing, but were convinced that the West Side was on its way back.

With their ten per cent down payment their contract to buy specified that the building be delivered vacant. With closing date set, they had three or four months to get plans ready and arrange a mortgage. The broker had offered his help in obtaining mortgages, but they felt that real estate brokers were about as trustworthy as used-car dealers, so they turned down his offer out of hand. They realized afterward that this was stupid: Brokers often expect to give this service, and there is nothing to lose by considering whatever financing they have to offer.

With the help of a friend in finance, the mortgage was obtained from a savings and loan association. Based on plans for the house, it would pay one third at closing, one third halfway through construction, and the final third on completion.

Meanwhile, work had begun with an architect, who had assured them that the renovation could be done within their budget. They had only considered a one-family house, but as there was a superfluous room on the ground floor front, it occurred to them that they could have a small efficiency apartment there.

The architect's preliminary sketches presented three plans: one for a one-family house; one with efficiency rental apartment; and a third, which provided a three-and-a-half-room duplex rental apartment, using only the one room on the ground floor plus half the cellar. This clever scheme involved digging out the rear garden to the cellar-floor level (which was three quarters underground)

Identical before and after views of garden apartment—fireplace replaces furnace.

and opening the back wall with French doors onto the garden. This plan created a thirty-foot living room and small kitchen in the cellar, with bedroom, bath, and private entrance under the stoop upstairs. The Stanforths would have access to the garden by a stairway from their kitchen, which they planned with French doors and balcony across the rear. The architect's inventiveness was impressive—the house had been thought too narrow (fifteen feet) to be income-producing, yet he had created an apartment out of nothing.

The income potential from this attractive apartment seemed too good to resist, and besides, it made the house more flexible. If they ever needed smaller quarters, they could move into the apartment and rent the house for enough to support them. It was like built-in insurance.

A contract was signed with the architect to start work immediately so that construction could begin as soon as

the house was theirs. But it was not until four months after the closing that demolition actually began. Two months after closing, plans and specifications finally went out to contractors for bids—and bidding took another two months. Actually, more time should have been taken, but knowing they faced impending eviction from their apartment, they felt they could not afford to waste another day. (It is vital to take time at this stage, because a mistake in choosing a contractor can be fatal.)

The bids came in as high as four times the amount they had set as their limit. Shocked, they sat down with the architect to cut out everything not absolutely necessary before negotiating with the two lowest bidders, whose price was merely twice what they were prepared to spend.

They chose one of the two and tried to check on him. He was far from solid financially, but at least seemed to be honest. They were on the verge of signing with him when the second contractor dropped his bid by several thousand dollars to get the job. Naïvely, they felt they had achieved a tremendous bargain.

Their worst mistake was the innocent assumption that it is always possible to make a contractor keep to the terms of the contract. By then they felt so pressed for time that they did not check the second contractor beyond calling a few of his alleged suppliers and asking the bank to investigate his corporation. They did not wait for the result, but when they got it, it simply said that no record could be found of such a corporation. A corporation with no record and no actual place of business is one to avoid. The Stanforths' contractor was operating out of the addresses where his jobs were located, with no directory listing, only an answering service for a phone number. This was indicative of nothing but trouble.

Their next mistake was due to Jim's admonition to leave the workmen alone. He told Deirdre not to get in their way and made jokes about them colliding with her when they drew back their arms to saw. She forced herself to stay away, when, in fact, she should have been on hand to supervise at every possible moment. If she had been on the premises, she would have realized the contractor was a crook. The fact that the work came out as well as it did must have been due to the architect's supervision. However, something went seriously awry in his control of the payment schedule. They had to depend on him because they no more knew when twenty-five per cent of the carpentry was done than they knew whether the plumbing and wiring were being installed correctly. The only safe way to use a contractor is always to keep the work ahead of the payments.

The demolition went very fast, but it always does. Their contractor did not stop altogether after that, but worked long enough to set them up for the *coup de grâce*. He knew they would soon be homeless, and he knew how to use that to his advantage. The job he started in June was supposed to be finished in October. Some time after that deadline, fewer and fewer men were found working on the house, until at last, one weekday afternoon, the door was found chained and no one working at all. Panic set in, with the hot breath of the eviction marshall on their necks.

They consulted the architect, who advised against firing their contractor and getting another one, saying it would cost more in time and money (in the end that proved untrue). His plan was to send the contractor (who could not be found) a registered letter threatening to fire him if he did not perform. This tactic seemed to work: He reappeared at once. He explained that he was completely broke because the extended plumbers' strike (which had paralyzed union construction in the city for months) had prevented his finishing three jobs and collecting the large sums of money he was owed. Therefore he could not meet his payroll or buy materials for their house. If the Stanforths would agree to meet those costs as they arose, he could get on with the work. The architect thought the request sounded reasonable, and in desperation they agreed.

They made out checks directly to suppliers and met the weekly payroll, subsequently found to be heavily padded. The full amount of the contract price was exhausted, and with the aid of a lawyer they extracted notes from the contractor for several thousand dollars more, to be advanced as a loan to continue the work. There was still too much work to be done for that amount to complete it; but he insisted that he had money coming in with which he would finish. He even signed an extraordinary document in which he agreed to complete a staggering list of items before they moved in the following week or pay a penalty of two hundred dollars a day. They have never been able to collect on either piece of paper.

Fortunately, working all weekend, his men managed to install the furnace, so there was heat and hot water. There was also one nearly complete bathroom and two painted bedrooms on the top floor. Otherwise the house was a shambles.

Jim insisted the house was not fit to live in and they must go to a hotel or stay with friends, but Deirdre preferred to stay on the scene watching what was happening than to go somewhere else and worry about it. At the last minute Jim gave in on the condition that they would leave most of their belongings in storage. So they flew around frantically the night before moving, labeling cartons "Storage" or "West 83rd St."

One week before Christmas they moved into the top floor of the filthy, unfinished house, and the contractor departed the same day, leaving behind a full crew of unpaid workmen. The Stanforths had no choice but to pay them and keep them on to finish the house, and that is what they did. They were nice men, of varying degrees of competence, who owed no allegiance to the contractor. The Stanforths got to know them very well indeed, as they lived with them for the next two or three months and Deirdre became their foreman.

The Stanforths met with the architect in their new "home" to plan the salvage action. He was distressed about his part in the debacle and agreed to forego part of his fee and come around daily to instruct the workmen. He fulfilled his promise, and between them they managed to finish the house.

The men arrived before eight every day including Saturdays, and the plasterer even worked Christmas and New Year's Day. If Deirdre was not up before they arrived, they would knock on the bedroom door to ask for instructions. Jim retired at night with his father-in-law's sword cane under the bed, ready to rise to his family's defense at any strange sound, because the rear of the house was virtually wide open. Deirdre was seen in nothing but paint-smeared blue jeans and sweater for months, and she often used their old car as a truck to pick up extra bags of plaster and other assorted materials. She did not have time to worry about the disreputable-looking people who lived on the block, and she was probably accepted by the Eighty-third Street inhabitants because she looked just like one of them. Meanwhile, the Stanforths attended a few block association meetings. This too was very helpful, because they were soon on a first-name basis with several forbidding-looking characters whom they otherwise would have feared to meet on the street.

They felt like refugees that Christmas. When Deirdre's mother arrived for her annual Christmas visit, she described their town house as "a disaster area."

It was bad enough camping out with no kitchen for two months, but worse by far was finding the money to meet the payroll every week. Without financial help from the family, they would have been lost. They could easily have forfeited everything if they had had to sell the house in that condition, and had nowhere to live.

Meanwhile, with ever-mounting fury, they were discovering what a thief the contractor was and how little they could do about it. They were shocked to learn that the district attorney's and attorney general's offices would do nothing at all, and the contractor who cheated them is continuing to do the same, or worse, to others.

All kinds of people began calling at their house to find him (including policemen to whom he had given a rubber check for protection). They got calls from two different banks that had given him loans on the same car! But worst of all, there were the suppliers and subcontractors he had not paid, who were threatening to put liens on the house. Not only had they already paid him what was owed these people, but it was possible that some materials had not even gone into their house: When credit is exhausted at one job, dishonest contractors often have material delivered and charged at another—then simply move it to where they need it. (This practice even has a name: "kiting.")

They cleared up the liens themselves, by proving they

Garden before and after. Flagstones were found on and under the ground and laid by the Stanforths. Most plants were donated from friends' country property—forest ferns thrive in city shade.

had paid the full contract price on the house before the claims were presented and therefore were not liable. However, this is a situation that should never arise: Receipted bills, or a waiver of liens for all labor and supplies, should be presented by the contractor before he is paid.

The Stanforths completed the work on their house within three months after they moved in, and rented their newly created apartment with no difficulty a month later. In spite of the misery it had caused them, they began to enjoy their house even before they got rid of the last workman.

They already had envious friends dropping in, one of whom bought the rooming house next door even after hearing of their disasters. They had no difficulty rounding up prospective homeowners for the improvement of the neighborhood, because people kept coming to them. And remembering what a difference the Caigans had made in

their lives, they welcomed every interested stranger. Although there were already four private houses on the block, there had been little change until their highly visible renovation. Probably the timing was right, but after that the trickle became a tidal wave. The prices of similar houses nearly tripled in three years, as approximately fifteen renovations got under way on their block alone.

Though they certainly never meant to, they became very involved in their community; through their efforts twenty-two trees were planted on the block. There is an enormous feeling of pride and accomplishment in making such a visible improvement in one's city. Another benefit, the most obvious one, is economic. Though cheated of a large sum of money, they could now sell the house at a profit. (They are bombarded with offers from real estate brokers and get much pleasure from refusing to sell at any price.) And they live in nine spacious rooms with a garden for less than the rent on most one-room apartments in the city today.

They are tremendously pleased with the informal and casual life, rather like a country town in the city. Though they originally scorned the stoop-sitters of slum neighborhoods, they find themselves indulging in the same sin occasionally, discovering it is impossible to remain there long without attracting a friendly group of gossipers. They find that people do not hesitate to drop in, something they would never have done when the Stanforths lived in an East Side apartment. As for the East Side, they scarcely ever go there any more. Aside from their delightful garden, they have the many pleasures of Central Park, including the Shakespeare Festival a couple of blocks away, where they can drop in on a free play or ballet on impulse. The Broadway theaters are a ten-minute bus ride away, and Lincoln Center is within walking distance, as are a half-dozen of the country's best museums. Though it is easy to describe the nightmare they lived through on the way to acquiring it, it is almost impossible for them to convey the pleasures of the totally different way of life in a city house.

As a renovator, one becomes part of a fraternity whose members anywhere have instant rapport. For example, one day in the midst of construction their doorbell rang, and Merle Gross introduced herself. It was obvious that the Stanforths were renovating a house, and so was she, on Seventy-seventh Street. So she came in and talked, comparing experiences. A short time later, the Grosses invited the Stanforths to a party. They must have had about a dozen couples—all of them brownstoners, all indulging in the game of one-upmanship over who had suffered the worst experience, whose house had looked the grimmest (rather like people comparing their operations). Everybody was having a delightful time. It was there that the Stanforths met the Stamms and began the friendship that led to this book.

What Kind of House Suits Your Needs?

THE HOUSE you decide to buy and how you choose to design the space inside will depend on your taste and pocketbook. But before you make the decision, you must understand your own needs and the limitations of the house you buy. First you must take stock of your family's needs and life style as well as your budget. The right house for one person may be the wrong house for another. And what is beautiful to look at may not be comfortable to live in.

What is the size of your family, and has it reached its limits? Do you need separate bedrooms for children or accommodations for overnight guests? If you have small children, you want their rooms close enough so that you can keep track of them, but at the same time you want them to be able to entertain friends without disturbing you. And what about access and storage for baby carriages and bicycles? On the other hand, children do not stay small forever, so you must plan for their future needs as well as your own. Here is a checklist of factors to consider:

1. Adequate and conveniently located baths
2. Adequate storage space
3. Privacy for every member of the family

4. Space for hobbies and family projects
5. Play space for children
6. Facilities for entertaining
7. Ease of maintenance
8. Flexibility for future growth or shrinkage of the family

Planning of baths, kitchens, and laundry equipment can make life either pleasant or difficult. A kitchen is an important personal consideration. For the family that is not food-oriented, a small kitchen can be perfectly adequate. But people who are interested in cooking and entertaining may spend a great deal of time in the kitchen and enjoy having company while they work. For them, the size and location of the kitchen and its relation to the dining space can be a vital factor in the successful planning of living areas.

Consider carefully where you want your laundry equipment. Some people want it in the cellar, others in the kitchen, and the latest trend is a preference for bedroom areas, nearest the source of dirty linens.

Most city houses involve vertical living. If you plan to live in the entire house, climbing stairs may be a problem. Be realistic about how much space you need. Most of us who have found space at a premium in city apartments are likely to be carried away, thinking we can never have too much of it. But we can. Cities are dirty: hauling cleaning equipment up several flights of stairs can be exhausting, and cleaning help may not always be available. If you do not plan to have rental apartments, select a house that is large enough for your needs, but not too large for convenient maintenance.

Though most of us tend to choose our homes on an emotional basis, because we like the staircase or the lovely marble mantel, you should think realistically about the kind of house that will work best for you. If you plan to create a whole new floor plan, do not pay a premium price for sound walls and architectural details that must be ripped out. There are plenty of houses without any— why not buy one of them and save the others for those who want to restore?

If you want to restore, you must be sure that what is in good condition is in a location where you can use it. Far too many renovators have been enthralled by marble-topped sinks and lovely paneling only to find that they must be ripped out to make a workable floor plan. If parquet floors or decorative ceilings are where a bath or kitchen must go or the position of walls must be changed, they will be destroyed in the process of renovation. When the condition of the house is wretched, with floors buckling and ceilings falling, a new floor plan is usually no more expensive than using the existing one and replacing all plaster and flooring.

Much can be done to alter the interior, but the exterior walls put limitations on what can be done inside. Although houses can sometimes be enlarged, most cities regulate the size of the house that can be put on a given lot, and getting permission to change the outside dimensions is usually not worth the effort.

The smaller the house, the more restrictions there are in terms of the number of rooms and the over-all layout. A wide house will allow you to have two rooms across either the front or rear if you wish. A deeper house allows you to use the interior space for baths and kitchens without cutting into the size of front and rear rooms. A house that is both wide and deep will accommodate on two floors the amount of space that would require three or four floors of a narrow, shallow house.

· POSSIBILITY OF RENTAL INCOME

Many people shrink from the thought of becoming landlords, of sharing their homes with tenants. However, renting part of your house has a great deal to recommend it.

In some cases it is quite possible to cover your entire monthly operating costs with rental income—to live rent-free. Of course, there are certain responsibilities and problems involved in being a landlord, but if your house is well planned and the apartments are designed to give tenants as desirable a place to live as you would want yourself, you will find that you have relatively little to do to earn that welcome extra income. In fact it can enable you to do more with your own living space than you could ordinarily afford. Whether you need or want rental income along with the amount of space you need for yourself should determine the size house you buy.

· HOW TO WORK WITH SPACE

Your budget is the main limitation on what you can do with the space inside the house. Generally speaking, the more you can use of the existing house, the less expensive the renovation. Skimping on basics such as plumbing, heating, and wiring is never wise, but it is often possible to save money by avoiding floor-plan changes. Take for example this floor plan of a two-story San Francisco Victorian house shown on the opposite page. As a private residence the house can remain essentially as it exists. Any modernization can be done within the existing plan, holding renovation costs to a minimum. However, when rental units are to be created, the floor plan must usually be altered. The amount of alteration will depend on the number of apartments being created.

The simplest conversion is the creation of a two-family house. A house with a high stoop makes an ideal two-family house because there are already two separate entrances, one under the stoop and another at the top of the stoop. The house merely has to be divided at the appropriate place to separate the two apartments. One apartment can be made on the ground floor by closing off or

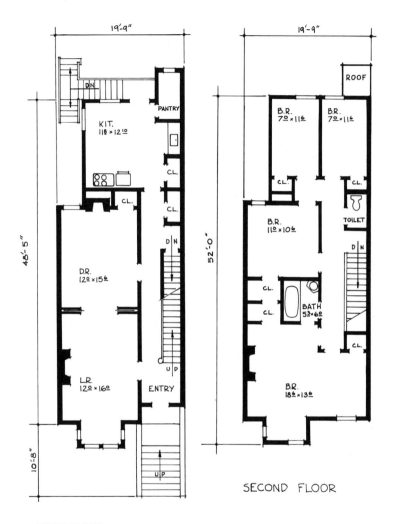

FIRST FLOOR

SECOND FLOOR

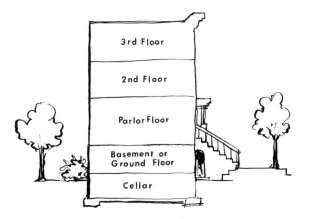

Cross section of typical high-stooped house.

removing the interior stair between the ground floor and
the one above, leaving the remainder of the house as a
second apartment. Should access to the garden be required
for the upper apartment, an exterior stairway can be
added at the rear of the building. The only interior change
necessary to complete the conversion is the addition of
kitchens and baths for both apartments.

If the house has more than two stories, a duplex (two-
story) apartment can be created on the lower two floors.
This is easily accomplished in a high-stooped house where
the staircase is in the right location. The main staircase
can be used as an interior stairway for the duplex by erect-
ing a partition beside the stair on the parlor floor to divide
the lower and upper apartments. If the house has three
stories, the lower two floors would become a duplex apartment, and the third floor would be a single floor-through
apartment. In a four-story house, two duplexes could be
created, and in the case of a five-story house, there would
be a lower duplex and upper triplex (three-story apartment).

In four- and five-story houses, many different combina-
tions are possible. Instead of two duplexes, or a duplex and

Circular iron stairway in this Park Slope, Brooklyn, garden shows how parlor floor may have access to garden when ground floor is rented as an apartment.

a triplex, you can have a duplex and two or three floor-through apartments or several studio (one-room) apartments. Though there is more income potential from two smaller apartments than one large one, there is likely to be more turnover in tenants, and the initial investment will be greater in terms of additional kitchens and baths and the necessary alteration of existing floor plans.

Since the upper floors of most houses were originally

bedrooms,* it is usually fairly easy to create a duplex or triplex on the upper floors. The pages following show the original plan (page 179) of the top two floors of a four-story house and the plans for two different renovations. Renovation Plan 1 (page 180) shows a simple conversion into a duplex. Renovation Plan 2 (page 181) shows the same two floors made into two floor-through apartments. As you can see, the duplex renovation required far less wall change and was therefore relatively inexpensive. The floor-through apartments cost substantially more.

However, floor-through apartments and studios can be created without gutting by clever use of existing space provided that the condition of most walls, ceilings, and floors is good. If all ceilings and walls must be replaced, it will cost very little more to remove the studs and put up new partitions.

City regulations sometimes limit the number of dwelling units permissible in a building. Be sure to find out before you buy the house whether your plans for it are feasible.

If you plan to create rental apartments, you must weigh the pros and cons of lower versus upper for location of your own living quarters. The lower floors would seem to have every advantage—a minimum of stairs to climb and access to garden and cellar. But there are disadvantages. The lower floors are much darker, and ground floor ceilings in many houses are low. If the house has a high stoop, floor space required for halls across the front on the first and second floors must be subtracted from the lower apartment. Many houses have rear extensions that provide additional space: some are only one or two stories, while others go up the entire height of the house.

---

* When these houses were built, families had more children and several live-in servants. Since most of us no longer have a dozen offspring, and electrical appliances have greatly reduced the need for servants, the average nineteenth-century house is larger than a single twentieth-century family needs.

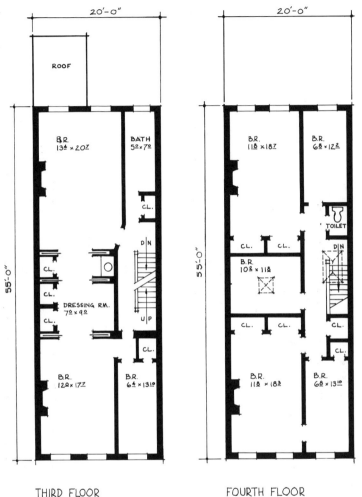

THIRD FLOOR   FOURTH FLOOR

Original Floor Plan
Victorian houses were often built in groups whose interior layouts
were identical though façades might vary. Here are the original
floor plans of the upper stories of a group of 1889 Manhattan brown-
stones. These plans were altered in two of the houses to create
the apartments shown on the following pages.

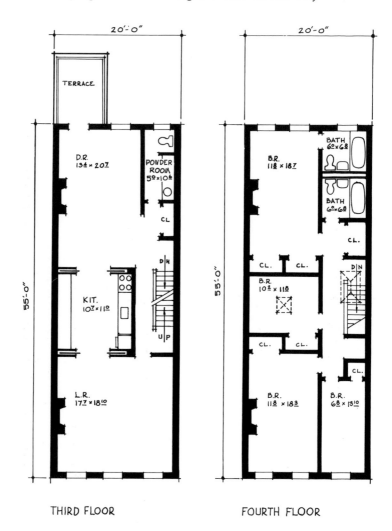

THIRD FLOOR   FOURTH FLOOR

Renovation Plan 1 (one apartment)
By knocking out a few walls on the third floor, combining two
dressing rooms to make a kitchen, and dividing a bedroom on the
fourth floor to create two baths, these two floors became a spacious
duplex apartment for a family with two active boys.

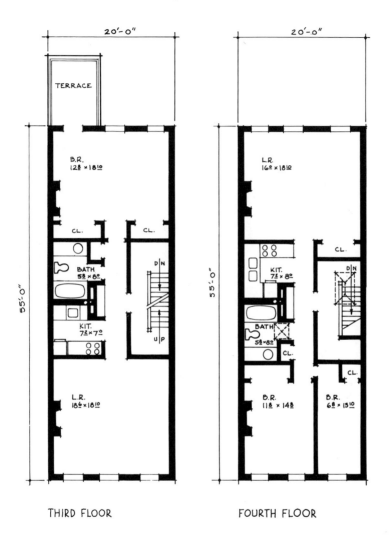

THIRD FLOOR

FOURTH FLOOR

Renovation Plan 2 (two apartments)
An almost total gutting was required to create two floor-through
apartments. Only the two bedrooms on the fourth floor remained
intact.

A rabbit warren of partitions and a large bathroom were removed to give a light, open feeling to the Stanforths' ground-floor kitchen. Ceiling height: eight feet, width: fourteen feet.

The upper floors have an abundance of light and lose no space across the front for hallways. If there is a rear extension that does not extend to the full height of the building, its roof can become a terrace for the upper apartment; or a large roof garden can be created on top of the house if the roof is flat.

Imagination can convert drawbacks into assets. Removing all unnecessary partitions can increase the flow of light, making low ceilings appear higher. Properly scaled furniture makes a small room seem larger.

There is no such thing as a perfect house: there are spatial and financial limitations, as well as those imposed by city regulations. The most successful houses are those whose renovators have recognized the limitations, creating an environment that works for them within that framework.

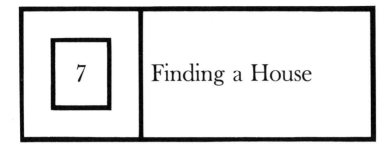

7 | Finding a House

THERE IS NO right or wrong way to find a house; some people buy the first or second house they see, and others have to look for a year or more. Buying a house depends in part on your frame of mind—your willingness to make the commitment—partly on your diligence, and sometimes on just plain luck.

Driving around your city is a good way to become acquainted with various neighborhoods you may never have considered. Wherever there are old houses, there is a potential for renovation. If a neighborhood interests you, get out of the car and walk around. (You may even spot a "For Sale" sign.) Do not be afraid to talk to people and ask questions. You can even ring the doorbell of a house that has obviously been renovated. A renovator is usually friendly and eager to have others follow his example—and he may know of nearby houses for sale.

If a house appeals to you from the outside, try contacting the owner to see if he wants to sell. His name and address are listed under the property address in tax assessment books open to the public at the tax assessor's office. This is a long shot, but worth the try.

You may even find a house by accident—like the Brooklyn couple who rang the wrong bell by mistake and found themselves talking to a family who had just decided to sell. They went through the house and liked it; the price was the lowest they had found in that neighborhood, and they agreed to buy on the spot.

But the obvious place to look for a house is in the classified section of the newspaper, where owners and real estate brokers advertise properties for sale.

· REAL ESTATE BROKERS

Real estate brokers must be licensed in the state in which they operate. Each person who acts as an agent for real estate (for management, renting, or selling) must have a license, either as a broker or as a salesman employed by a licensed broker.

A real estate broker (or agent) has one big advantage to offer the home buyer: He has listings for property that owners want to sell. It is far easier to find a house through a broker or his advertisement in the paper than trying to contact the owners directly.

Many people do not like the idea of using a broker because he receives a commission for his service which, although paid by the seller, is obviously included in the price of the house in most cases. However, if the broker finds you the right house, he will have provided a valuable service, and you should not begrudge him his fee. Can you imagine how difficult it would be to buy and sell property if there were no real estate brokers?

The broker acts as a third party between the buyer and seller, and his abilities as a negotiator are important. The broker is obviously interested in getting the highest possible price, because his commission (usually 5–6%) is based on the sale price; but more importantly, he is interested in making the sale and will negotiate on your behalf in order to consummate an agreement.

In buying through a broker, you can avoid contact with the owner, perhaps preventing embarrassing moments as well as saving money. Most of us are not good bargainers, and we often find it difficult to ask an owner to lower his price or take less cash. And in buying an old city house you could be dealing with an absentee landlord whom you may find offensive. If you should happen not to like the broker, grin and bear it—you are buying a house, not a real estate broker.

The renovation movement has given birth to a new breed of real estate brokers who live in the community in which they sell and have a stake in its development; in many cases, these are renovators turned brokers. They understand the problems of buying a house for renovation and go out of their way to be of assistance. Brokers of this kind take a sincere interest in helping you find the right house at a price you can realistically afford, and will bargain on your behalf as much as on the seller's. They will also often be helpful in advising about financing and the problems of renovation.

To get the most out of a broker or any professional, you must understand how to use him. Tell him exactly what your needs are and what you can afford. And do not waste his time. Too many people spend Sunday afternoons looking at houses they have no intention of buying.

House hunting can have many frustrations. The nonserious house hunters who waste the time of real estate brokers have a counterpart who can be a hazard to house hunters without a broker: the lonely aged who advertise their houses for sale in order to have visitors. There is an elderly doctor on the Upper West Side of Manhattan who offers his handsome house from time to time at a tempting price. After many frustrating visits, the prospective buyer

City house hunters must have the imagination to see the potential underneath the neglect, abuse, and additions that violate the original design. This derelict was restored to a charming brick colonial in Philadelphia's Society Hill.

eventually realizes he has no intention of selling. There is also a little old lady in Brooklyn who has lived in her house since she was a bride. She has nineteen cats, and one of the conditions of sale that she imposes on those eager buyers who answer her advertisement is that they find happy homes for the cats. She manages to get months of visits from prospective buyers before it finally becomes apparent that she is not going to sell her house.

A real estate broker may insist on showing you countless houses that are not what you are looking for. If this happens to you, tell him what you do not like about the houses and what you want instead. If he persists, find another broker. But you must be realistic about what you expect for your money. If you expect to find an elegant town house for the price of a run-down rooming house, brokers will avoid you like the plague.

The more brokers you deal with, the more you will learn. Many houses will be listed with more than one broker because the seller wants to reach as many prospective buyers as possible. On the other hand, some houses are listed exclusively with one broker and can be purchased only through him. Limiting yourself to one broker may prevent you from seeing a property that fits your needs.

Do not be too upset if you catch a broker in a misstatement of fact. Much of the information he gives you was given to him by the seller, and very few brokers have time to check all the data on each property listed with them. Also, many brokers feel that they will lose a sale if they admit that they do not know the answer to a question, and will take a stab at an answer. In every case, *let the buyer beware*—whether he is dealing with a broker or an owner—and check all critical information before agreeing to buy.

In working with a broker, be firm and straightforward at all times. Do not let him, or the seller, pressure you into a hasty decision by talk of another party who is interested in the property. It is far better to lose a good house than to buy and be sorry. And absolutely *do not sign anything until you consult a lawyer.*

Asking for a small deposit (sometimes called "earnest money") as a *binder* on a particular property in which the buyer has serious interest is common practice with real estate brokers. This deposit is made before negotiation for purchase is begun in earnest, and is sometimes accompanied by the signing of an agreement. This practice is a means of determining the intent of the buyer and is proof to the seller of serious interest.

It is advisable to discuss earnest money binders with your lawyer in advance so that you will understand the local practice and how to handle the situation when and if you are faced with it.

Earnest money should have no meaning other than to prove your intent to enter into serious negotiations for purchase, so be sure this is made perfectly clear to the broker when the deposit is made—and make certain the money will be returned if no sale agreement is reached. Make a notation on your check that it is earnest money. And never give a deposit to an unlicensed broker; if you do, you can probably kiss the money good-bye. If you are asked to sign anything, be sure you read every word—and it is best to have your lawyer read it first. If what you are asked to sign is unclear, do not sign it. It's better to be safe than sorry.

Besides selling you a house, real estate brokers may be able to offer help in obtaining financing and insurance. Since many sales are conditional on a new mortgage, brokers develop business relationships with lenders. Do not rely on a broker to get you a mortgage, but do not refuse his help if he offers it. In many cities, real estate brokers double as insurance agents. They can give you information about kinds and cost of insurance and write a policy for you if you wish.

Mark and Walter Lowrey's perceptiveness made possible this incredible transformation of a New Orleans French Quarter ruin.

· PROPERTY AUCTIONS

Property is auctioned for various reasons, one of which is a foreclosure sale brought about by the owner's failure to make mortgage payments or pay real estate taxes. A foreclosure sale may have complex legal problems because of the debts the property has incurred. And purchase at auction by a novice under any circumstances has potential dangers.

If you are interested in a property auction, discuss it with your lawyer so that you will understand all the problems involved. Property auctions can offer good opportunities to those who know what they are looking for. One young Philadelphia couple was able to buy a small three-story house at a sheriff's sale for $1,200 as recently as 1969.

Property auctions are advertised, usually a week or more in advance. Advertisements appear in legal and real estate publications as well as in local newspapers. A lawyer or real estate broker should be able to tell you where to find these advertisements.

In addition to foreclosures, cities sometimes have Urban Renewal property that they have purchased for resale to people who will renovate it. Renovators in New York, Boston, and New Haven have taken advantage of such city sales to buy houses below market prices. Property sold by the city in Urban Renewal projects is not truly auctioned because the price is set in advance; but buyers must submit an application for the property by a specified date, and the buyer is often selected on the basis of a priority system established by the city. Such properties are usually advertised for sale under an auction notice, but the wording is often so complex that most renovators would not recognize them as being of interest. However, your city's redevelopment agency or local Urban Renewal project office will be able to give you the specifics, such as what properties they will sell, when they will be sold, and how to apply for purchase.

A few words of warning before you begin the search for a house. The real estate business has its share of unscrupulous people. Owners and brokers have been known to deliberately lie about facts, causing unsuspecting buyers untold hardships. Then there are speculators who take advantage of inexperienced buyers by selling them houses at greatly inflated prices. There is no better protection against them than knowledge.

8

Is It a Good Buy and Can You Afford It?

BEFORE LOOKING at a single piece of property, you should make a thorough analysis of your own finances. The two most important questions to ask are:

1. How much cash do you have?
2. How much can you afford to pay each month for your living quarters (henceforth called rent)?

The amount of cash you have will determine the amount of financing you will need, and the amount of rent you can pay (along with rental income if there is any) will determine whether you can pay to operate the house. You may be able to purchase and operate the house as it exists when you buy it, but if you cannot pay for the necessary renovation or meet the expenses of the house after it is finished, you are in real trouble.

People usually know whether they like a house or not, but most do not understand how to evaluate anything beyond the purchase price. Any house you plan to buy must be evaluated in terms of your own needs and ability to pay for it. A house should be a pleasure, not a financial burden. Renovation should be a creative adventure, not a nightmare. Knowing your financial limitations and the realities of purchase and renovation can bring you the rewards of a successful accomplishment and a sound investment.

Following is a list of factors to take into account when evaluating what you can afford:

1. The price of the house
2. The cost of construction
3. The cost of professional services (lawyer, architect, etc.)
4. The cost of carrying the house while work is being done
5. How the purchase and renovation will be paid for
6. The cost of operating the house when it is completed

Far too many people think that a low purchase price means a bargain. However, the purchase price must be assessed in light of the finished cost of the house, because the finished cost will determine whether the house is a good investment for you.

As an example, take two houses of the same size—one priced at $10,000 and the other at $30,000. To the novice, the $10,000 would seem like the better buy. But if the $10,000 house costs $40,000 to renovate, is it still a bargain? If the $30,000 house will cost $10,000 to renovate, it will be a better buy than the cheaper one.

The cost of renovation is not limited to the price paid for the work. The cost of professional services, carrying costs (operating costs of the house while work is being done), and other expenses must be added to renovation costs to determine the cost of the finished house.

You must also consider how the renovation will be paid for. Financing must be obtained for the difference between the final cost of the property and the amount of cash you have. The availability of financing can also make a more expensive house a better buy than a cheaper one.

Lastly, you must estimate the operating costs of the

house to determine whether you can afford to live in it. On a private house, the rent you can pay must cover all operating costs. If the house has rental apartments, the money you receive from them will help pay operating costs. If you are particularly astute in the house you buy and the renovation you plan, it is possible for rental income from tenants to pay all operating costs, allowing you to live rent-free.

All of these items will be discussed in detail later in this chapter, with forms given for calculating the costs of buying, renovating, and operating a house. However, before you even look at houses, it is possible for you to do some rough calculations of what you can afford.

Start your evaluation with the cost of operating the finished house. The operating costs that you will have to pay are as follows:

1. Mortgage payments
2. Water and sewer charges
3. Heat
4. Utilities
5. Insurance
6. Maintenance and repairs

· How to Calculate Monthly Mortgage Payments

Mortgage payments are usually the largest single operating cost. To calculate the monthly payment on a given mortgage, you must know the interest rate and term. (The prevailing interest rate can be obtained by calling your bank and the term is the number of years you have to repay the mortgage debt.) Because interest is compounded, you cannot simply add 1% to the monthly payment on a 6% mortgage to find out what the payment would be if the interest rate were 7%.

If the mortgage is self-amortizing with equal monthly payments (as most bank mortgages are), you can use the table below to calculate the constant payment on mortgages with terms of 10, 15, 20, 25, and 30 years which have interest rates of 6%, 7%, 8%, 9%, and 10%.

This table expresses the constant annual payment as a percentage of the original amount of the mortgage. Thus a 10-year mortgage at 6% interest would have an annual constant payment of 13.33% of the original amount of the mortgage, whereas the same mortgage at 7% interest would have an annual constant payment of 13.94%.

To calculate the annual payment on any mortgage, take the appropriate percentage from the table and multiply the amount of the mortgage by that figure. Divide by 12 to get the monthly payment.

Constant Annual Percentage Table

Interest Rate	10 years	15 years	20 years	25 years	30 years
6%	13.33%	10.13%	8.60%	7.74%	7.20%
7%	13.94%	10.79%	9.31%	8.49%	7.99%
8%	14.56%	11.47%	10.04%	9.27%	8.81%
9%	15.21%	12.18%	10.80%	10.08%	9.66%
10%	15.86%	12.90%	11.59%	10.91%	10.54%

Until you have a specific property in mind you will have to make some assumptions on operating costs other than mortgage payments.

Let us assume that you have a $10,000 income and can afford to pay 25% of it in rent—that gives you $2,500 a year to operate a house.

Let us further assume that annual operating costs other than mortgage payments will run as follows:

Real estate taxes:	$300	Utilities:	$150
Water and sewer:	$150	Insurance:	$200
Heat:	$300	Maintenance:	$300

These costs add up to $1,400 a year. Subtract this from the $2,500 you have allotted for operating costs, and you will have the amount left with which to make mortgage payments on a private house—$1,100. What kind of mortgage can you carrry for this amount of money?

Assume that the prevailing interest rate is 6% and that 20-year mortgages are available. The Constant Annual Percentage Table on page 197 shows that annual payments on such a mortgage are 8.60% of the original amount of the mortgage. Your $1,100 represents 8.60% of the amount of the mortgage you can carry.

To calculate the amount of the mortgage that a given dollar amount will carry, you divide that amount by the appropriate constant annual percentage.

In the illustration given above, $1,100 ÷ .086 = $12,744, which is the amount of the mortgage you can afford.

To determine the price of the house you can afford, add the amount of cash you have to the amount of the mortgage. If you have $5,000 in cash, you could afford a private house worth $17,744 in the above illustration ($12,744 in mortgaging plus $5,000 in cash).

Assume that this house could accommodate your space requirements and still leave room for a rental apartment. Your rent would then be reduced by the amount of rental income you receive from the tenant. If you were able to get $200 a month in rent, it would cost you only $100 a year to live in the house.

If you want a more expensive house, rental income will enable you to have it. Assuming that you have the same $5,000 and can pay the same $2,500 in rent, what price house could you afford if you had rental income of $200 a month?

Using the same operating costs, exclusive of mortgage payments, as before, you will have $3,500 a year for mortgage payments ($1,100 of your rent and $2,400 in rent from your tenant). At 6% interest for 20 years, this will pay for a mortgage of $40,697 ($3,500 ÷ .086 = $40,697).

You can now afford a house worth $45,697 ($40,697 in mortgaging plus $5,000 in cash). Thus rental income of $200 a month more than doubles the price of the house you can afford.

Using the procedure explained in the above example, you can determine what price house you can afford under various circumstances. You can determine the effect of varying terms, interest rates, and rental incomes. The knowledge thus gained will help you determine what you should be seeking when you begin looking for a house to purchase. Although these calculations are based on many assumptions, they are nonetheless valid because they give you a rough idea of what you can afford.

But remember, just because you can afford to carry a large mortgage does not mean that a bank will be willing to give it to you. Chapter 9 gives you information about various kinds of financing. Keep this information in mind when you begin looking at houses. And be sure to do a thorough financial evaluation of any house before you buy it.

• PRICES ARE RELATIVE

Prices are indeed relative. A price that may be low in one city may seem high in another. And rental income can make an expensive house inexpensive to live in. We have purposely avoided using prices whenever possible because they vary so widely and because yesterday's high price may sound like a bargain tomorrow.

The price of the finished house is important to you, but the price must be judged and evaluated in terms of your ability to pay for it—i.e., how much cash you must invest and how much it will cost you to live in the house. If a house meets your financial requirements and gives you the amount of space you need, it is a good investment.

Generally speaking, the house with a low cash investment and low rent to the owner-occupant is the best investment. This means that you can realize maximum property appreciation either through selling or refinancing without pricing yourself out of the real estate market.

Although few people contemplate selling a house when they buy it, you should think about resale when choosing a house and planning the renovation, because five years from now you may be offered a better job in another city or for some other reason want to move. Your buyer will be just as concerned as you are about how much cash he will need to purchase and how much it will cost him to live in the house he buys. Low operating cost to the owner will make the house attractive to a large number of people —and if your cash investment was low and the mortgaging long-term, you can make a profitable sale without requiring an unreasonably high cash payment from your buyer.

The following are actual operating statements on renovated houses in different cities. They are given to show you how prices vary and how much it costs these renovators to live in their houses. If you study them carefully, you will see that prices are indeed relative and that each of these owners has a large amount of space for a limited cash investment, living at reasonable rent regardless of the total price of the house. In addition to all of these benefits, there are tax advantages in home ownership. See Appendix, page 389, for a discussion of tax advantages.

· *Boston, Massachusetts.* A young city planner whose income was $8,000 a year bought a five-story row house for $12,000. Using a general contractor and doing the finishing himself, he created a rental duplex on the upper two floors and a triplex for himself on the lower three floors. Following are the particulars:

Size of house: $17\frac{1}{2}'$ x 30'

Description of owner's apartment: two-story living room, dining room, kitchen, study, two bedrooms, two baths

Total cost of property: $33,000

Cash investment: $8,000

Operating expenses:

Mortgage payments:	$2,200
Real estate taxes:	850
Water and sewer:	50
Heat:	400
Utilities:	240
Insurance:	150
	$3,890
Less rental income:	3,000
	$ 890 per year, or $74 per month

· *Washington, D.C.* A lawyer and his wife whose income was $12,000 a year purchased a two-story house for $20,000. They moved into the house and did the renovation over a four-year period, doing some of the work themselves. The owners occupy the whole house themselves, with their 2,000 square feet of floor space giving them a double living room, dining room, kitchen, four bedrooms, and one and a half baths.

Total cost of property: $29,500

Cash investment: $15,500

Operating expenses:

Mortgage payments:	$1,350
Real estate taxes:	450
Water and sewer:	35
Heat:	335
Utilities:	240
Insurance:	30
	$2,440 per year, or $200 per month

• *Savannah, Georgia.* A young salesman with a wife and small daughter bought a three-story house for $4,000. The renovation took two years, with the rental unit completed by the end of the first year. This couple used contractors for all the work and did not move in until their apartment was completed.

Size of house: 20′ x 45′

Description of owner's apartment: living room, dining room, kitchen, three bedrooms, two baths

Total cost of property: $35,000

Cash investment: $9,000

Operating expenses:

Mortgage payments:	$2,520
Real estate taxes:	315
Water and sewer:	65
Heat:	150
Utilities:	270
Insurance:	172
	$3,492
Less rental income:	1,500
	$1,992 per year, or $166 per month

• *Chicago, Illinois.* A young Chicago executive purchased a two-and-a-half-story Chicago "cottage" for $16,000. Living in the house from the time of purchase, supervising contractors and doing some of the work himself, he created a two-family house.

Size of house: 25′ x 50′

Description of owner's apartment: living room, dining room, kitchen, two bedrooms, family room, and bath

Total cost of property: $25,000

Cash investment: $13,000

Operating expenses:

Mortgage payments:	$1,584
Real estate taxes:	
($280 included in mortgage)	—
Water and sewer:	50
Heat:	400
Utilities:	400
Insurance:	
(included in mortgage)	—
	$2,434
Less rental income:	2,400
	$ 34 per year, or rent-free

· EVALUATING A SPECIFIC HOUSE

When you have found a house you like, do not agree to buy it until you have evaluated the property. Following is the basic information you need for this purpose:

1. Address of the property
2. Name and address of the owner
3. Width and depth of the lot
4. Width and depth of the house
5. Number of stories, excluding cellar
6. Whether there is a cellar
7. The current use of the building and its legal classification (private house, multiple dwelling, rooming house)
8. Whether the house is to be purchased with or without tenants
9. If purchased with tenants, the rental for each unit
10. The type of heat (steam, hot water, forced air) and the type of fuel (gas, oil, coal)
11. The current tax assessment, divided into land and total assessment where applicable
12. The current tax rate
13. The water and sewer charges
14. The amount and kind of insurance on the property, and its cost
15. The existing mortgages on the property—the principal owed, date due, whether they are self-amortizing and if not the amount of the balloon payment, the interest rate, the amount and date of payments, conditions of prepayment, and if there is a subordination clause
16. The asking price and cash required to purchase
17. The amount and terms of any mortgage the owner plans to give (take back)

Insist that the broker or owner provide all this information before serious negotiations are started.

The asking price of the property should be assessed in terms of the market value of other houses in the area. This can be done by looking at other houses for sale, by talking to owners in the neighborhood, or by checking past sales at the city recording office. Remember that prices differ from area to area. What may seem absurdly low to the inexperienced buyer may in truth be a high price for the neighborhood. This is not to say that you should never buy when the price of the house is inflated. If the cost of the finished house makes sense, it does not hurt to pay a premium price for the property, particularly if the house cannot be purchased otherwise. However, a buyer armed with information about neighborhood prices can often bargain more successfully. It is upsetting to learn after the house has been purchased that it could have been bought for less money. No one likes to be a sucker.

Before you go any farther, do not fail to check the zoning regulations to make sure the house can be used for your intended purpose.

Tana and Eddie Galob owned a building in downtown Philadelphia that had been a bakery. They had an architect draw up exciting plans to convert it to a home only to learn that the zoning laws would not allow anything remotely approaching what they had in mind. They sold the bakery and bought a brownstone instead.

Hugh Patrick Feely, executive director of Chicago's Lincoln Park Conservation Association, says that his office constantly receives calls for help from people who have bought property only to find that zoning prevents them from doing what they had in mind. "If only they'd check zoning before they buy," says Feely. "I don't know what they think we can do to help them afterwards."

Another word of warning: Do not buy a house just because it seems to be a bargain. The Lee Murphys bought a New York brownstone primarily because of its bargain price. However, unlike most Manhattan houses, it had no cellar. The furnace was located in the front of the ground floor—space needed for their apartment. The Murphys planned to dig a partial cellar to house the heating equipment. They soon discovered why the house had no cellar; it was built on solid ledge rock. Abandoning the risky idea of blasting under the foundation, they finally got special permission for an addition on the rear of the house for the heating plant, thereby sacrificing half of their small garden. They are pleased with the results, but there is little doubt that the Murphys spent more than it would have cost to buy a house with a cellar in the first place.

· INSPECTING THE HOUSE

Do not take the word of either broker or owner concerning the condition of the house. They are interested in selling the property and have no obligation to point out its defects. The house should be checked first by you and then by someone technically qualified to evaluate its condition. Here are the things you can check for yourself:

1. Is there water in the cellar or signs of a water problem there? A wet cellar can be difficult to remedy, can prevent the use of the area for storage, and can lower the value of the renovated house.
2. If you plan to keep the existing plumbing, check to see that water lines are brass or copper. The water lines are the small pipes that run along the ceiling in the cellar and are often exposed in the bathrooms of old houses. Use a magnet and ice pick (or other sharp instrument) to determine the kind of pipe. A magnet will adhere to galvanized iron pipe but not to lead, brass, or copper; lead is soft and will dent and scratch easily when probed with an ice pick. Also be sure to check water pressure by turning on all faucets full force, leaving them on below while trying the ones on the top floor. (See pages 266–76 for a complete discussion of plumbing.)

3. How sturdy is the staircase? Does it sag badly? Although stairs can be jacked up to make them level, beware of a staircase with excessive sag, because severe sag indicates structural problems associated with settling. Jump on the stairs to determine how solid they are.
4. Are there signs of recent water damage from a leaky roof or around windows or on exterior walls?
5. Are floors fairly level? Place a marble on the floors and see if it rolls.
6. Check the general condition of floors and ceilings. This is important only if you plan to salvage them.
7. Are the windows in good condition? Open and close each one if necessary.
8. Check the wiring. How many outlets in each room? Are overhead lights operated by switches or pull-chains? Ask to see the fuse box. Are there ample fuses in addition to adequate main service for the size of the house? If there are few outlets, pull-chains, and an inadequate number of fuses, you can assume that you will have substantial wiring to do. (See pages 276–88 for a complete discussion of wiring.)

If you still want to buy the house after inspecting it yourself, call in an expert to check it further. Most older houses do not have serious structural problems, but why take a chance? It is quite a shock to the renovator who has bought a house thinking that it only requires modernizing kitchen and baths to discover that the plumbing is worthless and the foundations are crumbling.

Occasionally real estate brokers or owners are unhappy when you suggest having the house professionally inspected. Do not let this reluctance deter you. The commitment you make when buying a house is not to be taken lightly. You should know what you are buying because you cannot take it back and demand a new one when you discover a defect later.

A professional inspection of the house can be done by a home inspection service, a licensed professional engineer, a reputable contractor, or an architect who is knowledgeable about the structure and mechanical systems. Inspection cost is nominal (usually under a hundred dollars), and it provides invaluable information. If it prevents you from buying a house that could be a disaster to your budget, the money has been well spent. If the inspection turns up no serious problems, you will be reassured in knowing what you are buying.

Home inspection services and professional engineers are usually listed in the Yellow Pages. The service they provide is generally the same: a complete inspection of the house from top to bottom, with a written report of the conditions found. However, your professional inspector should be familiar with old houses, and if he is to do the proper job, you must tell him what you plan to do with the house. For instance, if you plan to relocate all the plumbing, he will only need to check the pipes in the cellar and the main water and sewer connections. He should thoroughly inspect the heating system, the foundations and exterior walls, the roof, leaders, and gutters, the stairs, and the beams. The plumbing and wiring are important only if you plan to reuse them. It is a good idea to accompany him on his inspection to see that he does a thorough job, but do not get in his way. You will also learn a great deal that may be of value to you later.

Most professional inspectors use a standard checklist form as the basis of their report. This form lists every aspect of the house with a rating (excellent, good, and so on) to be checked by the inspector. Some inspectors use only this standard form for their report, and others supplement the form with a written report of their own. Sometimes the report will give suggestions for remedial work and may include estimates for the cost of this work. As with everything else, you should check on the estimates given. Inspection reports are usually received three days to a week after the inspection is made. If you should need the report sooner, so stipulate when you hire the professional. If you use an architect or contractor to make the inspection, ask him for a written report and pay him for the job so you are under no obligation to him.

Although the kind of report issued will vary in detail, every report will provide valuable information about the condition of the house. An evaluation by an expert is essential if you are to know how much work must be done. His written report will also give you an advantage when negotiating the purchase: Being aware of flaws will put you in the best bargaining position.

If you are satisfied with the condition of the house, you should then estimate the cost of renovating and operating to see if you can afford to buy it.

· ESTIMATING RENOVATION COSTS

If you are satisfied with the condition of the property, it is time to think about the feasibility of renovating it. Without plans and specifications for the renovation, the best that even an expert could do is a "guess-timate" of construction costs. You could talk to an architect or contractor about the house and ask him what he thinks your job should cost. Renovation costs are often calculated on a price-per-square-foot basis and sometimes, when house sizes are fairly standard, on a cost-per-floor basis. Renovation costs can vary widely, even within the same city. Prices in Brooklyn run substantially below those charged in Manhattan, and as neighborhoods become more affluent, prices will often rise far in excess of increased costs.

If you have friends who have done renovations, ask them about the cost of their jobs and compare their scope to the one you are planning. A call to a plumber, electrician, or other craftsman may give you rough prices of specific costs, and a visit to appliance dealers and lumber yards will acquaint you with prices of appliances and fixtures. Add 10–15% for contingencies to estimates in order to be realistic.

There are costs other than construction that must be included when figuring the cost of the finished house. Since lawyers are necessary when purchasing property and are often used for legal assistance in financing and other areas related to the house, their fee is part of the cost of the property. The same is true of architects, home inspection services, and closing cost of purchase and refinancing.

Carrying costs are seldom considered by renovators, and yet if the owner is not living in the house while the work is being done, he will have to pay to operate the house as well as the place where he is actually living. The longer the renovation takes, the higher the carrying costs. Carrying costs on a vacant house consist of the following:

1. Mortgage payments
2. Real estate taxes
3. Water and sewer charges
4. Electricity (needed for construction)
5. Heat (must be provided in winter to keep pipes from bursting)
6. Insurance

When the owner does not move in until the renovation is complete, it is not unusual for a year to elapse before the house is occupied: six months for planning and obtaining necessary financing, six months for construction. In such cases, carrying costs can be substantial.

The following form shows what items to include in estimating the cost of completing a house:

PURCHASE AND RENOVATION SUMMARY FORM

Costs:

Purchase price of property:	$_____
Professional inspection fee:	$_____
Legal fees (purchase and refinancing):	$_____
Architectural fees:	$_____
Construction costs:	$_____
Contingency on construction:	$_____
Carrying costs (if not living in the house during construction):	$_____
Financing costs (points, mortgage broker's fee, etc.):	$_____
Closing costs (purchase and refinancing):	$_____
Tenant relocation costs:	$_____
Total Cost of the House:	$_____
Less owner's cash:	$_____
Amount of Financing Needed:	$_____

The Purchase and Renovation Summary Form is used to determine the cost of the finished house and the amount of financing the owner must obtain.

Financing costs (mortgage broker's fee, points, or discount on the mortgage) may be deducted from the amount of the mortgage and not paid directly by the owner. However, these costs will affect the amount of cash an owner must have. If the owner obtains a new mortgage of $20,000 from which $1,000 is deducted for financing costs, he will receive only $19,000. If he needed $20,000 in financing to accomplish the purchase and renovation, he will have to come up with an additional $1,000 in cash.

Not all of the costs listed are applicable to every renovation project. If the house is purchased vacant, there will be no tenant relocation costs. If you do not use an architect, there will obviously be no architectural fees. However, if the new financing is not obtained at the time of purchase, there will be additional legal fees and closing costs at the time of refinancing.

When estimating the cost of construction, be sure to add something for contingencies to be safe. If you are able to hold construction costs to your original estimate (a rare occurrence in renovations), you can use the contingency allowance for new furniture. On the other hand, it could prove a financial disaster to have construction costs come in well above estimates, so be prepared for this eventuality by not making construction estimates too low.

When all the costs of the renovated house have been totaled, subtract the amount of cash you have to determine the amount of financing needed to complete the project. You must then find out whether necessary financing is available. (If a bank will not give you a large enough mortgage, you will have to look to the seller or elsewhere for additional financing. See Chapter 9 for a complete discussion of financing.)

· ESTIMATING OPERATING COSTS
ON THE FINISHED HOUSE

Once you have estimated the price of the finished house, you must determine whether you can afford to live in it. Use the following form to estimate operating costs and the amount of rent you will have to pay:

INCOME AND OPERATING SUMMARY FORM

Operating Costs:	Annually
Mortgage payments	
1st mortgage:	$_____
2nd mortgage:	$_____
Real estate taxes:	$_____
Water and sewer:	$_____
Heat:	$_____
Insurance:	$_____
Utilities:	$_____
Maintenance and repairs:	$_____
Total Operating Costs (including amortization):	$_____
Less rental income:	$_____
Cost of Owner's Apartment:	$_____

· *Mortgage Payments.* When you filled in the Purchase and Renovation Summary Form, you figured how much mortgaging you would need to buy and renovate the house. Now you will have to calculate the payments on this financing. If you can reasonably expect to get all the needed money from one mortgage, you can calculate the payments by using the Constant Annual Percentage Table on page 197. If you will need two mortgages, the term and interest rate may be different on the two, so you should calculate the payments separately. If the second mortgage is from the seller, you should know the interest rate he will charge and the term he will give.

· *Real Estate Taxes.* You can get this information from the owner. You should know the tax assessment and the current tax rate so you can calculate the amount yourself. This information should be checked at the tax assessor's office. There is a chance that your taxes will go up after you complete renovation. See Appendix, page 393, for a discussion of real estate taxes.

· *Water and Sewer Charges.* Sometimes this cost comes in the form of a tax paid once or twice a year, and sometimes the water is metered. The seller will be able to give you information on what these costs have been in the past. If you will have a different number of kitchens and baths, his costs should be adjusted to reflect the change. A call to the city water department will tell you how these charges are made.

· *Heat.* The seller will also be able to supply you with his past heating bills. Often heating costs are reduced when the house is renovated because all windows and doors are repaired and the house properly sealed. A call to a fuel supplier should give you an idea of the cost to heat a house the size of the one in question. And if the owner is unable or unwilling to supply you with his costs, you can call his fuel supplier to get last year's cost.

· *Insurance.* You can also get the cost of his insurance from the seller. Be sure that the amount and kind of insurance is adequate for your needs. See Appendix, page 397, for a discussion of insurance.

· *Utilities.* The electricity and gas (for cooking) that your tenants use can be separately metered so they pay their own bills. However, you will have to pay for what you use and for any public areas. You can use the owner's past bills or call the utility company for an estimate of costs.

· *Maintenance and Repairs.*   These bills should be minimal for at least five years because the house has been completely renovated. However, you must make some allowance because there will always be minor problems such as a clogged toilet.

Once you have estimated operating costs, you must figure the amount of rental income you can expect before you know how much it will cost you to live in the house.

· RENTAL INCOME

If you are presently renting, you will have an idea of rents being charged in your city. However, there can be a wide variation in rents depending on location, apartment size, and other features. For the purpose of estimating how much it will cost you to live in the house, it is best to set rents at a reasonable rate, even though you may be able to get more—disaster may result from basing your purchase on unrealistic rental income.

If you are not familiar with the rental market, spend a day apartment hunting to acquaint yourself with the kinds of apartments available and the rents being charged. You should then be able to set realistic rents for your apartments.

· THE VALUE OF ESTIMATING
  OPERATING COSTS

Once you have filled out an estimated income and operating statement for the house you are interested in buying, you will know whether the cost to you falls within the rent you have set for yourself.

If the operating cost is too high, you must do one of the following:

1. Raise rents to cover costs above what you can afford to pay.
2. Reduce the amount of mortgaging by increasing your cash investment.
3. Reduce the amount of mortgaging by reducing the purchase price and/or the cost of construction.

All other costs are relatively stable, and reductions in them would be slight and not sufficient to make a meaningful reduction in operating costs.

If this economic evaluation shows that the project is within your budget (that you can afford to live in the house with no more cash invested than you have available), you are ready to begin negotiations for purchase. If the house is beyond your budget, forget it and start looking again. If you were thinking of a private house, you may have to consider rental income to help defray the operating expenses. If you were planning only one rental unit, maybe you should consider a larger house to maximize income.

After doing an economic evaluation, you should know what needs to be negotiated in purchasing the house. The price may have to be reduced, or you may have to buy for less cash than is being asked. Perhaps the seller will have to provide some of the necessary financing.

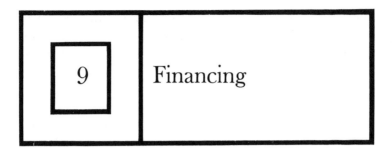

9 | Financing

WHETHER YOU CAN AFFORD to buy, renovate, and live in your house without financial strain is the question you must ask when considering the purchase of a house for renovation. Yet the average home buyer knows little or nothing about the various kinds of mortgages available and how to evaluate his ability to pay for the house in terms of anything beyond the purchase price, which may be only a small part of the finished cost.

Did you know that a good mortgage is an asset, not a liability? That the terms on which you arrange to buy a house may be more important than the price? You must know all about mortgages before being able to determine whether you can afford to buy a house, and the best possible means of financing the purchase and renovation.

· HOW TO GET A MORTGAGE

The major sources of mortgage money are savings banks, savings and loan associations, building and loan associations, and FHA-approved lenders. Commercial banks occasionally make mortgage loans as a special service to customers, and they are beginning to show an interest in providing money for urban housing. Insurance companies and some private individuals are also sources of mortgaging.

Phone calls to local banks (the term "bank" referring to all types of lending institutions) will give you an idea of their willingness to provide a mortgage. You can get additional information by personal visits to mortgage officers of the more receptive banks. Of course, no commitment for a mortgage will be made until an application is submitted.

You should learn all you can about the availability of mortgaging before you even begin to look for a house. Each bank has its own particular lending policy. Some put heavy emphasis on the borrower's income. Some are only interested in one-family homes, while others prefer income-producing property. The location of the property may be a critical factor.

Because getting a mortgage in an emerging neighborhood can be extremely difficult, the preferences of banks may be a factor in determining the house you buy. If the bank prefers a multiple dwelling to a two-family house, you should consider this factor when looking at houses to buy. And the amount of mortgage money you can get from the bank will determine whether you will need additional financing to purchase and renovate a house.

When seeking a first mortgage, you should pull any strings that you can. If you have business, personal, or family connections in the banking world, use them. Leave no stone unturned. You want to get the best mortgage at the most favorable terms possible.

One Brooklyn couple had several discussions about mortgages with a large New York City bank. Not only was their application for a mortgage rejected, but in an arbitrary and high-handed manner. Shortly thereafter, the chairman of the board made a speech about bankers needing to recognize their responsibility to help solve urban problems. Irate, the couple wrote him a letter explaining how they had been treated by his bank. Within ten days the couple received a commitment from the bank for the mortgage they needed.

Spurned by banks, homeowners in Brooklyn's Park Slope gave a cocktail party for local bankers to convince them that their area is undergoing a renaissance and is a worthwhile investment. The party was such a success that one bank completely reversed its lending policy. The bankers' cocktail party is now an annual event in Park Slope.

Renovators in Brooklyn's Boerum Hill tried another approach. Furious at rejections by scores of banks, they talked to a reporter at *The New York Times,* who wrote an article about their problem. It worked so well that homeowners actually had banks courting *them.*

Not all renovators have the time or inclination to make a "cause" of getting a mortgage. For them, the *mortgage broker* may be the answer.

A mortgage broker specializes in placing mortgages. He charges a fee for this service (usually about 2% of the amount of the mortgage), but you pay him nothing unless he obtains a mortgage for you.

The idea of paying someone to get you a mortgage may seem ridiculous until you find out how difficult it can be to obtain adequate financing. A mortgage broker keeps abreast of the mortgage market and has developed a relationship with many lenders. He knows what banks have mortgage money (including out-of-town banks that you would not know about), what kind of property they are interested in, and the best way to present your case. An application from a mortgage broker will often receive more favorable attention than the same application submitted by the owner, because the lender feels that he can rely on the broker to bring him a sound investment, whereas he knows nothing about the owner. (A mortgage broker would not stay in business long if many mortgages placed by him had to be foreclosed.)

Martha and Charlie Stamm have relied exclusively on mortgage brokers to get financing for the houses they have renovated. After spending months trying to obtain an adequate mortgage on their first house, the Stamms contacted a mortgage broker, who two weeks later got them a mortgage for ten thousand dollars more than the only mortgage they had been able to find. The Stamms now devote their time to planning the most economical renovation possible, which they feel saves them far more than the commission they pay the mortgage broker for finding them a mortgage.

Mortgage brokers are usually listed in the Yellow Pages under "Mortgages." Or you could ask your lawyer or real estate broker for the names of mortgage brokers who handle mortgages for the type of property you plan to buy.

· THE APPLICATION FOR A MORTGAGE

If you want a mortgage, you must submit an application first. It is better to apply to more than one bank so that hopefully you will have several mortgages from which to choose. Processing a mortgage application can take time, so be sure to get yours in as soon as possible. A large mortgage will be more difficult to obtain than a small one and will frequently require approval of a mortgage committee that does not meet often.

The more you know about your own finances, the kind of mortgage you need, and the particulars of the property to be mortgaged, the more receptive the mortgage officer and the bank will be to your application. Here is the kind of information most banks require:

1. A financial statement from you
2. Description of the property—location, size, number of apartments, rentals from each, estimate of operating costs (all of this on the finished house even if the house is yet to be renovated)

3. Description of renovation (with floor plans if the house is to be substantially changed) and estimate of the cost of the work, if the mortgage is to be based on the renovation

Be realistic in estimating rental income and operating costs, because the bank will adjust whatever they feel is inaccurate. (Lenders usually figure the former on the low side and the latter on the high side.) When estimating renovation costs, it is usually a good idea to pad them a little unless you have actual bids for the work—you will probably find the costs higher than you expected. On pages 212 and 214 you will find forms for estimating renovation costs and operating expenses. These will be helpful in presenting your case to the bank.

Ask the bank how long it will take to process your application. Then you must sit back and wait until you receive an answer. During the wait, keep your fingers crossed, rub your rabbit's foot or other good-luck charm, and pray for the best.

· THE IDEAL MORTGAGE

Ideally you want one mortgage to provide the entire amount of money you need to purchase and renovate your house. This mortgage must have payments you can meet without financial strain, and if it is not to be a burden to you at some future date, it should be transferable and have a prepayment clause.

If you need financing in order to purchase, you can obtain the mortgage before you buy, so that you will receive all or part of the money at the time you take title to the house. It can be obtained after you purchase, and placed on the house before renovation begins if you need money to pay for the renovation. And if you are lucky enough to have sufficient cash to pay for the house and renovation (but do not wish to tie up all this cash permanently in the house), you can wait until the renovation is complete to look for a new first mortgage. In this case, you are in an ideal situation: You will have time to shop around, and because the bank will be able to see the finished house, judging it on its own merits rather than from plans, you will probably be able to get a more favorable mortgage.

Because an ideal mortgage is often difficult to obtain in transitional neighborhoods, renovators can make their lives easier by fully understanding all the financing options open to them. If you have no financing problems, skip the following section. However, if you have a limited amount of cash and want to make the most of it—this detailed explanation may be helpful to you.

· A MORTGAGE PRIMER

A *mortgage* is a loan for which your house is the security. The amount that the lender (*mortgagee*) will give you is based on the value he could easily recoup on the market by selling the house if you (*mortgagor*) failed to meet your obligation and repay his loan. If you did fail to repay, he would have to go through the legal procedure of *foreclosure* in order to sell the house and recover his loan. The amount of the mortgage loan is called the *principal* and must be paid back by the end of the mortgage period. The *term* of the mortgage is the number of years you have to repay it.

· SELF-AMORTIZING MORTGAGES

The most common type of mortgage is the *self-amortizing* (self-liquidating) mortgage, which has payments designed to repay the full debt over the term of the mortgage. The mortgage payments are made up of interest plus amortization. *Interest* (stated as a percentage of the debt) is the amount you pay to the lender for the use of his money. *Amortization* is the amount of the loan you repay yearly, thereby reducing the principal owed. Mortgage payments are normally made monthly and are based on the rate of interest and the amount of amortization to be paid. In self-amortizing mortgages, the term determines the amount of amortization. The longer the term, the more the amount can be spread out, and consequently, the smaller the monthly payments. The following chart gives an example of monthly payments for varying terms, on a self-amortizing mortgage of $10,000 at 6% interest:

Term	Constant Monthly Payment
5 years	$193.33
10 years	111.10
15 years	84.40
20 years	71.70
25 years	64.50
30 years	60.00

In the early years of a mortgage you will be paying a larger amount of the monthly payments in interest, because interest is based on a percentage of the principal owed. As the principal is reduced, the amount of the interest is likewise reduced. The total monthly payment remains the same; but the ratio gradually changes so that in later years you pay less in interest and more in amortization. The following chart shows the breakdown of annual payments on a five-year $10,000 mortgage at 6% interest whose monthly payments are $193.33:

	Annual Interest	Annual Amortization	Principal Balance
1st year	$551.91	$1,768.05	$8,231.95
2nd year	442.86	1,877.10	6,354.85
3rd year	327.07	1,992.89	4,361.96
4th year	204.17	2,115.79	2,246.17
5th year	73.67	2,246.17	—

The amortization payments represent your *equity* (or ownership) in the property. By the time the mortgage is fully amortized, you will own the house free and clear. Amortization can be considered as putting money into a forced savings account. If you should sell the property for the same price you paid for it, you will get back all amortization you have paid on your mortgage—whereas you get nothing back when paying rent on the place you live.

A mortgage states all the conditions of the loan: year placed, amount borrowed, rate of interest, term, amount and date of payments, and other conditions. The mortgage is then recorded with the city and becomes a *lien* (claim) against the property. Mortgages are a matter of public record and can be checked at the city recording office. The mortgage debt is not automatically removed when the mortgage is paid off. In order to remove the mortgage a document (called a satisfaction piece) must be filed when the debt is paid.

· MORTGAGE BOND

A mortgage is attached to the property, not to the borrower. At the time the mortgage is placed, the lender requires the borrower to sign a mortgage bond, an instrument in which the borrower promises to pay off the mortgage debt. Bonds make the borrower personally responsible for the debt—which means that in the event of foreclosure, if the house is sold for less than the amount still owing, the borrower must make up the difference. (Personal responsibility for the mortgage debt can be avoided by the use of corporate ownership.) However, if the amount and conditions of the mortgage are favorable, a personal guarantee should not be a deterrent. The homeowner does not plan to allow the mortgage to be foreclosed because he would lose his house and destroy his credit rating.

- Mortgage Conditions

The conditions of the mortgage are important to you. Your mortgage payments usually are the most expensive item in the operating cost of your house. In addition, the mortgage conditions may be important when and if you ever want to sell or refinance your house.

• *Transferability.* If the mortgage is *transferable,* it remains on the property even if it is sold, which means that the buyer can take over your mortgage. But if your mortgage is *not transferable,* it must be paid off when you sell the property. This may make selling more difficult, since the buyer must either pay all cash for your house or raise the money by getting a new mortgage on the property himself.

Some mortgages require that the mortgagee approve the buyer before the mortgage can be transferred.

• *Prepayment Clause.* Ideally, you should be able to pay off your mortgage at any time before the end of its term, if you wish to. To assure this right, your mortgage should have a prepayment clause.

It costs the lender money to place the mortgage. He usually does not recover this cost until the mortgage has been in effect for several years. Therefore, some mortgages will not allow prepayment without an interest penalty. Some states limit a lender's right to prepayment penalties.

A large prepayment penalty can be a burden; but a small penalty (such as three months interest on the early payment) will not be an undue hardship. The real hardship can come from a long-term inability to prepay without a large penalty. If you wish to sell, your buyer will be unable to raise cash by getting a new first mortgage himself unless he pays the penalty. And should you ever need cash, you will be unable to get a larger new mortgage to replace the reduced existing one unless you pay the penalty.

· *Interest Rate.* The interest rate is important only as it affects the operating cost of the house. A higher interest rate obviously increases the amount of the mortgage payments, thereby increasing operating costs. However, high interest rates alone should not prevent you from borrowing money. A house can be a good investment even with a high-interest mortgage; and if the mortgage contains a prepayment clause, it can later be refinanced favorably if the interest rate drops. In the meantime, you are paying off the mortgage and also stand the chance that the property will appreciate in value.

If, on the other hand, the interest rate on your mortgage is well below the current rate, you have a real asset. One young couple insisted that an old low-interest mortgage of $3,000 be removed before they took title to their house. They then had to borrow against securities they owned in order to finance the purchase and renovation. But they would have needed to borrow $3,000 *less* if they had left the existing mortgage; what they did, in effect, was to re-borrow the $3,000 at a higher interest rate.

· SECONDARY FINANCING

There is no limit to the number of mortgages that can be placed on a property. Mortgages are referred to as first, second, third, and so on, to designate their place in line as liens against the property. The first mortgage is called *primary financing* and is the first claim against the property in foreclosure; all subsequent mortgages are *secondary financing* and have subordinate claims in foreclosure—the first mortgagee must collect his debt in full before the second mortgagee can lay claim to the property, and so forth down the line. A second mortgage is thus subordinate to the first, and a third subordinate to the second as claims against the property. As you can easily see, there is more risk involved in holding a second mortgage than a first mortgage, because if a foreclosure sale does not bring in enough money to cover them both, the second mortgagee may be left holding the (empty) bag. For this reason, banks and other lending institutions generally place only first mortgages. Second mortgages are available from individuals or firms specializing in secondary financing.

The conservative mortgage policies of most lending institutions have denied city homeowners the liberal terms and amounts available to suburban home buyers. This situation is in part understandable, because the decay that has infected many city neighborhoods has caused mortgagees to lose a great deal of money as property values declined. Nonetheless, this negative attitude has penalized city renovators and has made it difficult and sometimes impossible, to obtain anything but minimum bank financing. For this reason, second mortgages are common to city property owners and have become a necessary means of financing for many renovators.

As a renovator, you must consider not only the financing of the purchase, but the financing of the renovation as well. Therefore, it is doubly important to know how to get secondary financing under the most favorable terms.

· DISCOUNTING

Because secondary mortgaging involves a risk, it is usually more expensive financing than a first mortgage, with a *discount* (premium) charged by the lender. This discount is a percentage of the loan deducted from the principal at the time the money is borrowed; the loan is then repaid as if the borrower had received the full amount. Although second mortgages are generally written at the prevailing interest rate, the discount has the effect of raising the interest rate.

The amount of discount charged will vary according to the area and the availability of money. A second mortgage might be discounted at a rate of 5% a year, which means that a three-year mortgage would be discounted 15%.

This means that on a $10,000 mortgage, the mortgagor would receive only $8,500 (or $10,000 minus 15%) but would pay interest on the full $10,000.

Second mortgages are often short-term loans, with terms of from three to five years. If a short-term mortgage were to be completely self-amortizing, the payments would be extremely high. Therefore, many second mortgages are not self-amortizing and have a large principal payment owed when the mortgage term is ended.

Consider the above mortgage of $10,000 at an interest rate of 6% plus an amortization rate of 4%—a total of 10% annual constant payment. In three years the borrower would have reduced the principal by only $1,373.44. Subtracted from the $10,000 debt, that leaves $8,726.56. Since he received only $8,500 from the lender to start with, he would now owe $226.56 more than he had received. He has paid $1,726.56 in interest and is indebted for more than he borrowed.

As you see, the amount of amortization is important, and a favorable rate should be negotiated when the mortgage is placed.

Not all second mortgages are so unfavorable as the one just mentioned.

· PURCHASE MONEY (P.M.) MORTGAGES

In neighborhoods where banks are unwilling to provide sufficient financing (which is generally true of renovation areas as they begin their comeback), it is not uncommon for the houseowner to give (take back) a mortgage himself if he is anxious to sell. In other words, instead of receiving the entire amount of the purchase price in cash, he takes part of it in monthly payments with interest. This mortgage is called a *purchase money (P.M.) mortgage*—so called because the loan was given in order to make the sale possible.

A P.M. mortgage can be a first, second, or third mortgage, depending on the existing mortgaging at the time of sale. If the seller owns the house free and clear, the P.M. would be a first mortgage. If there is already mortgaging on the property, the P.M. would take its proper place behind existing mortgages. In some neighborhoods it is not uncommon for a property to have several mortgages—each a P.M. held by a previous owner.

Unlike previously mentioned second mortgages, a P.M. mortgage given by the seller is not discounted—the premium the seller receives is the sale of his property at a price agreeable to him. If he had to depend on a bank to give his buyer a new first mortgage, he might not be able to sell his house at all.

· SUBORDINATION

If the seller gives you a P.M. mortgage, try also to get subordination. *Subordination* means that the mortgage does not have to be paid off first if a new first mortgage is placed on the property, but will instead revert to a secondary (or subordinate) position behind the new first mortgage.

To illustrate how subordination works, assume that a house has two mortgages, a first of $10,000 and a second of $5,000. If these are consolidated in a new first mortgage in the amount of $15,000, $10,000 of this money goes to pay off the existing first mortgage, and $5,000 goes to pay off the second mortgage. However, if the original second mortgage contained a subordination clause, it would not have to be paid off; it would revert to a secondary position behind the *new* first mortgage, and the owner would thus receive $5,000 in cash.

Subordination of a P.M. mortgage is the most favorable way to obtain the necessary money to purchase and renovate a house where adequate first mortgaging is not available. However, the seller most likely will want to place some restrictions on his subordination. For example, to protect his loan against overfinancing, the mortgagee will probably want to limit the size of the first mortgage that takes precedence over his P.M. so that he can reasonably expect to recoup his investment in case of default. He may also want to approve of the first mortgagee. Subordination is a complex matter, and terms must be worked out in advance with the assistance of a knowledgeable attorney.

The value of a subordinated P.M. mortgage can be illustrated by the example of the John Does. They found a house that could be purchased for $10,000, and estimated that it would cost $20,000 to renovate—a total of $30,000. They had $5,000 in cash and no other convertible assets. Their bank was willing to provide a mortgage of only $18,000 on the finished house. That left the Does $7,000 away from the amount needed. Their seller then agreed to give them a $7,000 P.M. mortgage as part of the purchase agreement—and to subordinate that mortgage to their new $18,000 bank mortgage. With a total of $25,000 in mortgaging, plus their $5,000 cash, the Does were able to buy and renovate the house.

· BALLOON MORTGAGE

An owner may agree to give a P.M. mortgage for only a short period, such as three to five years; thus if the mortgage is self-amortizing, the monthly payments will be extremely high. In such a situation, you might consider a *balloon mortgage*—a mortgage that is not self-amortizing, requiring a large principal payment (balloon) when the term expires. (The second mortgage discussed on page 229 was a balloon mortgage.) In such a loan the amortization can be very low or nonexistent. If you are paying interest only, you will have the entire principal to repay at the end of the mortgage term. Obviously a balloon mortgage is not wise unless you are fairly certain that the cash will be available to meet the debt, but in some circumstances it can make sense.

As renovation improves a run-down neighborhood, the neighborhood becomes more desirable and property values rise. Banks then become willing to give larger mortgages. Thus three to five years after you complete your renovation, your bank may give you a new mortgage large enough to cover both mortgages when your balloon mortgage comes due.

For example, in 1965, the John Smiths bought a rooming house on Manhattan's Upper West Side for $25,000, which cost them an additional $25,000 to renovate to a three-family house. At the time, banks would lend no more than $25,000 regardless of how much was invested in the property. So the Smiths negotiated with the seller to give them a P.M. mortgage of $15,000, which he agreed to subordinate to the new $25,000 first mortgage. The seller set a term of five years for his P.M. mortgage, but he agreed to the low amortization figure of 2% a year so that the Smiths could hold down their monthly costs. This meant that in five years the mortgage would be reduced by only $1,500, leaving a debt of $13,500 to be paid in 1970.

During that five years many houses in the area were renovated, and the purchase price for unrenovated houses more than doubled. With each year the Smiths' property became more valuable. By 1970, banks were willing to place mortgages of $50,000 on renovated property. The Smiths were able to refinance the entire cost of their house, recouping not only the amortization payments they had made, but their initial cash investment as well. You cannot necessarily assume that this will happen, but the situation is certainly not unique. In renovation neighborhoods across the country property values have soared as the renovation movement snowballed.

· THE VALUE OF REFINANCING

The property appreciation factor is a prime attraction to the real estate investor. Property appreciation enabled the John Smiths to refinance their house, consolidating two mortgages into one larger mortgage that had been unattainable five years before.

But refinancing also allows an owner to realize cash from his past amortization payments—plus an additional amount of money representing the appreciation value of the property. Of course, if you refinance for a larger amount, your mortgage payments will probably increase. But the mortgage can be replaced by a new one for the original amount (providing the interest rate and term remain the same) with no increase in monthly payments.

The experienced real estate investor may often refinance every ten years in order to reinvest his cash elsewhere. Refinancing allows you to recoup your cash investment and realize appreciation without selling your house. What an easy way to pay for the children's college education, buy a summer house or take a trip to Europe!

· FINANCING RENOVATION

You must first purchase the house and then pay for the renovation. Unless you have a substantial amount of cash, you will need to finance both. If you get a new mortgage in order to purchase, where do you get the money for renovation?

· THE CONSTRUCTION LOAN (BUILDING LOAN)

Construction loans are temporary financing designed to take you through construction to the finished product, on which a long-term permanent mortgage can be placed.

They are normally first mortgages, which means that all existing mortgages must be paid off or must become subordinate to the construction loan. The term of the construction loan will depend on the complexity of the project. For renovation it is normally from six to eighteen months. The construction loan must be paid back in a lump sum when the term expires.

These loans are only for construction, and the money is advanced in stages as the work progresses. Interest is paid monthly on the total sum that has been advanced: There is no amortization, so the owner's costs are kept to a minimum during the time the property is unusable.

· *Take-Down Schedule.* The lender will provide a schedule of payments (take-down schedule), showing what percentage (or dollar amount) will be released as each phase of the work is completed. The following is the take-down schedule from a New York savings and loan association:

1. Enclosure (of walls)—45%
2. Brown mortar—15%
3. White plaster—15%
4. Trim—15%
5. Completion—10%

As you can see by this take-down schedule, no money is given by the bank until a substantial amount of construction has been done.

Each lender has his own take-down schedule; there is no standard form. However, what must be completed at each payment stage is specified exactly, and an inspector is sent to verify that the work has been done before a payment is released. Obviously, this system protects you as well as the bank, because the inspector will not authorize payment for work that has not been done. However, do not depend on his judgment of quality, because he may not be an expert in construction techniques.

• *Points.* A construction loan involves a risk to the lender, because there is no guarantee that the job will be completed or that it will be done well. Because of the risk, usually either a bonus may be charged or the interest rate may be higher than the prevailing rate on mortgages. The bonus charge on a construction loan is called *points* and is similar to the discount rate on second mortgages. The number of points means the percentage deducted from the amount of the loan: Two points would mean a 2% discount. Points are not limited to construction loans. When money is tight, points are often charged on first mortgages as well.

• COMBINATION MORTGAGES

The ideal type of financing for renovation is the *combination mortgage.* On this type of mortgage the lender agrees to give you a new first mortgage upon completion of construction, but meanwhile will give you a certain percentage (usually 90%) in the form of a construction loan. When the job is complete, the amount advanced for construction will be incorporated into a new first mortgage along with the final payment you will receive at the time the permanent mortgage is written. In the take-down schedule on page 234, the first four payments would be for the construction loan, and the permanent mortgage would be written at the time of the fifth payment.

A more simplified form of the combination mortgage is used by many banks when the amount of money needed is not large. No construction loan is used, but the permanent mortgage is advanced in three or four stages, the first advance at the time of purchase and the final advance on completion of the renovation. Most often these mortgages have amortization payments during construction; and sometimes the full mortgage is recorded at the time of the first advance, with payments based on the full amount even though the balance of the mortgage is held in escrow by the lender until the next payment is released. This type of mortgage is tailor-made for the particular situation, so there is no standard procedure.

Some banks will not give construction money because of the risk. However, if a permanent mortgage commitment has been obtained from a bank, the owner can often get a construction loan from firms that specialize in construction financing. A construction loan, whether it is a separate loan or part of a combination mortgage, has a time limit, and the job must be completed within the specified time. The commitment for a permanent mortgage usually has a time limit also, after which the lender is not obligated to honor his commitment to provide the mortgage. Some renovators who were not aware of the importance of this time limit have found themselves in difficulty when construction work was not completed by the deadline. In two cases, one in New York City and another in Atlanta, the mortgagee was willing to extend the mortgage commitment, but raised the interest rate on the mortgage.

Furthermore, you must remember that permanent mortgage commitments are based on the renovation you describe to the lender. If you make changes as the renovation progresses, the lender is not obligated to honor his commitment. So any major changes, particularly omissions of work previously planned, should be approved by the lender.

· HOME IMPROVEMENT LOANS

Another kind of financing available to help pay for renovation is the *home improvement loan*. This is not a mortgage, and only a limited amount can be borrowed. It is a short-term loan, usually no more than three to five years, and it is discounted. It is relatively easy to obtain from most banks, but because the term is short, the monthly payments are higher than those on mortgages. However, when an additional one to five thousand dollars is needed to finish a renovation, a home improvement loan can provide the solution.

· ADDITIONAL MORTGAGE INFORMATION

· *Escrow for Taxes and Insurance.* Mortgagees are concerned that their loan be secure, that the property be adequately insured against fire, and that real estate taxes are paid—since an uninsured fire can wipe out the lender's investment, and unpaid taxes can bring foreclosure proceedings by the city. Many lenders require monthly mortgage payments to include a pro-rated amount for taxes and insurance, with this money held in a special (*escrow*) account from which the lender makes payments as they are due. Mortgagees realize that it is often difficult for an owner to set aside money each month for bills that must be paid only once or twice a year. When the mortgage is placed, the cost of real estate taxes and insurance is determined and then divided by twelve to determine the monthly amount that must be added to the regular mortgage payment. If taxes or insurance premiums rise, the escrow payment is increased to cover the additional costs.

Escrow payments for taxes and insurance are not always a condition of a first mortgage. When the borrower pays these bills himself, the lender normally requires proof that they have been paid.

· *Grace Period.* Each mortgage specifies the date on which payments are due, but there is a period of grace, usually specified in the mortgage, during which no foreclosure action can be taken because payment did not arrive on the date it was due. However, once the grace period has passed, the mortgagor is in default and the mortgagee can institute legal action for payment (foreclosure).

· A Mortgage Can Be an Asset

Some people have the mistaken notion that a mortgage is something bad, to be gotten rid of as quickly as possible. No doubt this notion comes from the melodrama in which the villain (twirling his big black mustache) threatens to foreclose the mortgage and drive the heroine out into the snowstorm. This feeling about mortgages is also expressed in the custom of the mortgage button, found in old New England houses: When the mortgage was paid off, it was burned and the ashes placed inside the newel post in the front entrance hall. The small wooden "button" in the center of the top was replaced with an ivory button so that guests would know that the owner had paid off the mortgage.

However, if your mortgage is self-amortizing and at a favorable interest rate, you have nothing to gain and possibly a great deal to lose by paying it off ahead of time simply to remove the debt. If you would like to lower your operating costs, you can do so in ways other than paying off the mortgage. The money you would use to remove the mortgage can be invested, and you can use the return on that investment to make your mortgage payments. You would then have two investments instead of one, both of which could appreciate in value. And your favorable mortgage could be an asset if you wanted to sell the house.

· GOVERNMENT FINANCING PROGRAMS
AND PURCHASE IN PROJECT AREAS

In addition to conventional financing, there are government mortgage programs (federal, state, and city) that provide money for building and/or renovation of housing, for which conventional lenders are unwilling or unable to give mortgages.

- FHA MORTGAGE INSURANCE PROGRAMS

Under these programs, the federal government itself does not give mortgages. It insures, or guarantees, mortgages made by approved lenders—banks, building and loan associations, and so on. There are many different FHA mortgage insurance programs, each with its own qualifications designed to carry out the various objectives of the federal government. The FHA and its first programs were created to encourage and make home ownership possible for large numbers of American families who had good credit but insufficient capital to purchase homes.

Prior to the establishment of FHA in 1934, most mortgages were short-term balloon mortgages with average terms of three years and no set amortization payments. Usually all an owner could do was keep up with interest payments and periodically renew the loan. Therefore, people saved for years, often well into middle age, to pay cash for their homes so there could be no danger of foreclosure.

FHA-insured mortgages were self-amortizing and extended the debt over a long period of time. This FHA policy helped make the low down payment, fully-amortized loan the standard mortgaging practice of lending institutions.

Under the FHA mortgage and loan insurance system, a buyer makes a small down payment and obtains a mortgage for the rest of the purchase price. The mortgage loan is made by an FHA-approved lender and insured by FHA, which means that the lender has a guarantee that his loan will be made good. Because he has no risks, the lender can allow more liberal terms than would otherwise be possible.

FHA-insured mortgages offer more liberal conditions than their conventional counterparts. Conventional mortgages are normally for 50–75% of appraised value, whereas

FHA-insured mortgages can cover up to 100%. Though the maximum term of conventional mortgages is currently twenty-five years, FHA-insured mortgages can have terms of up to forty years. FHA-insured mortgages not only lend larger amounts but through longer terms can keep monthly payments to a minimum.

FHA charges a mortgage insurance premium of $\frac{1}{2}\%$ a year on the average outstanding balance. This premium is in addition to the interest and amortization payments, but is included in the monthly mortgage payment and is disbursed to FHA by the lender. Considering the liberal terms, the premium charged by FHA is worth paying.

FHA mortgage insurance programs cover financing for new and used houses, for new construction and renovation, for purchase and refinancing, for private homes and multiple dwellings, for property in urban, surburban, and rural areas. There is hardly a category of residential housing not covered by some FHA program.

Each FHA program has a set of minimum property standards that must be met, and a ratio of loan-to-value (or cost) used to determine the amount of the mortgage to be insured. Each program has a maximum loan amount and a maximum mortgage term: The amount and term of a mortgage are determined by FHA when an application is received.

In order to qualify for FHA insurance, the borrower must have a good credit record and enough steady income to meet mortgage payments and other operating expenses of the property without difficulty. In addition, the property must meet the requirements set by FHA for the particular program involved. Information on all FHA programs can be obtained from the following:

1. U. S. Department of Housing and Urban Development (HUD), Washington, D.C.
2. Regional HUD office for your area (address can be obtained from HUD in Washington or from FHA)

3. Federal Housing Administration, Washington, D.C.
4. Local FHA office in your city (check phone book for address and number)

· Pros and Cons of FHA-Insured Mortgages

If you want a mortgage for the purchase of a house or a mortgage on a property once the renovation is complete, you can generally get an FHA-insured mortgage from a bank very quickly. Or, if you want an FHA-insured home improvement loan, that too is easy to obtain from a bank. The difficulty comes if you need a combination mortgage —where FHA insures a construction loan as well as a permanent mortgage. This is a complex and lengthy procedure, because FHA must approve your construction plans before it will agree to insure them. FHA requires much information before it will approve an application: detailed floor plans, elaborate estimates of construction and operating costs, and complicated applications filled out in triplicate. In order to apply properly, you will need a lawyer and an architect who are thoroughly familiar with FHA requirements and procedures. In addition, FHA has a number of requirements that may or may not be good for you:

1. FHA must approve the contractor, and requires a performance bond or other guarantee that work will be completed.
2. FHA construction requirements often do not allow an owner to save money by salvaging existing features of the house. Therefore, FHA-insured combination mortgages make more sense for houses that are to be gutted and rebuilt.
3. FHA requirements often increase renovation costs and preclude most do-it-yourself projects.
4. The maximum mortgage loan is sometimes available only if you create a number of apartments in the house.

5. Many banks are unwilling to provide money for some FHA programs. You may have difficulty finding a lender even after FHA approval has been obtained. The Federal National Mortgage Association (Fanny May) can solve this problem, but the amount of its funds is limited, so you may have to wait until Fanny May gets more money.

Requirements of FHA should be compared with those for conventional financing. Liberal amounts and terms are meaningful only within the framework of your own budget. If FHA requires you to spend more money, the advantage of a longer term may be wiped out. The monthly payment on a $10,000 mortgage at 6% interest for twenty years will be the same as that on a $13,100 mortgage for forty years at 6% interest: Twice as long to pay does not mean that you can carry twice as large a mortgage, as you can see.

· FEDERAL PROJECT AREAS

One result of the first FHA programs was the boom in suburban home building. As the boom grew, builders began to buy up and develop large tracts of land and build homes specifically for purchase through FHA-insured mortgages. This trend created a large and unforeseen result. As the middle class began its mass exodus from the cities to these new suburban homes, the cities began to decay more rapidly. The federal government then became concerned with the plight of the cities, and in 1949 Congress enacted legislation establishing the Urban Renewal Program.

· THE URBAN RENEWAL PROGRAM

This was the beginning of a joint effort between federal and city governments to renew America's cities. It works in two ways: (1) through conservative and rehabilitation (renovation) of existing structures, and (2) through demolition and redevelopment (new construction). Urban Renewal deals with the total physical environment of the project area: buildings, both residential and nonresidential, and community facilities, such as streets, sidewalks, parks, and lighting.

Urban Renewal has been justly criticized for demolition of hundreds of worthwhile (even historically valuable) buildings that need not have been destroyed and for displacing countless needy families. Its planners have sometimes been insensitive to the needs of residents and have made colossal blunders in the execution of projects. But its impact cannot be denied: Urban Renewal has resurrected dying cities. The commitment on the part of federal and municipal governments to rebuild the center city and combat the rampant decay infesting so many urban areas has inspired new confidence in our cities and has been responsible directly and indirectly for the investment of hundreds of millions of dollars of private capital in formerly abandoned and hopeless urban areas. It has also had spill-over effects, causing surrounding neighborhoods to renew themselves.

• *Buying Property in Urban Renewal Areas.*   One of the aspects of Urban Renewal that may interest the renovator is city sale of property for renovation. The city buys and vacates the property, and then sets a sale price that makes the property economical to renovate. Often this price is less than the city paid. Besides the low cost, there are other advantages to buying property from the city in an Urban Renewal project. It is not necessary to take title until plans for renovation are drawn, financing is arranged, and a contractor is obtained, which means a substantial saving in carrying costs. The new owner can take title one day and start work the next. The city will not sell to anyone who cannot afford to complete the project, and therefore works very closely with the prospective buyer to make certain the investment is a sound one that can be completed within the allowed budget. The buyer has all the resources of the project office at his disposal and a great deal of assistance from the staff.

However, you must convince the city that you are the right purchaser. It often takes the city a year or more to select a purchaser, and it may take another year before the buyer can take title to the property. Only a small percentage of property in most Urban Renewal projects is resold by the city for rehabilitation, with sales usually spread over a long period of time. Because the property is often held vacant by the city for so long, it may be in wretched condition by the time the new owner takes title, and require complete gutting.

Property for sale by the city in Urban Renewal projects is normally advertised in local newspapers, but the advisements are written in such a way that the renovator would scarcely recognize them as pertinent to his needs. The best way to obtain information about houses the city has for sale is to go to the local project office. There you can learn about city-owned properties in the area, when they will be for sale, and how to go about applying for purchase. Usually you are required to submit an application, including a description of your plans for the property, and a personal financial statement. Each applicant is screened, and those considered worthy are interviewed; an interview does not mean that the applicant has been selected, merely that he is being considered.

Just because an area has an Urban Renewal project does not mean that property cannot be purchased on the open market. The city does not own all property in project areas, and remaining owners are free to sell at any time they choose. The free market prices of houses in a project area are generally higher than those sold by the city because of the city write-down policy. However, many renovators prefer to pay the additional price so that they can get on with the job, avoiding the bureaucratic red tape.

· OTHER FEDERAL PROGRAMS

Besides Urban Renewal, the U. S. Department of Housing and Urban Development (HUD) has two other programs that may be of interest to the renovator: Concentrated Code Enforcement and Model Cities.

· *The Concentrated Code Enforcement Program.* Authorized by Congress in 1965, this program is designed for predominantly residential neighborhoods that have code violations in at least twenty per cent of their buildings. The Concentrated Code Enforcement program is a neighborhood conservation program which emphasizes the retention of the essential character of the area. Under this program the owner is encouraged to rehabilitate the property himself or to sell it to someone who will.

· *The Model Cities Program.* Enacted by Congress in 1966, Model Cities is designed to attack the social, economic, and physical problems of deteriorating neighborhoods, upgrading the total environment and improving the lives of residents through education, employment, and medical and health facilities as well as housing.

Both Urban Renewal and Concentrated Code Enforcement projects have local offices providing assistance to property owners and tenants. There you can get information about all types of financing. Staffs of these offices are familiar with most of the programs and availability of money from local sources, and will assist in preparing applications for financing, help with planning, and information on renovation. To locate Urban Renewal and Concentrated Code Enforcement projects in your city, call your local redevelopment agency, which can be found under city government listings. In New York City, call the Housing and Development Administration.

- ### ADVANTAGES AND DISADVANTAGES OF FEDERAL PROGRAMS

Urban Renewal, Concentrated Code Enforcement, and Model Cities programs may interest the renovator because they deal with housing and the upgrading of decaying neighborhoods, offering opportunities for renovation with the assurance that the city is committed to improvement of the project area. However, there are disadvantages. It takes an incredible length of time to get these projects started, and in the interim, those who live in the area must resign themselves to the depressing environment of vacant buildings and bombed-out landscapes for long periods. The Urban Renewal plan itself can be a source of bitter contention. In the past, planning was sometimes subject to arbitrary decisions by bureaucrats who lived in other parts of the city or suburbs and had no genuine understanding of the needs of the community. Recognition of this fact has brought a change: residents may participate in planning for their area, but satisfying all elements in the community can cause long delays.

Private renewal of an area can move as rapidly as people are willing to invest their money in it, whereas federal projects are full of red tape and interminable delays; and city commitments to make improvements may not be made when they are needed to stimulate private investment. However, there are many neighborhoods, such as Boston's South End, that are too large with problems too immense to be solved by private renewal alone. Individuals can renovate old buildings and construct new ones, plant trees and repair sidewalks, but only the city can repair streets, improve transportation and other public facilities, and enforce building codes. Often Urban Renewal or Concentrated Code Enforcement is the only means to get the commitment for government spending necessary to re-vitalize a neighborhood.

• *312 Loans.* Renovators should also know about 312 loans. Limited to Concentrated Code Enforcement and Urban Renewal areas, they are federal loans direct from HUD authorized by Section 312 of the Housing Act of 1964), bearing an interest rate of only three per cent, with terms up to twenty years. They are used to bring buildings up to local code requirements and may be either promis-sory notes (for loans less than thirty-five hundred dollars), second mortgages (when there is an existing mortgage), or first mortgages (combining the existing debt with the cost of rehabilitation).

312 loans have been available in Urban Renewal (as well as Code Enforcement) areas for six years, but it is only recently that renovators have become aware of them and taken advantage of their extremely favorable terms.

• STATE AND CITY PROGRAMS

In addition to federal programs, there are also some state and city programs for upgrading and financing of run-down property and neighborhoods. You may want to find out whether there are helpful programs in your city that may be applicable to your own situation. Contact appropriate government offices to make inquiries.

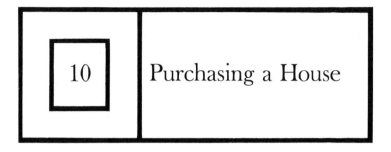

10 Purchasing a House

Due to a lack of knowledge, the inexperienced buyer usually does very little negotiating when purchasing a house. There is often little to negotiate when buying a relatively new one-family house—the price of the house and the amount of cash needed are the major concerns, and even these may be accepted without negotiations. But the purchase of a city house is often complex, particularly when the buyer plans to renovate it; and the terms of purchase can be as important as the price. When buying a house to renovate, one must consider financing, city regulations and restrictions, and many other problems.

There are three steps involved in buying a house: negotiating the purchase; signing the purchase contract (going to contract); and taking title to the property (closing).

Once the buyer and seller have agreed on the price and terms of purchase, a contract that details this agreement is drawn up and signed by both parties. Even though a verbal agreement has been reached, either side can back out with very little liability prior to signing a contract. If, however, a broker is involved in the transactions, he can sue for his commission once a verbal agreement has been reached, because he has fulfilled his responsibility to find a buyer who is ready, willing, and able to purchase. Once the sale contract has been signed, the buyer usually forfeits his deposit if he reneges on the contract. Therefore, do not go to contract unless you are sure you want to buy the property.

Once all the conditions of the sale contract have been met, a closing takes place, in which the title to the property changes hands. The closing is a mere formality. The signing of the contract is the critical phase in purchasing.

· HIRING A LAWYER

An attorney is needed in all real estate transactions, but a competent and knowledgeable real estate lawyer is a must when buying city property. You should consult a lawyer before entering into serious negotiations for purchase, and it is probably best to find a lawyer as soon as you consider buying a house. You not only want the smartest lawyer you can find, but one who will take an interest in your affairs and is thoroughly familiar with the kinds of problems you will face.

You are not drawing up a will, so for heaven's sake do not depend on Aunt Jane's lawyer, ever so nice though he may be. You are buying a city house, which often encompasses a multitude of sins and building violations. You need an astute real estate attorney who is familiar with the type of property you are buying and the renovation you will undertake. You are a novice in city real estate, and you need someone to represent you who will insure that you get everything you bargained for. Talk to several lawyers, if necessary, until you find one you have confidence in.

Make an appointment to go to the lawyer's office before you begin negotiations to purchase. Tell him what you have in mind, and ask for his suggestions. Discuss with him the services he can provide and the fee he will charge.

There is a general rule of thumb that an attorney will charge one per cent of the sale price, but the fee may be more or less, depending upon how much work is necessary.

Do not pinch pennies with your lawyer. He will work diligently for you and your interests only if you are willing to compensate him for his efforts. The experience of the lawyer can often save you the cost of his fee, and perhaps more.

A good lawyer should be consulted throughout the entire project. He will not only handle the legal work for purchase and financing, but he should be consulted on the contracts for renovation, and he can advise you on tax problems concerning the property, the kind of insurance you should carry, and the form of ownership the house should be in.

Ownership of property can be individual (one person), multiple (two or more people), or corporate (a corporation having title to the property with individuals owning shares in the corporation) or otherwise. Each type of ownership has advantages and disadvantages. In individual and multiple ownership, the owner(s) is personally responsible for the expenses and operation of the property; in corporate ownership, the corporation (rather than the officers or shareholders) is responsible for the property. In individual or multiple ownership, all expenses can be deducted from the personal income of the owner(s); in corporate ownership, the corporation, not the shareholders, receives any tax benefits of ownership. (See Appendix for discussion of tax benefits.)

Sometimes, particularly during construction, it may be advantageous to have the property in a wife's name or in a corporation to protect other assets such as salary or investments. Although property ownership can be transferred, there are legal and tax considerations in such transactions as well as in the decision about the form of ownership. These should be discussed with a lawyer and/or accountant.

An attorney's job is to be your legal representative. He should point out potential problems, but it is not his job to make decisions for you. His knowledge of city regulations, codes, zoning, restrictive covenants, and mortgaging can prevent unforeseen disasters.

His job is to see that you are protected legally in every way possible. If he is to represent you properly, he must have all the facts. He must see that the contract for purchase contains everything that the seller has agreed to, that it has no hidden provisions of which the buyer is unaware, and that the purchaser will be given a clear title to the property.

· NEGOTIATING THE PURCHASE

In negotiating a purchase, you should attempt to buy under the most favorable conditions. The price to be paid for the house is only one of the terms of purchase. Other terms that may be important are:

1. The amount of cash needed to purchase
2. The financing available (either existing mortgages or P.M. mortgage provided by the seller)*
3. Whether the sale is conditioned on the buyer's ability to get new financing (conditional sale)
4. Whether the house is purchased occupied or vacant
5. Whether the property is sold in as-is condition
6. The contents of the house that are to be a part of the sale
7. The amount of down payment, and how this money will be handled
8. The closing date, and interim access to the property for the buyer

The buyer should determine in advance the key items that must be negotiated. Negotiations are usually a matter

* See Chapter 9.

of compromise, with neither party getting everything he asks for. The buyer should know which items are non-negotiable. If the key item is financing by the seller, the buyer may have to pay the asking price or even a little more, whereas if the sale is for all cash (or cash over existing mortgages) the buyer can expect to bargain on the price. At the beginning, the buyer should clearly state to the broker or owner those terms that are absolutely necessary for purchase. If no agreement can be reached on these, there is no sense wasting time on other points.

· THE CASH NEEDED TO PURCHASE

The amount of cash may or may not be critical to the seller, but it definitely is important to the buyer. When renovation is planned, the buyer cannot afford to put all of his cash into the purchase. He must have enough money to pay lawyer, architect, and other miscellaneous costs involved in starting the renovation. Generally speaking, the less cash paid, the better for the buyer. It is always a good idea to have more cash available than you think you will need in case unforeseen difficulties arise during construction. You may need more cash during periods of construction than you will have invested in the house when it is completed: money may be owed before the bank releases it to you for payment. Keep this in mind when negotiating the cash required for purchase.

The cash payment for the house can be lowered by the use of financing. If the price of the property is $15,000, the amount of cash needed will depend on the financing. If there is an existing $5,000 mortgage, the buyer must pay $10,000 in cash for the house unless the seller is willing to take back a mortgage or the buyer can obtain a new mortgage for a larger amount. If the seller is willing to hold an additional $5,000 mortgage, the buyer will need only $5,000 in cash to purchase.

If the owner is inflexible in the amount of cash he requires, and that amount falls within your budget, get him to negotiate on other points.

- EXISTING MORTGAGES, P.M. MORTGAGE,
  AND SUBORDINATION

The property you are planning to buy may or may not have existing mortgages. If it does, you should be given information about them. (See page 205 for the information you will need.) The current mortgages on the property will remain when you take title unless you or the seller chooses to pay them off. Thus, if a house selling for $10,000 had $7,000 in mortgaging, you would pay the seller $3,000 in cash and take over the $7,000 worth of mortgaging. If the mortgage has no provision for prepayment, you will not be able to refinance the property until the mortgage expires unless you pay penalties. (If there is a prepayment penalty, you may want to negotiate with the seller to compensate you for the amount of the penalty.) If the payments on existing mortgages are extremely high, you may want to get a new mortgage for a longer term to lower payments. If the interest rate on the existing mortgages is below the current rate, you may want to keep them on the property as long as possible. You will be unable to make a judgment about existing mortgages until you have all the facts about them.

Often the asking price of the property is more than the combination of asking cash and existing mortgages. In such cases, the seller may plan to take back a P.M. mortgage. (See page 229.) All the terms of the P.M. must be negotiated—amount, interest rate, term, and so forth. Be sure that you understand what you need when negotiating the P.M.

It is a good idea to try to get subordination of this mortgage (see page 230), even if you do not think you will need it. You do not have to use the subordination clause, but it is generally impossible to obtain subordination once the mortgage has been written.

Subordination is a very complex matter and should be discussed in detail with a lawyer before any agreement has been reached. The subordination agreement must be meaningful and legally enforcible. Only a lawyer can assist you in negotiating proper subordination of a mortgage.

· CONDITIONAL SALE

If the seller is unwilling to take back a mortgage when the amount of cash asked is more than you have, you must get a new mortgage in order to purchase the house. In such a situation, you should insist on a *conditional sale*. This means that the sale is conditioned on your ability to get a mortgage of a specified amount. The sale price and all other terms of purchase are agreed upon and incorporated into a sale contract that is binding on you only if you are able to get the necessary financing. Your down payment is refunded if no mortgage can be obtained. If you do not have a conditional contract and are unable to get a mortgage, you will lose your down payment deposit and may be liable for damages.

A conditional sale is binding on the seller: His property is taken off the market while you look for a mortgage. You have a specified amount of time to get the mortgage, which must be negotiated in the conditional sale terms.

· THE PROBLEM OF VACATING

Vacating a house may be a problem, depending on whether the tenants have leases, the type of tenants involved, and city regulations dealing with vacating. For the inexperienced, the process is neither easy nor pleasant. In

New York City vacating is very difficult and often impossible because of the city's unique rent control regulations.*

The seller is in a much better position to vacate than you are because he knows the tenants. Try to get him to sell you a vacant house. That way, you know that you can start renovation whenever you are ready and will not have to wait for tenants to move or supply them with services while they remain. It is often worthwhile to pay more for the house to have it delivered vacant. Discuss the problem of vacating with your lawyer before deciding to undertake the job yourself.

If you should decide to buy an occupied property, remember that there may be additional expenses for vacating that will add to the cost of the finished house. Many cities have regulations requiring the owner to pay relocation fees to displaced tenants. You will often have to find new homes for tenants in order to speed the vacating process. In some cities there are firms or individuals that can be hired to vacate property. (An owner's time is generally better spent in planning the renovation than in relocating tenants.)

Ask your lawyer or real estate broker for the names of people who can be hired to vacate your property for you.

· THE CONDITION OF THE PROPERTY WHEN PURCHASED

Most property is sold as is, with no guarantees given on its condition. Sometimes a seller is willing to give guarantees as to the condition of the property and occasionally you will find an owner willing to rectify certain conditions,

---

* If you plan to buy a house in New York, rent control can present serious problems. Not only does it affect your ability to get possession of your house in order to renovate, but it can also affect the amount of rent you can charge as well as future rent increases. It is therefore mandatory that you discuss the problems of rent control with a knowledgeable lawyer before buying a house in New York.

such as a leaky roof, before you take title to the house. (You may want to do this work yourself to see that it is properly done. If so, ask for a price reduction instead.) Any conditions in the property that are to be changed by the owner must be negotiated and incorporated in the sale contract.

Old city houses often have building violations, some of which may be on record with the building department as uncorrected. If you are planning to do a major renovation, they may not be important, since construction will usually remove them. However, your lawyer may insist upon having a record of any violations on file so that you are aware of the problems you face. This information is often a good bargaining point when dealing with the owner of a house in bad condition.

· THE CONTENTS OF THE HOUSE

The sale of a house usually includes built-in features of the property. However, the lovely dining-room chandelier that enticed you to buy the house may be missing the day you take title unless you negotiate for it to remain and include this agreement in the sale contract. On the other hand, the house may be full of furniture and debris. If you expect the seller to remove it, you must negotiate for this also.

· DOWN PAYMENT ON CONTRACT

The amount of down payment (paid on the signing of contract) must be negotiated and is often handled by the attorneys involved. The seller's lawyer generally asks for 10% of the sale price, with the buyer's lawyer usually insisting upon 10% of the cash payment. A settlement is normally reached somewhere between these two figures.

What happens to this down payment is important to you. If the money is given directly to the seller, you may have difficulty recouping it if the sale falls through and you are entitled to a refund. To avoid any problem, you should insist that the money be held in escrow by a third party (usually the seller's attorney) until the title to the property changes hands. If the seller reneges on the contract or is unable to deliver a clear title, the money is returned to you. If you back out of the agreement, the money may be turned over to the seller.

· DATE FOR TAKING TITLE

Most sale contracts call for title to change hands as soon as all the conditions of the contract can be met. This usually takes no longer than thirty days. Often, however, a buyer would like to have a longer period of time between contract and closing. Since a seller can terminate a contract if too many delays are requested, you should negotiate in advance for enough time. A sixty- or ninety-day contract is not unusual.

· RIGHT OF ACCESS

You should insure your right to visit the property during the contract period in order to start planning the renovation. Negotiate this right as a part of the sale agreement. It is not unusual to start drawing the plans for renovation before you have title to the property. In fact, you can save time and carrying costs by arranging to have the renovation planning done during the contract period so you are ready to start work once you take title to the house. There is always the chance that the sale will not go through, causing you to lose any money spent on plans. Whether to take this risk is up to you. However, under no circumstances should you perform any physical work on the property until you take title. It is extremely risky to invest money in a house you do not own. If the sale were not consummated, you would not only lose any money invested, but would be liable for damages as well.

· THE SALE CONTRACT

The sale contract is the legal document on which the sale of property is based. It contains the sale price and all terms and conditions of sale. Any agreement between you and the seller must be incorporated in the contract to be legally binding. (Verbal agreements normally cannot be enforced.)

A sale contract is written in legal jargon that is not only boring to read, but difficult to understand. It is your lawyer's job to see that the contract contains all provisions agreed upon, that these provisions can be enforced, that you will receive a clear title to the property, and that you are not being cheated.

The contract is normally drawn up by the seller's attorney and is approved or amended as necessary by your attorney. The ideal procedure is to have the contract drawn up in advance so that the lawyers can iron out the difficulties before signing day. When this is done, you are often unaware of the work the lawyer has done in your behalf.

When the contract is not drawn up in advance, your attorney has his first opportunity to see the document the day it is to be signed, and the session can be a long and noisy one. The contract will often look more like a doodle sheet than a legal document, with all changes and additions handwritten and initialed by both you and the seller. Once the contract is complete and approved by both attorneys, you and the seller sign it and you make a down payment.

· BETWEEN CONTRACT AND CLOSING

During this interval your lawyer will be preparing for the closing. The title to the property must be searched (a *title search* is an examination of public records to determine the ownership, encumbrances, encroachments, and rights of way affecting real property) and title insurance obtained. *Title insurance* is an insurance policy that indemnifies the holder for any loss sustained by reason of defects in the title. Although there is little prospect of difficulty once the title has been searched, there is no reason to take a chance when title insurance is available at such reasonable cost.

Your lawyer will have a *survey* of the property made (or the existing one updated), verify existing mortgages, and check the property for liens and violations. Your lawyer will make sure that the title is free of defects and that you are protected in every way possible.

Meanwhile, there are matters that you should take care of. You should notify electric and gas companies to have the utilities transferred to your name on the date of closing. If heat is provided by oil, you should make arrangement for fuel-oil deliveries and service of the furnace. You must also be certain that the property will be adequately covered by insurance when you take title. (See Appendix, page 397, for information on insurance.)

· THE CLOSING

When all the terms and conditions of the contract have been met, the closing takes place. It is here that the property changes hands. You give the seller a certified check for the amount you owe, and he gives you the deed to the property. The change in ownership is recorded and becomes a matter of public record.

At the closing, there are *adjustments* to be made on real estate taxes, mortgage payments, insurance, water and sewer charges, and fuel and utility bills. If any of these items has been paid in advance by the seller, he will receive a refund for the portion that does not apply to his owner-ship. If, however, bills are owing for debts incurred during the seller's ownership, you will receive credit.

In addition to adjustments, there will be *closing costs* for the purchase. These consist of title insurance, survey cost, tax stamps, recording fees, and other miscellaneous charges. These costs are normally paid by the purchaser, and your lawyer should give you an estimate of the amount in advance of the closing date.

The closing can be handled exclusively by the attorneys without the buyer or seller being present. However, most buyers want to be present at this official ceremony. When the closing is complete, the buyer has become the proud (and often poor) owner of a piece of real estate. It is not uncommon for buyer and lawyer to have a drink to cele-brate the transaction.

· KEEPING RECORDS

Now that you own a house, it is very important to keep accurate records of all money spent on it. Ideally all ex-penditures should be made by check, with a notation at the bottom relating it to the house. (At income tax time you may have forgotten who John Doe is, from whom you bought that old mantel to replace the missing one.) If pay-ments are made in cash, be sure to get a receipt and file it with other house records. Many people who insist on receiving cash can be paid by making out the check in their name, having them endorse it, and cashing it for them. Many contractors use this method of paying work-men so they have proof of payment in the canceled check.

It is amazing how many boxes of nails and miscellaneous items you can buy, and these trivial expenses can add up. You want to be able to get every tax advantage possible, and this can be done only if accurate records have been kept.

It is also important to know exactly how much you have invested in your house if you should sell it. Any improvements in your own apartment after the renovation is finished should be recorded, even though there is no tax deduction on your own living quarters: The expenditures *will* make a difference if you sell the property, for they may enable you to avoid a capital-gains tax at the time of sale.

If the property brings in rental income, it is mandatory that you keep a record book of income and expenses. At tax time you will have all the necessary information already recorded, making preparation of income tax returns much easier.

It is always best to discuss record keeping with either your lawyer or accountant, who can acquaint you with procedures and tell you what records must be kept.

11 The Basic Elements of a Renovation

· THE IMPORTANCE OF PLANNING

Having a total plan for your house before you begin is vitally important. *Do not tear out one wall or drive one nail before you have a plan for the finished house.* This is as important for a simple renovation as for a major one, and is perhaps more necessary for piecemeal, long-term remodeling than for a job to be completed in a matter of months, where a plan is more likely to be an integral part of the project.

Most renovators are so anxious to see work begin that they plunge in headlong without proper preparation. Some people have managed to muddle through on luck, but others find themselves with expensive kitchens or bathrooms immovably installed in places where they are not wanted.

A young couple bought a house in Brooklyn that had been renovated into several small apartments. They moved into the ground floor, planning to take over the parlor floor when their budget allowed them to create a duplex for themselves. The kitchen was miserably inadequate, so as soon as they were able to scrape together enough money, they remodeled it with new appliances and cabinets. When they took over the parlor floor, they discovered that the kitchen was in the wrong place and did not function within the framework of the newly added space, but they had invested too much money to contemplate ripping it out and starting over, since the cabinets and appliances could not be sensibly reused. Had they only formulated a plan for the finished duplex before they remodeled the kitchen, they could have worked out a solution that would have functioned well before and after. As you can see, the less money you have, the more important it is to have a total plan.

The most serious and costly problems that occur in construction are usually the result of inadequate planning and could be avoided by taking the time to think out every detail carefully in advance. The first step involves an assessment of the current condition of the house, both interior and exterior. The state of the existing plumbing and wiring must be evaluated: the roof, gutters and leaders, and exterior, including foundations. (If you followed advice urging professional inspection before purchase, you should already have a written report on these conditions. If you did not, have it done *now*.) Deficiencies in any of the above should be corrected before any other work is begun. While it is an entirely normal impulse to want to rush in and do things that show, such as painting and wallpapering or a new kitchen, it could be a heartbreaking mistake. If a room is decorated before the old plumbing is replaced, there is a danger of water damage as well as the possibility that walls must be ripped open for repairs. If the roof should leak, a ceiling may fall, or at the very least, plaster will crack and discolor. If the exterior walls have any cracks or gaps, there is a constant danger of water damage and the added expense of heat loss. Work done on a floor-at-a-time basis can result in an enormous waste of money, as completed work on lower floors may be damaged by construction above. This is not to say that you cannot renovate your house gradually; only plan carefully in advance so that work is done in the proper sequence.

Lack of planning may end well through sheer luck, as it did for a couple who bought an eighteenth-century house in Old Town, Alexandria, Virginia. Buying on impulse and having to sell everything conceivable to raise the cash they needed, they did nothing about having the house inspected by a professional, and felt they could not afford an architect or contractor. They were under the illusion that they could simply clean up and paint to make their house habitable. Like so many of us, they never considered those vital unseen elements whose functions we take for granted, such as plumbing, wiring, and heating. They had never even heard of a bearing wall.*

Since the kitchen was the worst room in the house, they decided to work on it first. They had their hearts set on a brick floor in their kitchen: when they ripped up the old flooring, they found they were standing on dirt. Further investigation revealed that there was nothing under the dining- or living-room floors either—the beams had been eaten away by dry rot, and all that propped up the floor were a few rocks under the center.

By this time they were aware that they needed new wiring, plumbing, and heating to replace the pipes that ran crazily around the walls. However, it was the bricklayer who advised them that the pipes and wiring must be installed first underneath before he laid the brick floor in the kitchen.

The living-room mantel was a later addition that did not conform to the period, so they ripped it off, only to discover bricks falling out of the wall and beaverboard propped in the gaps. Before they knew it, they had demolished the living room. The bricklayer reported that the

---

* A wall that is a structural component of the house and carries part of the load (weight) of the floors above.

chimney was a disaster, with scorched boards all around it. It had to be rebuilt from the top to bottom.

Fortunately, Alexandria is a tightly knit community with some excellent (and honest) craftsmen, so the couple survived and achieved a charming, beautifully restored house. However, they could have avoided their problems by having the house inspected before purchase. If they had bought it in spite of its defects, they would have known what to expect and been able to plan accordingly.

Begin to plan by looking carefully at the place you are currently living in. What do you like about it? What do you dislike? Look at your friends' homes, and evaluate how they would work for you. Make a list of what you would like to have in a house and what you would like to avoid. At all times you must keep finances in mind.

Before getting your plans on paper, you must understand the elements of a renovation and how they relate to one another. There are four general areas:

1. *Mechanical systems* (plumbing, wiring, heating, air conditioning, and mechanical ventilation): all of these systems are important because they provide essential services and conveniences. You may be able to use those currently existing in your house, but some, even if they are in good condition, may be inadequate for your needs and will have to be replaced or expanded. You should have an idea from the professional inspection what can be salvaged and what cannot.
2. *Room arrangement* (the floor plan)
3. *Equipment* (fixtures, cabinets, and appliances)
4. *Decorating* (flooring, painting, etc.)

You are probably familiar with the last three: The first seems a dreadful bore and is often swept under the carpet, either because the renovator is unaware of its importance or because he is too preoccupied with the kind of stove he will buy to think about whether there is a gas line that will make it work. While it is natural to be excited about the things that make a house attractive and pleasant, first things must come first, both in planning and construction. The mechanical systems must be considered first because they provide the necessary comforts that few of us are willing to do without—and you cannot decide where to put the dishwasher until you know where the plumbing and wiring will be. The dishwasher would be singularly useless without either.

· PLUMBING

Plumbing is a convenience that none of us would consider giving up. In addition to basic bath and kitchen facilities, it enables us to have such labor-saving devices as washing machines, dishwashers, and garbage disposals. Yet no other single item in a house can cause more annoyance, damage, and expense when it fails to function properly. Plumbing is an essential element of any renovation effort, and yet it is probably the least understood. If you are to plan and execute a renovation and hold your cost down, understanding the fundamentals of plumbing is essential. This knowledge will also enable you to see that your plumbing is installed properly when construction begins.

The plumbing system in any house consists of water pipes, which carry hot and cold water, soil (or waste) pipes, which carry water and waste to the sewer, and gas pipes. Most cities provide a public water supply and a public sewer system, each of which is usually located below ground in front of the property. (The local utility company's gas supply lines normally run in the same location.) The city also has a plumbing code, which is part of the Building Code: rules and regulations about plumbing—the kinds and sizes of pipes that can be used and how they must be installed and maintained. The code usually requires that new plumbing pipes be installed by licensed plumbers. Although plumbing codes vary from city to city, there are certain fundamentals of plumbing that apply everywhere.

· WATER LINES

There is a water line below ground that brings water from the city water supply (main) to the house; the installation and maintenance of this line is the responsibility of the property owner. Once inside the house, this supply line must be divided into two separate lines—one for cold water and one for hot. Hot water is obtained by feeding cold water into a *hot water heater* or into a *heating coil* that is part of the furnace. However the water is heated, you want to make sure that there is an adequate supply of hot water at all times by having a heater or coil large enough for the demands made on it. Water heaters can either be heated by the furnace or separately heated so that the furnace does not have to be on in hot weather.

A pair of water lines called *risers* are then run vertically through the house with pipes called *branches* connecting plumbing fixtures to the risers. The size of pipe needed for water lines will be determined by the number of fixtures and appliances serviced by the risers and by how high the risers must run. Risers are normally larger than branches, because constant pressure must be maintained in the risers even when one of the branch lines is turned on. If risers are too small, you will get a dribble when you should have strong pressure. Inadequate water pressure is a common problem in old houses. Many times the original water lines, which were installed to service only one bath, have been employed to serve several baths and/or kitchens, resulting in loss of water pressure at the top of the house when water is turned on below. This is usually the sign that water lines are too small for the use to which they are put.

When indoor plumbing came into use, water lines were made of lead (many old houses still contain some or all of the original lead pipes). Since then, water pipes have gone through an evolution of iron, steel, brass, and copper, with the latest innovation the introduction of plastic pipe. Although plastic piping has been endorsed as efficient and economical in certain situations by engineers and other professionals, many building codes do not allow its use— brass or copper is generally required for new water lines.

It is possible to continue using existing water lines when they are in the right location, are large enough, and are in good condition. However, you will often find that the water lines in old houses are a combination of various kinds of pipe, copper or brass mixed with lead or galvanized pipe. This combination of metals causes corrosion at the joints, resulting in leaks and broken pipes.

Do not take a chance on existing pipes that are in poor condition. A completely modernized and correctly installed plumbing system will give years of repair-free service. No one wants to go through the ordeal of major plumbing work once the renovation is completed. DON'T SCRIMP ON PLUMBING RENOVATION. Immediate savings will only increase the cost in the long run and cause headaches in the future.

· SOIL LINES

Each plumbing fixture must have a soil pipe, which takes water and waste to the sewer. It would obviously be very expensive to run a separate pipe from each fixture to the sewer; therefore, a vertical soil line, called a *stack,* is brought up through the house, and the fixtures in the house are attached to it by means of pipes called *branches.* Gases from the decomposition of waste are generated in the soil lines. To prevent these gases, odors, and actual waste from backing up into the fixtures, two things are done. First, each fixture has a *trap* connected to the drain pipe close to the fixture. This trap, an S-shaped pipe, holds a certain amount of water at all times through which gases cannot force their way. (The trap is the curved pipe you see under every sink.) In addition, the soil stack must be opened at the top so that sufficient fresh air can be supplied to the stack and branches through *vent pipes* to prevent back-up of waste material into fixtures and to dilute sewer gas. Every soil stack must go all the way through the roof. Each fixture must be connected to both the vent and the soil stack. The following illustration shows a soil stack, vent stack, and the branches of each.

Plumbing diagram

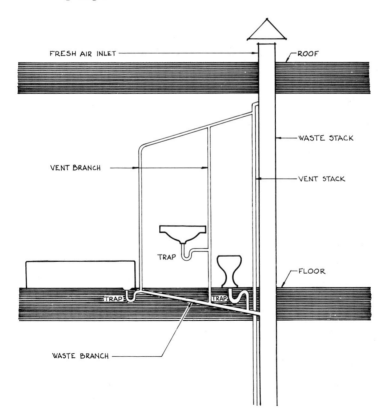

All of the pipes shown above would be hidden in the walls with the exception of the sink trap. Additional plumbing facilities could be installed on the other side of the stack and on the floor below by connecting these fixtures to the stack with additional branches. Notice that the above illustration shows the soil branch on a slant. If soil branches were horizontal, water and waste would not flow easily into the stack, but would tend to lie and accumulate in the pipe. All soil pipes that are not vertical must have a slope sufficient to insure immediate removal of waste to the sewer.

The soil stack is connected in the cellar to the *house drain.* The house drain is a large cast-iron pipe that normally runs (sloping) along a side wall, or along the floor, disappearing below ground at the front of the cellar. The house drain goes through the foundation wall and is joined to the *house sewer,* a large pipe connecting the house drain with the city sewer. (The installation and repair of the house sewer is the responsibility of the property owner.) The exterior gutters and leaders as well as the yard drains are connected to the house drain so that all water and waste is transported to the sewer.

Provisions must be made for cleaning out the drains and stacks in case of stoppage. This is done in the cellar by means of special plumbing fittings that have removable caps. These fittings are called *clean-outs,* and enough of them must be installed in the proper locations so that all lines can be properly cleaned out.

If soil lines are in good condition, are in the proper location for the baths and kitchens you need, and are large enough to service the fixtures and appliances you plan to install, there is no reason to replace them. Soil lines are generally cast iron, and the size required depends on the amount of waste they must dispose of. Be sure they are large enough to handle normal usage without clogging, and be sure that all lines are vented. Without proper venting you may find suds from the kitchen bubbling up in the bathroom sink, or possibly worse things.

· NEW PLUMBING INSTALLATION

If your plumbing is in the right location for the kitchens and baths you need and if it is in reusable condition, count yourself extremely fortunate indeed. (Do not forget to check the condition of the house sewer and water supply line from the street.) Being able to use existing plumbing can save a great deal of money.

If new plumbing is necessary, you must have more information before planning for it. Since the installation of new pipes is expensive, you should plan your room arrangement so that unnecessary plumbing costs are avoided. The location of baths, kitchens, and other plumbing facilities determines to some degree the price of the plumbing installation. One *line of plumbing* (soil stack, vent stack, and water risers) can serve many different plumbing facilities. The location of these facilities will determine whether more than one plumbing line is required. The examples shown on page 273 are an illustration:

Example A shows a situation where a separate plumbing line is needed for each bath because the distance between the two rooms is too great for both to be served by one line. The two plumbing lines are indicated by 000 inside the walls at either side of the plan. Example B shows how a simple modification of the plan will allow one line (located in the joint wall and indicated by 000) to serve both baths. From the point of construction, there is no difference between the two plans—each requires the same number of partitions. However, the difference in plumbing costs between the two is great.

Example B makes use of what is called *back-to-back plumbing*. When two rooms, both of which require plumbing, are placed back-to-back, one plumbing line located in the common wall can serve both areas. If the location of plumbing facilities is the same on two or more floors, the same line will serve each of these facilities. This is called *stacked plumbing*. In stacked plumbing, the plumbing facilities can be on either or both sides of the plumbing line. You can combine stacked and back-to-back plumbing to serve any number of needs. Thus it is possible to have all plumbing needs served by one plumbing line. This method of plumbing installation is the most economical and easiest.

Running the plumbing line vertically through the house is not always possible. Where the location of the plumbing line must change between floors, there may be problems. The soil stack must either be vertical or sloped sufficiently to allow waste to flow properly. If the shift in location occurs within a wall that can accommodate the necessary slope of the stack, there is no problem. However, if the shift in location of the stack involves crossing a room, there may not be sufficient space for the necessary slope of the stack. For this reason, baths and kitchens cannot be located on a mere whim—the problem of providing plumbing to these rooms must be considered.

This discussion of plumbing has been provided to prevent you from making costly plumbing mistakes—either by failure to replace inadequate or faulty plumbing, or by failure to plan the renovation to keep plumbing installation cost at a minimum. This is not to say that one plumbing line is always more economical than two. If two plumbing lines will enable you to renovate with no wall changes whereas the use of only one line would mean a complete alteration of the existing floor plan, by all means use two plumbing lines. In that case, the cost of the extra plumbing will probably be far less than substantial demolition and rebuilding. Plumbing cost must be considered in light of the total cost of renovation. However, when substantial rebuilding as well as new plumbing is required, the use of stacked back-to-back plumbing should be considered. The money saved by using one plumbing line instead of two can pay for an additional bath. The cost in relation to value received should be weighed in all decisions involv-

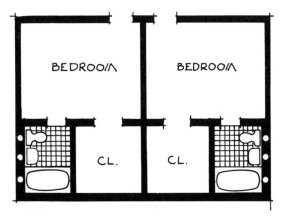

EXAMPLE A

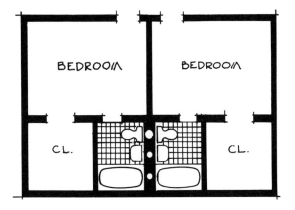

EXAMPLE B

o   o   o INDICATE PLUMBING LINES (OR STACKS)

ing plumbing. (This is true of all other elements of a renovation also.)

Keeping costs down is necessary, but sometimes the wrong things are sacrificed in the name of the budget. People often cut out plumbing facilities they want because they think they cannot afford them. When rough plumbing (the installation of pipes inside the walls) is being done, the cost of an additional branch or two is minimal. Installing the rough plumbing does not mean that the fixtures must be installed immediately. These branches can be capped off for use at a later date. Providing new branch lines when new plumbing is being installed is relatively simple and inexpensive; doing it later involves taking the whole line apart and inserting new fittings. The cost for such a job is often prohibitive, to say nothing of the mess involved. Make provisions in the new plumbing work for future additions you may not be able to afford now. A powder room, an extra bath, a washing machine or dishwasher may be out of the question now, but if the necessary pipes are installed, they can be added easily whenever the money is available.

Any large rental apartment should have provisions for installing a washer and dryer, even if you do not supply the appliances. These facilities are a big plus in renting. So is the provision for a dishwasher. Don't forget about outside faucets, front and rear. If you are planning to buy a refrigerator with an automatic ice maker, remember to have provision made for the water such an appliance requires. Plan for a sink in the cellar if it is used for a workshop—you can use one of the old sinks that are being removed.

· GAS LINES

Gas pipes are a very small part of plumbing installation. The gas company brings the necessary gas supply into the house, and the plumber takes the job from there. Gas lines are usually needed only for stoves and gas-fired clothes dryers; the gas lines for a gas furnace are a part of heating rather than plumbing. Old houses generally have gas lines, and these can be reused if they are in the proper location and are in good condition. If gas lines are in the wrong location, it is often easier and no more expensive to disconnect the old lines and run new ones than to trace out the existing lines and reroute them.

Gas was the source of light during the Victorian era, and houses built during that time often retain evidence of the original gaslights even though the fixtures have long ago been replaced. Many renovators use the old gas lines to install gas chandeliers in living or dining room. Another common practice of renovators is the installation of gas lamps on the exterior. If you want these, remember to make provision for the installation of gas lines for the fixtures.

The gaslight age also saw wide use of gas logs in fireplaces; the vestiges of these logs can be found in pipes protruding from the floors of fireplaces and in gas shut-off valves found on the floor beside many Victorian mantels. Some people who do not want to be bothered with wood have been reviving the use of gas logs in their fireplaces.

The gas supplied to the house passes through a meter so that the gas company can bill you for the amount you use. If the house contains rental units using gas stoves, it is possible to provide separate gas meters for each apartment so that tenants pay their own gas bills. However, the amount of gas used for cooking is minimal, and an owner can often provide gas for his tenants for very little money.

Be sure to consider any gas requirements when planning the renovation so that necessary pipes are provided. In many homes there is no gas at all. If you do not plan to use gas but gas lines exist in the house, have the gas company remove the meter or you will be billed the monthly minimum for a service you do not use.

· ELECTRICAL WIRING

The Building Code sets standards for electrical wiring, and most cities require that new wiring be installed by licensed electricians. Just because the wiring in a house meets city requirements does not mean that it will be adequate for your needs. City regulations merely set minimum requirements that must be met in order to insure the health and safety of residents. Current wiring may be adequate for current usage, but you may want additional equipment and appliances, and you must be sure that the wiring is adequate to service them.

The amount of electrical power available in any house depends on the *service line* that is brought to the house. The size of the service line determines the amount of electricity that can be used at any one time: The larger the service line, the more electricity available. The amount of electrical service is expressed in amperes (amps): Two-hundred-amp service is larger than one-hundred-amp service, and will therefore provide more electrical power to the house. The size service you need depends on your electrical requirements.

The electric company provides the service line for your house. A service line adequate fifteen years ago will scarcely be adequate for today's needs. The list of electric gadgets (toothbrushes, knives, can openers) grows each year, as do innovations such as self-defrosting refrigerators and self-cleaning electric ovens. This gradual electrification of our lives means that the average family in the United States uses many times more electricity than it did fifteen years ago.

Electric companies are aware of this rapid expansion of electrical needs and realize that older homes are not adequately wired for today's usage. For this reason, most electric companies provide some sort of *adequate-wiring survey* free of charge to property owners. This survey will determine whether the existing service is adequate for the owner's electrical requirements. If it is not, the company will determine what size service is required and will issue a report stating service size as well as the number of circuits needed inside the house and the size of wire to be used for each. This report can then be included in any contract for rewiring to insure that all work is done in accordance with the report. Many electric companies will send out inspectors during renovation to see that adequate wiring-survey requirements have been met.

The size of the service determines the amount of electricity that can be safely used; if more power is demanded than is available, the line becomes overloaded and can cause a fire. *Fuses* are a safety device to prevent overloading. When too much power is demanded, the fuse blows and shuts off the power. *Circuit breakers* are the modern substitute for fuses. Fuses require replacement when blown; the circuit breaker merely flips off to shut off power and prevent an overload. To return power to the area, you merely flip the appropriate circuit breaker just as you would a light switch.

The service line passes through a *master circuit breaker* just after it enters the house, thereby enabling all power to be turned off at the source. The service line is then fed into a *meter* so that the electric company knows how much electricity is being used. If the house contains more than one apartment, a meter can be installed for each apartment. Separate meters allow each occupant to pay his own bill so that landlords do not have to estimate how much electricity a tenant will use when setting the rent. The tenant can then regulate how much electricity he uses and must pay for.

From the meter, wiring is divided into *circuits,* which

are then carried to the various areas of the house. Each circuit has its own circuit breaker (or fuse). These circuit breakers are housed in a *circuit-breaker box,* which is installed either in the cellar or inside the apartment. (There will be at least one circuit-breaker box for each meter.) The division of wiring into circuits enables power to be turned off in one circuit without turning off power everywhere in the house. Each circuit should be clearly labeled so that you know what area it services.

It is the electrician's job to install the proper size of wire for each circuit and to divide the electrical requirements among the various circuits available, making certain that the demands made on each circuit can be met. Certain electrical equipment such as room air conditioners and electric stoves require separate lines because they use so much power, whereas several lights or plugs can be placed on the same line. It is mandatory to give your electrician all of your electrical requirements in advance of rewiring so that he can plan his installation properly. One renovator forgot to tell the electrician that he was planning to use an electric stove; when the stove arrived, it could not be installed.

If a professional inspection of the house was made, you will have a report on the condition of the existing wiring in the house. If the wiring is safe (that is, the existing circuits are not overloaded) but inadequate to supply all of your needs, it is often possible merely to add to the wiring already present. This can be done even when the size of the service must be changed in order to install new circuits. Bringing in a new service line involves no work on the wiring inside the house.

You may have a problem reusing existing wiring when separate meters are to replace the one currently in use. Let us give a simple example to illustrate the point:

A two-story house currently has one meter. A renovation of the house will create two apartments, one on each floor of the house, and each apartment is to have its own meter. The existing wiring is good, but it must be separated and fed into the appropriate meter. If the wiring was installed so that each circuit only supplied electricity to one floor, there is no problem. If, however, one circuit supplies electricity to parts of both floors, the separation of wiring is difficult.

Tracing out existing wiring is often arduous and time-consuming. Many electricians will refuse to do the job if it is a complex one. Tracing the existing wiring to reuse it may be just as expensive as disconnecting it and running all new wires.

Electrical work involves running wires inside the walls and ceilings. These wires are run into *electrical boxes* to which switches, outlets, fixtures, and special electrical appliances are attached. Where existing plaster is to remain, the job involves breaking small holes and snaking the wires inside, and making holes large enough to house boxes at specified locations. Where new partitions are being erected, installing new wiring is a simple matter. Since more time is involved in snaking wires inside of existing walls than in running wires in open partitions, electricians often charge more for the former. Therefore, all necessary wiring should be done at the beginning of renovation rather than after new walls have been closed up and existing ones patched and painted.

Renovators are generally more familiar with the need for adequate wiring, possibly because of the fire hazard of old electrical systems, than they are for the need for adequate plumbing, but often they do not carefully study their electrical needs when planning the renovation.

The planning of wiring is essential, but the renovator seldom realizes its importance until he suddenly discovers that there is no outlet in the bathroom for his electric razor or that the walk-in closet is unusable because it has no light.

Electricians often charge by the box—so much for each outlet, switch, fixture, and so on. The cost can mount rapidly, so keep it in mind when planning, but do not cut corners where you may regret it.

· OUTLETS

There are three types of electrical outlets: *convenience outlets,* the regular kind of double plug used for lamps, radios, and other small appliances; *utility outlets* for kitchens, workshops, and other areas where appliances drawing a lot of current are used: and *heavy-duty outlets* for such equipment as air conditioners, electric stoves, and electric dryers. Several convenience outlets can be placed on one circuit, whereas utility and heavy-duty outlets require their own lines, with heavy-duty outlets requiring the use of heavier wire than the other two.

The first thing you must consider is how many outlets of each variety you will need. Most electrical codes specify a minimum number of outlets for each room (according to its size and use), but you may want more. Next consider their location. You may have a sufficient number of outlets, but if they are not properly located, they can be frustrating. Consider the following when planning outlets:

1. Outlets should be no farther than 6 feet apart, because that is the standard length of appliance and light cords.
2. Provide enough outlets in the kitchen for all your appliances—then add another for future acquisitions.
3. Do not forget about outlets in the bathroom.
4. If the cellar is to be a work area, provide outlets there too, although they can be added later since exposed wires there are not a problem.
5. Provide outlets at the top and bottom of stairs and in or near halls for vacuum cleaning.
6. Wire for dishwasher, washing machine, and dryer even though you do not plan to install them immediately.

7. Do not forget weatherproof exterior outlets in the garden.
8. Wire for gadgets such as timer, light, and clock on stove; this line is different from the one that provides electricity for oven and burners, and must also be provided for gas stoves with such equipment.
9. There are outlets with special covers to protect children: Consider these if there are toddlers in your house.
10. Many building codes now require an air conditioning outlet in every room when central air conditioning is not being installed. If this regulation does not apply in your area, it is a good idea to consider it anyway unless the climate precludes the need.

· FIXTURES

The next consideration is the placement of fixtures. Fixtures are either surface-mounted on wall or ceiling, or recessed. In surface mounting, only the electrical box is recessed; but in recessed fixtures, the fixture must also be inside the wall or ceiling, and a wooden frame to hold it must be made and put in place by the carpenter before the electrician installs the fixture. Location of recessed fixtures depends on the position of beams. Beams normally run the width of the house, and there is less space between them in old houses than in new ones. It takes several recessed fixtures to give as much light as many surface-mounted fixtures using the same size bulb. Recessed lighting can be extremely effective, but you should be aware of the added installation cost (more fixtures required to produce enough light, extra cost of framing out) before deciding to use it. Also think twice about putting many recessed fixtures in a twelve-foot ceiling if you mind getting out a tall stepladder whenever a light bulb needs replacing. Recessed lights are ideal for low ceilings, where surface-mounted ceiling fixtures make ceilings seem even lower.

There are two kinds of light bulbs used in fixtures: fluorescent and incandescent. Fluorescent bulbs are more economical, and bulbs last far longer, but this kind of lighting is so often associated with institutions and unattractive fixtures that many renovators do not consider it. There are, however, very attractive surface-mounted and recessed fixtures available for use in baths and kitchens. Strip fluorescent lights can be used effectively when concealed under kitchen cabinets or used behind decorative moldings around the ceiling of any room. Another attractive solution is to conceal fluorescent strips behind translucent fiberglass panels. An entire fiberglass ceiling can be hung in baths and kitchens that have ceiling heights of ten feet or more. Seal all holes and cracks, leave pipes along the ceiling exposed (or do not bother to recess new ones). Paint the ceiling all white to reflect light, install enough fluorescent strips to give proper light, and then hang the luminous ceiling (metal strips hold the fiberglass panels). These can be installed by a handy homeowner and are available from Sears Roebuck or your local supply house. The effect is of a skylit room, and the bulbs last a year or more without replacing.

The exact location of all fixtures must be known when the electrician does his wiring, so that boxes can be installed in the proper places. Adequate lighting is difficult to achieve, as most of us are sadly aware. In a renovation, you have an opportunity to remedy the situation. Take the time to plan it properly. You may even want to consult a lighting expert. At any rate, be sure to consider the following:

1. Although specific fixtures (except those that are recessed) need not be selected at the time the location of electrical boxes is planned, the kind of fixture to be used may influence the location, particularly in wall-mounted types, where the size of the fixture may determine its placement.

2. Fixtures using several candelabra-type bulbs are lovely, but changing the bulbs, each of which inevitably burns out at a different time, can be a real nuisance. Limit the use of such fixtures for sanity's sake.

3. The location of the ceiling fixture in a dining room can be critical, since most people want it centered over the dining table. If there is any doubt about the location of the table or if you contemplate shifting its location occasionally, you may want to omit the overhead fixture and instead use wall fixtures with candles on the table.

4. If you plan to use heavy chandeliers or ceiling fixtures, be sure to let your contractor know so that he can make any necessary provisions. An electrical box will not carry the load of a heavy fixture—usually a pipe or small beam must be put in to support the weight.

5. Do not forget about lights for the cellar, attic, and inside closets.

6. Lights should be provided for the exterior of the building, both front and rear. If an extension roof is used for a terrace, put a light there, too. If the house has a high stoop, you may want a light at the top of the stoop as well as at the ground floor entrance.

7. Electricians often object to drilling through masonry walls, and will run exposed exterior wires to avoid it. Insist that no wires be run along the exterior of your house even if it does cost extra to recess them, so that exposed conduit does not detract from the beauty of the façade.

8. If you want a gaslight in front of your house, provision must be made by the plumber.

· SWITCHES

Once you have located all fixtures in the house, you can plan the location of switches controlling them. Some observation of your current residence will start your thinking in the right direction. Have you ever lived in a place where the bathroom light switch was behind the door, so that you had to go into the dark room and partially close the door before you could turn on the light? Or have you found light switches placed so high that your children had to be seven or eight years old before they could reach them? Sometimes this can be an advantage, but more often it is a nuisance. Whatever you want, plan deliberately, so that you will not have to live with the accidental whim of the electrician. Architect Benjamin Kitchen, designing his own Philadelphia town house, put the switch by the front door low enough so that it could be turned on with his knee when he came home loaded with packages. As soon as all new partitions are erected, mark the exact position of each outlet and switch with a felt-tipped pen so that there can be no doubt about where you want them to be. Insist that all switches and outlets be placed at the same height and absolutely vertical, or you may find yourself with some absurd variations.

One switch can control one or more fixtures. Sometimes it is pointless to have a switch for each fixture. On the other hand, you want to be able to control the number of lights illuminated at one time, so that four lights do not go on when only one is needed. In some cases you should be able to turn lights on and off at more than one location: This can be done with three-way switches. You will probably want three-way switches at the top and bottom of all stairs and possibly at either end of large rooms. It is even possible to control lights all over the house from a central location, such as the master bedroom or front door. Remember however, that when you pay by the electrical box, a switch is separate from the fixture it controls, and a three-way switch counts as three boxes.

When planning switches, consider the following:

1. Dimmer switches can be used in living and dining room to alter the intensity of light. There is an additional charge for these, and if money is tight, they can be installed later by a handy homeowner familiar with wiring. There is no saving in electricity when lights are dimmed.

2. The budget-conscious renovator should be aware of the combination outlet, where switch and outlet are installed for the price of only one box. However, you get only one outlet, so do not use it where you may have two appliances in constant use, such as an electric toothbrush and an electric razor. This type of outlet is ideal for a guest bath or powder room.

3. Exterior lights can be controlled by a photoelectric cell that automatically turns on lights at night, especially convenient for those who often return home after dark.

4. Closet lights can be operated by an old-fashioned pull-chain or switches that automatically turn on the light when the door opens and off when the door shuts.

· OTHER WIRING

Another electrical system that should be considered is an *intercom*. Urban apartment dwellers are accustomed to the convenience of being able to ask who is calling when the front doorbell rings without going downstairs to answer it. These systems can be equally important to a house that has more than two floors, and can be useful inside the house to communicate with family members who are several floors away. An adequate system need not be prohibitively expensive, and should be included in your wiring plans.

Another idea borrowed from the apartment house is the installation of a *door buzzer system,* used to let visitors into a locked building. When combined with an intercom, the buzzer system can save the homeowner countless steps, because he can release the lock merely by pushing a button at the intercom box. The location of intercom boxes and door buzzers is important. There should be at least one on every floor, located so that it is easily accessible. Do not forget the cellar if it is a work area; the one on the entrance floor is more useful at the rear than close to the entrance. Be sure that intercoms are placed at the proper height for the family—better too low than too high. This system is virtually a necessity where rental units are on top floors of four-story and five-story houses.

In summation, a rewiring job should include the following items where applicable:

1. New service line from the street
2. New meters when more than one meter is used
3. Replacement of fuses with circuit breakers
4. A circuit-breaker box inside each apartment
5. Adequate and properly located outlets, fixtures, and switches
6. Air conditioning outlets or electrical wiring for a central system
7. Heavy duty lines for electric stoves and other appliances
8. Wiring for heating and air conditioning thermostats
9. Wiring for dishwashers, washing machines, and clothes dryers
10. Intercom and door-buzzer systems
11. Wiring for special requirements, such as a central stereo system

For a discussion of preparing and reading electrical plans, see pages 313 and 318.

• *Prewiring for Telephones and Cable Television.* Telephones require wiring also. In old houses a maze of wires is often found around door and window moldings, along baseboards, and on the exterior of the house. These wires are telephone installations that have accumulated over the years. Telephone installers usually find it necessary to put in new wires with each installation, but they seldom, if ever, remove those no longer in use. The need for so many exposed wires can be greatly reduced or eliminated altogether by *prewiring for telephones* during renovation. When the walls are open during construction, telephone wires can be placed inside. Telephone wires must run from a box that provides the service to each location in the house where a telephone is desired. In prewiring, these lines are run through the house vertically and/or horizontally, and connecting blocks (those square plastic boxes from which installations of individual phones are made) are located on each floor. Any installation is then made from these blocks without requiring wires brought all the way from the telephone box. In the case of New York City houses, the New York Telephone Company runs the wires up through the center of the house and puts two connecting blocks on each floor—one to service the front area and the other to service the rear. Thus, a telephone can easily be installed in any location with a minimum of wiring. If the exact location of telephones is determined in the renovation planning, it is possible to have the connecting blocks placed in the exact location where they are needed when prewiring is done.

The use of *telephone jacks* will enable you to use a telephone in more than one location by simply unplugging the phone and moving it to another jack. You are billed monthly for each phone you have; you pay for a jack only once, when it is installed, and one phone can then do double service. If you plan to use jacks, it is a good idea to have them installed in both the cellar (if it is used as a work area) and the back yard. That way you can take a phone with you and avoid the frantic rush to answer it when it rings.

The location of the telephone box can often be a problem to homeowners. Not every house has a box, because many different lines are fed through one box. If yours is a row house and the telephone box is in your back yard, the repair man may have to troop in and out of your house to make repairs on any phone serviced by the box. Having the box located in the cellar instead of the back yard can save wear and tear on your house as well as your nerves, particularly in bad weather. Your local telephone company should be contacted about the relocation of the box as well as about the availability of prewiring. Prewiring is only done where the necessary walls will be open.

The demand for telephone service has increased so rapidly that in many areas there is a delay in installation, or in getting a phone number assigned. It is a good idea to reserve your phone in advance to be sure you get it when you need it.

If you plan to use cable television, the necessary wiring should be done during construction so that these wires can also be hidden in the walls.

· HEATING

There are three kinds of heating systems in use in older city houses: forced air, steam, and hot water. Each of these systems requires a furnace, which is generally fired by either oil or gas, although coal-fired furnaces are sometimes still in use. Steam and hot-water systems usually require radiators—steam or hot water is produced by the furnace and moves through pipes to the radiators. In forced-air systems, heated air moves through metal ducts to outlets (registers) in the floor or walls of each room. The ducts for forced-air systems can also be used for air conditioning.

Before you make any decision about a heating system, you should determine the condition of the one that currently exists: It may be in good condition. If it works, leave well enough alone. You may have problems with a new one. Old furnaces may need attachments added to make them easier to operate, but such work is minor.

Often pipes and radiators or ducts are in good condition but the furnace is old and inefficient (that is, burns too much fuel for the amount of heat produced). If so, you need only replace the furnace. The price of a new furnace is small compared to the cost of a whole new heating system. Furnaces can sometimes be converted to use another fuel (coal to oil, or oil to gas) without having to install a new furnace.

Old-fashioned radiators are not the most attractive things, but they can often be cleverly camouflaged, recessed, or even replaced with the newer baseboard type of radiation. People can often learn to live with radiators and exposed heating pipes when they learn the price of installing a new heating system.

However, there are times when a new system makes sense. If the existing system does not provide sufficient heat for the house, you must change the system if you cannot expand the current one to supply demand. If you are installing central air conditioning with ductwork, it may make sense to use the same ducts to supply heat, which will enable you to get rid of the old radiators and exposed heating pipes.

When deciding on a new heating system, consider electric heat as well as the types already mentioned. Electric heat eliminates radiators as well as furnaces. Upkeep on electric heat is just about nil, and each room can have its own control. If the house has several apartments, the heat can be separately metered so that tenants pay their own heating bills. There is one big drawback: In most areas, electrical rates are high by comparison to other fuels, and the house must be well insulated if heating costs are to be kept at a reasonable level. When considering electric heat, check with people who have installed it to see if they are satisfied and how their heating costs compare with other systems. The electric company should be willing to give you the names of such people.

When selecting the type of system to install, you should consider not only installation and operating costs, but also be sure that there are competent people to install and service the system. The following example, though not a case of new installation, illustrates this point:

Carol and Larry Hulack bought a house in Manhattan that had a hot-water heating system. The engineer who checked the house praised the condition of the system and told them how lucky they were to have hot-water heat. The Hulacks were delighted, until the renovation was finished. They could not get any hot water until the furnace was turned on since the hot water was provided by a heating coil on the furnace. The plumber could not make the furnace work. After a week of bathing in cold water, they found someone who knew something about hot-water heating systems. They were well into the winter before the system was made to function properly, not because anything was wrong with the system, but because hot-water heat is rare in Manhattan and not many people understand how it works.

The same is true of gas furnaces. In Manhattan most furnaces are oil fired, and therefore many people service the equipment. It is very difficult to find someone to service a gas furnace, because the gas company, unlike fuel oil companies, provides only fuel. Although Brooklyn Union Gas gives its customers free service, Con Edison, serving Manhattan, provides no service at all.

If you install a new heating system, carefully select the person who designs it. He should be familiar with the peculiar features of old houses, the cost of installing and operating (in old houses rather than new ones) each type of system, and the availability of service for each. Before you let anyone design your heating system, check on him as thoroughly as you would an architect. (See page 327 on checking an architect.) If your architect is to design the system, be sure he is qualified to do so. As for the person who will install it, check him as carefully as you would a general contractor (see pages 342–46), and be sure he gives an adequate guarantee of the work.

· AIR CONDITIONING

Air conditioning, once considered a luxury, is rapidly becoming so prevalent that many people take it for granted and many building codes require installation of air conditioning outlets when rewiring. Air conditioning can be provided by individual window units or installation of a central system. In either case, there must be adequate electrical service to the house and electric lines inside the house to service it.

Window units are far cheaper than a central system when only one or two are needed. However, if very many window units are required, you should compare their cost (plus cost of necessary wiring) with the cost of a central system. If the cost is close, the central system is preferable.

Since central air conditioning requires a network of ducts that usually should be hidden in the walls, they must be installed during the early part of the renovation, while walls are still open. If you have a forced-air heating system, the ducts can sometimes be used to service central air conditioning by simply adding the necessary equipment or replacing the furnace with one designed to serve both heating and cooling. If the central system must be designed from scratch, it should be designed by an air conditioning specialist. Two sets of ducts (one to circulate cool air and the other to remove warmer air) are needed, and they must be located so that an even temperature is maintained throughout each room as well as throughout the house.

Locating ducts within the framework of a house where floor joists (beams) and partitions are in place before the system is designed is much more difficult than when the system is a part of the design of a new house. Make sure that whoever designs your air conditioning system is familiar with the problems of installation in old houses.

If the cost of a central air conditioning system is more than your budget will allow, it is possible to install ducts and necessary wiring during the renovation, postponing the purchase and installation of equipment until a later date. The cost of opening walls to install ducts later is far greater, and ducts are often difficult to locate properly because of pipes, etc., inside. The installation of central air conditioning is almost a matter of now or never.

In an installation where more than one apartment is involved, you can have either one system for the whole house or a separate system for each apartment. The latter is obviously more expensive initially, because it involves duplicating equipment; but since tenants can pay their own air conditioning bills, the extra cost may be justified. And of course you can always provide central air conditioning for only the part of the house that you occupy.

Make certain that you thoroughly check the credentials of the person who designs and installs the air conditioning system. A guarantee of installation and equipment is mandatory.

· MECHANICAL VENTILATION

Building codes regulate the size of rooms and the amount of air each must receive. Most cities require that living rooms (any room used for living or sleeping) must have natural ventilation from windows. However, rooms such as baths and kitchens can have ventilation provided by mechanical means. Mechanical ventilation is supplied by ducts with fans attached that provide and circulate necessary air. There is either a central fan on the roof, controlled by a clock (usually located in the cellar), or individual room fans that start automatically when the light is turned on. (The building code sets requirements for mechanical ventilation—sizes of ducts and fans, installation methods, and sizes of rooms so ventilated.)

Mechanical ventilation enables the renovator to use space that might otherwise be wasted. In the case of the row house, interior space can be used for kitchens and baths; and if the house is a deep one, this space can often provide two such rooms on each floor. (See floor plans on page 181.)

· ROOM ARRANGEMENT

As you can see, the mechanical systems in your house will affect your floor plans. The location of plumbing determines where kitchens, baths, and laundry equipment can be placed. Once you have determined the location of these rooms, you can begin to think of their size and the most desirable, convenient arrangement of other rooms in relation to them and to each other. Ideally, each room should function well within the total plan. Rooms should flow into each other so that the house has an open and spacious feeling while still providing needed privacy.

When planning room arrangement, apply all of your earlier thinking on present and future family needs and living patterns, and what you do and do not want in your house. Start thinking about details, because they must be considered when planning the location and sizes of rooms.

Think about traffic patterns when planning rooms. Avoid bottlenecks at main entrances and other areas such as halls and kitchens. There should be easy access to each room without impairing its function.

Consider the moving of furniture when planning. It is frustrating and costly to find that you must discard your sofa because you cannot get it through the door or down the hall. Halls and front doors should be three feet wide, as should doors to rooms that will have large pieces of furniture. Avoid, where possible, the use of long halls, which tend to become a maze of doors. Where a long hall is unavoidable, a width of three and a half to four feet will make it seem shorter and allow the use of decorative pieces of furniture to avoid a bowling-alley effect.

Ceiling heights are an important consideration. A ten-by-fifteen-foot room with a ten-foot ceiling seems more spacious than the same room with an eight-foot ceiling. Creating wide entries, using double doors or eliminating doors altogether, helps give visual space to areas with low ceilings. On the other hand, avoid small, narrow rooms where ceilings are high, or you may have an upended-coffin effect. (Ceilings should be lowered in such areas.)

The standard-height door for today's construction is six feet eight inches or seven feet. Using these in rooms with twelve-foot ceilings, particularly when combined with original doors nine to ten feet tall, can be very disconcerting. New doors over seven feet high must be custom made and are very expensive. When old doors are not available, clever solutions can be found. Borrow from the Victorian era and install transoms (fake) above stock doors to create the illusion of height. Transoms can be solid wood painted to match the door or decorative panels, with door molding going around door and transom to the desired height.

Room sizes can be important. A living room and dining room must be large enough to accommodate needed furniture, but the use of built-in furniture can make a small room seem spacious. When the number of rooms is important and the amount of space you can afford is limited, do not rule out small rooms. One room can be divided, either permanently or temporarily, to make private areas for two children.

To make the best first impression, plan the entrance to your home so that it makes an impact. A tiny entrance hall can cause a traffic jam. Direct entrance into a major room detracts from its usefulness and subjects it to more than normal dirt and traffic. When planning the entry, remember the conveniences of coat closet and powder room for guests.

There can never be too much storage space, so be sure to plan enough. In rooms with high ceilings, utilize the space above the height of closet doors. Built-in wall cabinets or niches for open shelves can be made very easily and inexpensively between the studs in bathrooms if they are included in the plans for construction. Use the studs themselves for the sides of the cabinet or niche, with a horizontal piece for top and bottom installed at the proper height. The interior must be finished, but in most cases the sheetrock on the wall behind can serve as the back. Add a door and molding to finish the cabinet. Old shutters make lovely doors for such cabinets and, when used on either side of the bathroom mirror, can be a custom-made detail on a very modest budget.

Pay careful attention to doors, not only their width and height but also the direction in which they open. There is nothing more annoying than having two or more doors placed close together that collide with each other, or having one open door block the use of another when the problem could be avoided by merely placing the hinge on the other side.

Think about furniture placement when planning room arrangement. The location of doors can chop up a room or create a hall within it, making furniture arrangement difficult. Be sure that there is sufficient wall space for furniture. Sometimes it is a mistake to keep an old mantel for decorative purposes when the wall is needed for a bed, desk, or sofa.

· EQUIPMENT

When you have determined the location of all rooms, you can begin to think about plumbing fixtures, cabinets, appliances, and other items that must be selected and installed in your house. Obviously, some of these things will determine the size of rooms and should be considered when planning room arrangement. For example, if you need a lot of kitchen storage space, the kitchen must be large enough to accommodate it. However, the details of the kitchen cabinets should not be a major concern until the total floor plan of the house has been worked out.

If you want the construction bids to come within your budget, choose stock (or standard) items wherever possible. Stock items can be used creatively—you don't have to pay a custom price to achieve a custom look. Clever use of inexpensive materials and equipment can create a spectacular effect. This is true of everything from doors and floors to cabinets and fixtures. White bathroom fixtures combined with distinctive wallpaper can be as attractive as colored tile and fixtures, and you have the option of changing the wallpaper when you get tired of the color. Stock kitchen cabinets can often be improved with a change of hardware. And an old dresser can become a vanity by replacing the top with formica in which a basin has been inserted. The dresser can either be stripped to the natural wood or antiqued in any number of marvelous colors.

Pay close attention to details because they can give your house a custom look. Take time to look at styles and samples of hardware, moldings, tile, and so forth well in advance of your final plans and specifications. They can be more important than you think. If you simply specify plain white tile for your bathroom floor, you may regret the choice for years if the tile man chooses to give you the unglazed type that absorbs dirt like a blotter. Think about the placement of towel bars and toilet-paper holders— trivial things that are so inconspicuous if they are right and so maddeningly annoying if they are wrong. If you think things will just appear in their proper place if left to the discretion of workmen, you may be in for an unpleasant shock.

· PLUMBING FIXTURES

You may be surprised at the infinite variety of plumbing fixtures available. There are four major plumbing fixture manufacturers (American Standard, Crane, Kohler, and Rheem) and numerous other small ones. American Standard, for instance, makes eight different styles of toilet for residential use, and each is available in a variety of colors. Plumbing fixtures consist of toilets, bidets, tubs and shower stalls, lavatories and sinks, as well as the trim (faucets and so on) that goes with them.

Each of these items should be selected and designated by manufacturer, style number, and color before the work is begun. One of the prime considerations in selecting plumbing fixtures should be their availability from local plumbing supply houses. The newest and most expensive items often require a special order, as do many colored fixtures. If a special order is necessary, it may take weeks and even months, holding up construction in the process —and the contractor may charge a higher markup for special-order material than he would for stock items. Remember that this year's fashionable color may date your bathroom five years from now, or be difficult to replace should damage occur. White fixtures are more readily available at supply houses and are less expensive than colored ones.

All major plumbing fixture manufacturers have showrooms in New York, Chicago, and other large cities. You can write to them for brochures and catalogues of all their equipment or get the information from local supply houses.

Some city building codes do not allow the use of certain plumbing equipment, such as garbage disposals. Be sure to check city regulations before ordering. Your architect, plumber, or plumbing supply house should know, but a call to the building department is always wise.

Bathtubs come in two heights, fourteen inches and sixteen inches. The fourteen-inch tub is the cheaper builder's model and is ideal for small children who have difficulty stepping over the additional two inches and for those who prefer showers, for the same reason. However, for people who like to soak, the sixteen-inch tub is preferable. If

Bathrooms like this are a familiar sight to renovators (sometimes there are as many as six or eight in one house). New plumbing fixtures, taste, and imagination can transform them.

the exact tub is not specified, the contractor may install the builder's model to save money.

Standard rectangular tubs are five feet long. (Tubs are available in five-and-a-half- and six-foot lengths, but they are expensive and usually require a special order.) Modern tubs are normally recessed into a niche and are finished

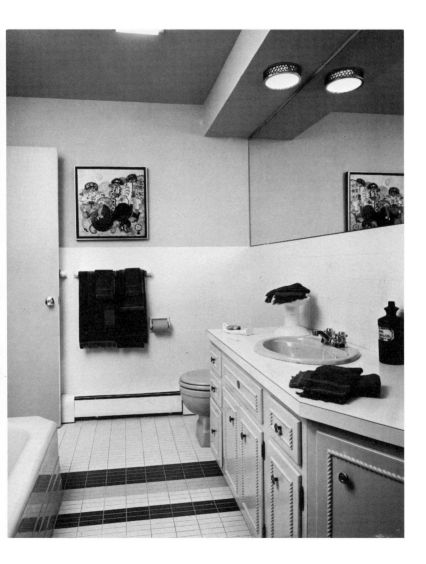

along only one side; you must specify which side is to be finished. If the end of the tub is to be exposed because it is fitted into a corner instead of a niche, you must buy one with a finished end.

Always install a shower body in at least one tub, even if you do not take showers. Its cost is nominal, and it will add to the value of your house. On the other hand, have at least one tub in the house even if you always take showers, for the same reason. If you plan your plumbing facilities exclusively for your own idiosyncracies, you may have difficulty selling, when and if that day should come.

Lavatories are made of enameled cast iron or vitreous china. There are pros and cons for each type—enameled cast iron chips, and china cracks. It is not a good idea to use china lavatories in children's areas.

Lavatories come in a variety of sizes and shapes, in wall-hung, free-standing, and counter-top models. Be sure that at least one lavatory in the house is large enough for washing lingerie, hose, and other items.

There are two kinds of installation for counter-top lavatories, one for formica tops and another for marble. You must specify the type of installation when ordering the lavatory in order to get the proper fixture.

Many toilets come in standard and elongated models. Be sure the room can handle the additional length when ordering the latter for a small bathroom. Wall-hung toilets are becoming popular, but special provision must be made for reinforcing the wall that carries their weight. Toilets do not usually come equipped with seats, so be sure to order them.

Most plumbing fixtures do not come equipped with trim (faucets and so on), so this must be selected separately. The new single lever and push-pull faucets are becoming popular, but remember that they are difficult for small children to operate.

A wide variety of shower heads is available. Those with adjustable head and spray are worth the slight additional cost. There are even thermostatic controls that can be installed on the shower body, enabling the bather to set water temperature and have it maintained. For real luxury, you can have a shower body installed at both ends of the tub so that the backside does not get cold while the frontside is warm.

· KITCHEN CABINETS AND COUNTER TOPS

There is infinite variety in both the design and cost of kitchen cabinets, from mail-order catalogue to custom cabinetmaker. You can order stock, ready-made cabinets and have your contractor or carpenter install them. Or you can go to a kitchen planning center, which will help you design your kitchen, sell you what you need, and install everything. And if stock cabinets do not appeal to you, you can hire a carpenter or cabinetmaker to build your cabinets exactly to your liking.

Most stock cabinets do not come with counter tops—those must be provided separately. Formica counter tops can have edges finished with metal strips or be self-edged; you must specify which you prefer. Butcher-block counter tops, usually of maple, are a great asset to any kitchen, allowing you to chop and cut at random. They can be installed in special areas or used for every counter top. Or if you prefer, you can have counter tops made of ceramic tile.

Back splashes are normally part of the counter top, and their height must be specified. With back splashes more than six inches high, you may want to have electrical outlets recessed into them. The outlet can be installed the usual way, or with plugs side by side instead of one above the other.

When using stock cabinets, you can seldom buy them to fit your space exactly. Filler pieces to match wooden cabinets are used in the spaces between cabinets and walls. Be sure to order these filler pieces when you order cabinets.

A

A. *Inexpensive stock cabinets, a butcher-block counter top, and economy vinyl asbestos floor combined with original brick hearth in Stanforth kitchen.*

B.-C. *Many renovators have converted shabby rooms like this to attractive kitchens.*

B

C

When selecting cabinets, think about such features as adjustable shelves in overhead cabinets, roll-out shelves in base cabinets, and drawers on rollers.

· APPLIANCES

Everybody is familiar with appliances, even people who have never bought one. Every city is full of appliance dealers. *Consumer Reports* regularly gives ratings to the various models, and you might want to check their back issues before making your selection. Be sure to purchase appliances easily serviced during the warranty period because a guarantee means nothing if there is no service by the manufacturer in your area.

The cost of appliances is directly related to the number of gadgets they contain. A "stripped down" stove is often half the price of the same stove with automatic timer, rotisserie, and other options. If your budget is tight, consider the cost of extra features in relation to their usefulness before deciding you need them. Also, when a new model first comes out, it is usually more expensive than one that has been in use for some time.

Do some window shopping and comparative pricing before selecting your appliances. (If you have several apartments, you may be able to get a discount from a dealer-distributor. Ask.) You should have the manufacturer's model number of every appliance you have selected. And remember to check the measurements of each appliance to be sure it will fit into the space allocated for it and can be moved through doorways and up or down stairs where necessary.

Wall ovens and counter-top burners take more space than a regular stove and limit counter area. There are regular stoves (forty inches wide, as opposed to the standard thirty- and thirty-six-inch models) with two ovens and six burners. If you like to cook and the size of your kitchen is limited, consider one of these.

Built-in dishwashers normally do not come with a front panel; it must be ordered separately. You can have one made to match your cabinets.

Self-defrosting or frost-free refrigerators are becoming almost standard. They cost a little more to buy and operate, but are worth every penny. Use them in tenants' kitchens also, so you don't have to worry about the appliance wearing out because your tenant did not defrost it regularly.

Refrigerator doors can be hinged on either the right or left. To prevent having the door open against a counter instead of a wall, be sure to specify which you want.

Refrigerator sizes are expressed in cubic feet, which tells you nothing about the width, height and depth of the appliance. Be sure to check dimensions so that the refrigerator fits into your kitchen.

It is often difficult to find space for a washing machine and dryer. The appliances that fit one on top of the other (stacked units) are often the answer, because they can be placed in a small, deep closet. Remember that dryers must be vented.

· DECORATING

"Decorating" is used here to describe that part of renovation related to interior decoration—painting, flooring, lighting fixtures, hardware, and other miscellaneous items. This stage of the planning is so much fun for most people that they fail to recognize the importance of what goes before.

All decorating is a matter of taste. What pleases me does not necessarily please you. Our only concern in this area is to point out the practical considerations to be taken into account. One that is often overlooked is maintenance. A white vinyl floor may be ever so lovely when laid, but the job of keeping it spotless is endless.

Cost is another consideration. Be sure that you get a dollar's worth of value for every dollar you spend. It is often possible to achieve the same look for a lower price if you are willing to spend some time looking at products and thinking about the desired effect.

If you are having difficulty making a decision, let it wait for a while. You can hardly do without a refrigerator; but if your kitchen is not painted for a time, it will not interfere with normal living. Better to wait than to be sorry.

· CITY REGULATIONS AFFECTING RENOVATION

Just because you plan to do a renovation does not mean that you are free to do whatever you choose. Each city has rules and regulations designed to protect its citizens. The two basic areas of concern are (1) zoning laws and (2) building codes. Any new construction or renovation of existing structures falls under the jurisdiction of both areas, and the renovator must acquaint himself in advance with these regulations to be sure he is not breaking the law.

· BUILDING CODES

Building codes vary from city to city, but each city has one. The building code is the compilation of all laws relating to building (new construction, alteration of existing conditions, and maintenance). These regulations have been passed over the years in order to insure the health and safety of citizens.

The renovator must find out how the local building code affects the work he intends to do. You need the answers to the following questions (if you plan to use an architect or a general contractor, he should know; if not, phone the building department):

1. Must plans be filed with and approved by the city?
2. Is a building permit necessary?
3. Does the city require the use of licensed contractors?
4. Does the city inspect the work?
5. Is a certificate of occupancy or a certificate of completion required when the work is complete?

Many renovators do not adhere to building code regulations, either because they are ignorant of them or because they do not want to be bothered. Failure to comply with the building code is never a good idea—the penalty for getting caught is not worth the risk. City regulations concerning approval of work, permits, inspections, and so on are all very valid. The city wants to insure that all buildings are structurally sound and free of fire and health hazards. These regulations protect you against faulty work and are written for your benefit. To ignore them is to leave yourself wide open for problems.

· APPROVAL OF PLANS

Not all renovation work requires the submission of plans to the building department. Generally, city approval is required when there are wall changes and/or a change in occupancy (the number or composition of apartments). City approval is usually required for any new plumbing, wiring, or any other change affected by building code regulations.

The filing (submission) of plans is usually required where city approval must be obtained, and approval must be obtained before any work is started. If the only changes to be made are plumbing and wiring, the contractor doing the work can file the necessary papers with the building department. If there are to be structural changes (removal or addition of walls) or a change in the number of apartments, a complete set of floor plans usually must be filed. In some cities, like New York and Chicago, these plans must be stamped by a licensed architect or professional engineer. In other cities, like Washington, plans can be drawn and filed by either the owner or the contractor.

Codes vary so from city to city that you will have to find out what is pertinent in your area. However, do not work without needed city approval. If a city inspector discovers illegal work in progress, he can shut down the job as well as impose a fine. An owner should doubt the honesty of any contractor willing to do work illegally: Is he trying to get away with improper work?

Although the city may never realize that illegal work has been done, the owner may have problems if he wants to sell a house that has been altered illegally. An astute lawyer will insist that a house his client purchases is a legal residence. Trying to obtain approval after the fact can often be difficult and sometimes impossible. Why take a chance?

Joan and Lloyd Slomanson found a house they wanted to buy in Greenwich Village. The sale had been negotiated, but their lawyer discovered an illegal renovation had been done on the property. The seller was advised to make the house legal before the sale could go through. After six months the owner still did not have the necessary city approvals, and the Slomansons had to look elsewhere for a house. They were disappointed, but not nearly so much as the owner must have been.

· BUILDING PERMITS

Building permits are generally required for any alteration and are issued only after any necessary city approval. The building permit, which usually must be displayed on the premises while construction is in progress, is certification that work is being done. The job is recorded, and inspectors are usually sent out to see that work complies with the building code.

Building permits are obtained at a nominal fee from the department of buildings by the owner, architect, or contractor. It is generally better to have one of the latter get the permit, since he is familiar with the procedure.

There are instances when permits are necessary but filing of plans is not needed. In such cases, the risks involved in not obtaining a permit are the same as those for not filing plans.

· LICENSED CONTRACTORS

Generally, new plumbing and electrical work must be performed by men licensed in those trades. A few cities even require the licensing of general contractors. These contractors are familiar with the building code and risk losing their licenses if the work is not performed properly. (Plumbers and electricians do not have to be licensed to do repair and maintenance work.) Licensed contractors know they must obtain permits and will usually be sure they have all necessary approvals before they start work.

In some cities licensed tradesmen sell the use of their licenses so that nonlicensed men can do the work. Martha and Charlie Stamm had an experience with an unlicensed plumber working with a borrowed license. The man was not familiar with new installations and, furthermore, did not know how to read floor plans. When plumbing pipes began appearing in strange places, the Stamms got very upset. It was then that they learned that he was using someone else's license. He was thrown off the job, and the new plumber had to replace practically all the work that had been done. There was a loss of time and money, to say nothing of the annoyance to the owners. Such an experience points out the hazards of using unlicensed plumbers and electricians.

· CITY INSPECTION

The building department has a staff of inspectors whose job it is to inspect new construction and renovation as well as the conditions in existing structures. Often the inspectors are put in charge of one specific trade, such as plumbing, electrical, or plastering. How often and by how many inspectors a renovation must be checked will depend on the city's policy, but each job requiring a permit must usually be inspected at least once. Many cities require the inspectors to approve the job when it is complete.

Building inspectors can be terribly helpful and co-operative, or they can be a nuisance. In some cities it is the deplorable custom to give "gifts" to inspectors in order to make life easier for everyone. When this is expected and not forthcoming, the building inspector can make life miserable by finding endless faults with the work.

· CERTIFICATE OF OCCUPANCY

The certificate of occupancy (C.O.) is a document given by the city at the completion of construction, certifying that the house complies with all building department regulations and is ready for occupancy. This document may also be called a certificate of inspection, a certificate of completion, or any of various other names. Some cities issue no document at the end of the job. If, however, such a document is part of city procedure, it is mandatory that the owner obtain it, since it certifies the work as legal and prevents later problems.

Take the time to find out about zoning regulations and building codes in advance of making final plans. "But I didn't know . . ." will not solve problems brought about by ignorance or failure to comply with the law.

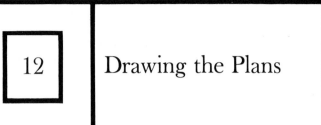

12 | Drawing the Plans

THE PURPOSE OF floor plans is to put down onto paper a picture of the house as it should be when finished, so that contractor and workmen will know what walls to remove, what to leave, and what to build. If plans are accurate and detailed, there can be no mistake about where things are to be located and what must be done. Many renovations have been done without floor plans; some have been successful, others have had problems that could have been prevented by a set of plans. You must understand all about floor plans before determining whether you need them and whether you should hire an architect or do the plans and other architectural work yourself.

The best way to start planning your renovation is to obtain a set of floor plans of the house as it exists when you buy it. These are often available from the building department. You can ask the seller to supply you with a set or go down and check what is on file yourself. (If you want to get plans of a building you do not yet own, you generally must have a letter of authorization from the owner.) You can either trace the plans or have the city make a copy for you for a nominal charge. Make sure the plans you have are accurate. Measure actual room sizes, and compare them to the plans according to the scale indicated. (The most common scale used is a quarter of an inch to each foot.) If plans of the house as it presently exists are not available, have some made by a competent draftsman or your architect.

Floor plans not only show room sizes, but also the relationship of one room to another. You may have difficulty visualizing a decrepit bathroom free of fixtures and tile and converted into a small study or guest room. With plans of the existing house you will be able to see rooms in perspective without being prejudiced by their current condition.

Scale rulers (available at stationery stores) are very useful in reading and making floor plans: You do not have to translate inches into feet—the ruler does that for you. Also available are scale templates (stencils for bathroom fixtures, kitchen cabinets, appliances, and furniture). By drawing a bed or chair on a floor plan, you can get a feeling for the size of a room.

It is mandatory that you become familiar with floor plans and know how to understand them. This is true whether or not you are having an architect design your renovation: You want to be sure that the plans include everything you had in mind.

A complete set of floor plans should provide the following information:

1. The location of all walls (those to remain, to be removed, and to be built)
2. The location and size of all windows
3. The location and size of all doors and the way they are hinged
4. The location of all plumbing fixtures
5. The exact size of all rooms and closets
6. The location of all stairs

7. The location of plumbing lines, radiators, fireplaces, cabinets, appliances, mechanical ventilation and air conditioning ducts, and wiring

In addition, the floor plans can contain a *finish schedule* that gives information about floors, walls, ceilings, and so forth. The simple finish schedule on the next page was used for the renovation of a New York City brownstone.

Most city house renovations do not require elaborate floor plans (plans are usually two or three pages), but the plans for complex renovations can run ten pages or more. The plans for a simple renovation can include electrical requirements on the floor plan, but more complex jobs should have a separate set of electrical plans. Electrical plans are simply a set of floor plans, minus all written details, that show the location of each switch, outlet, fixture, intercom, or other electrical device. The following electrical symbols are used on floor plans:

ELECTRICAL SYMBOLS

Ceiling outlet

Wall bracket

Wall switch (single)

Wall switch (double)

Wall plug (single)

Wall plug (double)

Telephone

It is often impossible to get enough detail on floor plans to give workmen information needed to do the proper job. In such cases, *detail drawings* may be necessary. Details may be shown of custom bookcases, a fireplace to be built, or a kitchen with exact dimensions of cabinets and appli-

Finish Schedule

AREA	FLOOR	WALLS	CEILING	CEILING HEIGHT	REMARKS
Hall	carpet	repair existing	existing plaster	8′ 6″	repair existing floor for carpet; repair existing walls for wallpaper
Bedroom (north)	repair existing	repair existing	new plaster	8′ 6″	remove existing wainscoting & patch plaster
Study	new strip oak	repair existing	new plaster	8′ 6″	strip oak laid east–west
Passage	carpet	new plaster	existing plaster	8′ 6″	repair existing floor for carpet
Bathrooms	ceramic tile	ceramic tile & plaster	new plaster	8′ 0″	ceramic tile around tub to ceiling
Bedroom (south)	repair existing	new & existing plaster	new plaster	8′ 6″	remove mantel & patch plaster
Dining room	new strip oak	new & existing plaster	existing plaster	11′ 0″	strip oak laid east–west
Kitchen	vinyl tile	east wall exposed brick	new plaster	10′ 0″	drop soffit* to 9′ at east wall
Living room	repair existing	new & existing plaster	existing plaster	11′ 0″	patch & repair existing parquet floor & wood paneling

* A soffit is a built-out section of wall or ceiling, usually made to conceal pipes or ducts.

ances in relation to the way they fit into the floor plan. If there is any doubt about the clarity of necessary information, a detail drawing is in order.

· SPECIFICATIONS

Floor plans and detail drawings alone are not adequate to describe every aspect of the work to be done; a certain amount of written description is necessary to supplement the floor plans. This written material is called *specifications (specs)*. Specifications describe the work to be done, the methods of construction, the standards of workmanship, the manner of conducting the work, and the quality of materials and equipment to be used. Floor plans, detail drawings, and specs together are called *construction documents*. The construction documents enable contractors to bid construction costs accurately so that the owner can have a fixed price for the job. Ideally, a qualified contractor can build from the information given in the construction documents with no questions as to dimensions, materials used, or the slightest detail in construction.

Specifications should include all pertinent information and instructions in the following categories:

1. Demolition
2. Rough carpentry
3. Masonry
4. Plumbing
5. Wiring
6. Heating and air conditioning
7. Mechanical ventilation
8. Roofing
9. Plastering (or sheetrock)
10. Finish carpentry
11. Tile work
12. Ironwork
13. Cabinets, appliances, and other equipment

14. Hardware
15. Flooring
16. Painting

Following is a sample from actual specifications for a renovation so that you can see the kind of information given:

Bathroom and toilets shall have vitreous ceramic tile "Mosaic" pattern #200 cinnamon set in cement over M.L. and waterproof membrane or laid in waterproof mastic over ¾" waterproof plywood. Bathrooms shall have ceramic tile wainscot of selected color 48" high and to ceiling around tubs, glazed trim at all edges. Wall tile around tub shall be set in waterproof adhesive over cement plaster or set in wet cement. Supply recessed vitreous china accessory sets to match tile in baths.

Since the specifications are the instructions given to the contractor about what is expected, they must include everything you have in mind. Many problems in construction develop because there are no specifications or because the specs are not detailed enough. Even the simplest renovation job needs specifications. Make sure that every detail is down on paper.

· DEMOLITION

Demolition specifications include everything that must be removed (walls, ceilings, floors, cabinets and appliances, and so on), including all rubbish and debris. Any items that must be removed but are to be reused must be clearly specified, along with instructions for special care of these and other items to remain.

· ROUGH CARPENTRY

In the building business there are two kinds of carpentry: rough carpentry and finish carpentry. Rough carpentry is the work not visible to the eye when the job is complete because it is hidden behind plaster or sheetrock. The materials used during this phase of the job affect the finished product. If inferior-grade lumber is used for studding, it will warp, causing plaster to crack or sheetrock to pull away from the studs. If partitions are framed with two-by-threes instead of two-by-fours, or if studs are placed too far apart, the new walls will not be sturdy.

Specify that all new partitions be plumb. It is absolutely amazing how many modern carpenters do not seem to know how to use a level. If you do not know how to use one, now is not too soon to learn. Get a level, and practice using it at home. You will probably be surprised to find how few level surfaces there are in your present residence. The level should be your constant companion once construction begins. Use it on all surfaces, and insist that the workmen use theirs. They may think you a pest and complain, but they will have a new respect for you when they know you understand their tools.

• MASONRY

The term *masonry* applies to all work in brick and stone. In renovation, it applies to both new construction and repair of existing conditions. If plaster is to be removed to expose a brick wall, this work would come under the heading of masonry, because not only must the plaster be removed, but the brick must be repaired, cleaned, and either sealed or painted. Any repair to foundations or exterior masonry surfaces must be detailed. You might even put any concrete work to be done under this heading.

• PLUMBING

Plumbing is not limited to soil, water, and vent lines. It includes any plumbing in connection with the heating system, sprinkler system, yard drains, outside faucets, connections to city water and sewer systems, and gas lines. It also includes plumbing fixtures and trim. Everything should be clearly specified, from pipe size and material (brass, copper, cast iron, and so on) to the kind of toilet seat you want. You must make perfectly clear what plumbing is to remain, what is to be repaired, and what is to be new. The fixtures and trim should be designated by manufacturer, style number, and color—that way there can be no mistake. A provision should be made for cut-off valves in each bath and kitchen so that if a repair must be made, only the area to be worked on will be deprived of water.

· WIRING

If a total rewiring job is to be done, there should be an electrical plan for the entire house, showing the location of every fixture, switch, and outlet, along with all other wiring requirements. In addition, the quantity of each of these items (such as twenty-five outlets, thirteen switches) should be listed in the specs. Wiring includes new electrical service (usually done by the electric company but arranged for by the electrician), meters, circuit-breaker boxes, wiring for thermostats, air conditioning, special appliances, intercom and door-buzzer systems, and the installation of lighting fixtures.

If lighting fixtures are to be supplied by the electrician, they must be selected in advance and specified by manufacturer, style number, and color. In the case of recessed fixtures, these must be specified because the carpenter will have to frame out the opening in which they are housed.

Planning for wiring is not an easy job, so take the time to do it properly. Then make sure that everything is down on paper.

· HEATING AND AIR CONDITIONING

Like all other categories, this one includes new installation as well as repair of the existing system. All required work must be put in writing.

If a new system is to be installed, you will have an expert design it for you, and he will write all necessary specifications. Be sure he includes all work done by the various trades, such as electricians, plumbers, and carpenters.

The specs for the upgrading or repair of an existing system are usually more difficult. You may want to include a catch-all phrase such as "repair of existing system and installation of all necessary controls to have the system operate properly and efficiently." Older furnaces often do not have controls (such as an automatic hot-water cut-off valve) that make them easier to operate. Remember radiators or ducts, and registers. Old radiator valves should be replaced during renovation to prevent leaking after the floors are finished; with forced-air systems, ducts should be cleaned and registers replaced if they do not work. These things, and any others, must be specified if you want them done.

· MECHANICAL VENTILATION

You must specify the ductwork needed and fan size, etc. (see page 292 for discussion) .

· ROOFING

Roofing and flashing, leaders and gutters, and skylights and other protrusions in the roof are included under this category.

The roof must be made watertight so that no leaks ruin your renovation. In houses with flat-topped roofs it is generally a good idea to replace the roof, since the expense in relation to potential damage is minimal. (Do not forget roofs on extensions.) Pitched roofs are much more expensive to replace, and a careful inspection should be made to determine whether they must be repaired or replaced. Leaders and gutters must be repaired or replaced, and skylights repaired to prevent damage to the interior.

The roofing business is notorious for fly-by-night operations. The kind of roof you wish to have installed, the repairs you want made, along with the size and material for leaders and gutters, must be precisely specified to insure that you get what you want. You should also receive a guarantee of the work.

· PLASTERING OR SHEETROCK

Which you use is a matter of choice—plastering is usually more expensive, but unless you literally gut the house, some plastering will be required, if only for repair of what exists.

The job of new plaster is done in three stages: (1) Lathing is applied to the studs; (2) brown mortar is applied to the lathing; and (3) white plaster is applied over the brown coat once it is thoroughly dry. The thickness of the white coat as well as whether you want smooth or textured plaster must be specified.

When using sheetrock, the thickness of the material and the way it is installed and finished is of utmost importance. Five-eighth-inch sheetrock is required by many building codes, but contractors may try to save money by using half-inch material. Waterproof sheetrock should be used in baths and around kitchen sinks. Use of sheetrock nails and corner beads, along with proper taping of seams and spackling of nail heads and sanding, are important for good results. You want smooth new walls, whether they be plaster or sheetrock.

Make sure that existing plaster is properly repaired and joints between old and new plaster smooth. Also, you want no holes or cracks around moldings, baseboards, lighting fixtures, electrical face plates, and so forth.

· FINISH CARPENTRY

This work is a bag of worms and a constant source of homeowner's headaches everywhere. Finish carpentry includes installing and repairing existing doors, windows, moldings, baseboards, cabinets, medicine chests, hardware, or any other built-in feature of the house that requires the use of hammer and nails. The list of the finish carpenter's responsibilities is endless. The problems he can cause are bad enough in new construction, but they are even worse in renovation, where old things must be repaired and new things matched to the old.

Each item to be repaired must be specified, as well as where the new is to match the old. Each door and window should be described by size and design, using manufacturer's style numbers where possible. The kind of moldings around windows and doors should be specified. You cannot afford to miss a single item, since omission will either bring added cost or the lack of the item in the finished house. Go over the plans with a fine-tooth comb when writing specs for finish carpentry. When you have an architect write the specs, peruse his work equally diligently to see that he has forgotten nothing and has made no mistakes—architects are subject to errors and omissions like the rest of us humans.

· TILE WORK

Tile work refers to ceramic tile; other types of tile come under flooring. All tile should be specified by manufacturer, style number, and color. In making your selection, try to select a tile readily available from local suppliers, or you may be in for problems.

Tile can be installed in two ways. The old method is

called a mud job. In wall installations, wire lath is nailed to the wall. Wet cement is applied to the lathing, and the tile is applied to the wet cement. When the cement dries, the wall is grouted. In laying tile floors, wire lath is nailed to the floor. A thick layer of dry cement is applied over the lathing and leveled. The tile is laid on the dry cement, with the whole floor wet down when the tile is complete. When the cement dries, the floor is grouted.

The newer method is called a glue job. In wall installations, tile is merely glued to the wall and grouted when the glue dries. In floor installation, the same process is used, but often a concrete floor is poured first, to which the tile is glued. The glue job is obviously less expensive than the mud job.

Specs for tile work should include the method of installation, the color of grout to be used (gray, white, or white tinted to a specified color), the tile base around floors when there is no wall tile above, ceramic accessories (such as soap dishes, toilet paper holders, towel bars) if they are to be used, and details for custom-made shower stalls, tile counter tops, and so on.

· IRONWORK

Ironwork includes railings, burglar bars, fire escapes, metal stairs, and any repairs requiring welding. If you have a high stoop with a metal gate underneath, you may need an iron man to help with the installation of a new lock. Any ironwork, whether new work or repair, should be specified. Any new work, such as railings or stairs, should have a detail drawing. Ironwork can be expensive, so remember this when planning your renovation.

· CABINETS AND APPLIANCES

All appliances should be designated by brand name, model number, and color. They should be carefully chosen to make sure they will fit and function properly in the space designed for them.

Stock kitchen cabinets should be specified by manufacturer, style name, and finish, and each cabinet should be designated by size and number. A detailed plan of their location should be drawn so there can be no confusion.

If you are using custom-made cabinets, plans for them will have to be drawn by you, your architect, or the cabinetmaker and should include the materials to be used, the hardware, and the finish.

Specifications must also include information about counter tops.

· HARDWARE

Hardware includes a multitude of items: doorknobs, locks and latches, hinges, magnetic catches, door closers, sliding-door tracks, towel bars and other bathroom accessories when not ceramic, and so forth. Do not leave their selection to the contractor. Specify each item by manufacturer and style number, and be sure that selections are available locally if they are to be supplied by the contractor.

· FLOORING

It must be made clear whether existing floors are to be retained; if so, specifications should be given for their repair and finishing. Details about all new flooring should be given: grade and width for straight oak flooring; manufacturer and style number for parquet, vinyl, vinyl asbestos, and other tile and linoleum; and grade, color, and thickness for slate and marble. Methods of installation and finishes required should be specified.

· PAINTING

Painting refers to both interior and exterior work, and in the latter case includes steam cleaning and sandblasting as well as painting.

Preparation for painting in renovation work is almost more important than the painting itself. Painting will truly hide a multitude of sins, but it also points up flaws if proper preparation is not done. All nails and old wires should be removed, and cracks and holes filled with spackle and sanded smooth. Cracked or peeling paint should be scraped and sanded. Windows should be caulked and puttied inside and outside.

The brand name as well as the type (oil base or water base; flat, semigloss, or high gloss) and color of paint should be specified, along with the number of coats to be applied. Include also finishes for surfaces not to be painted. (See page 378 for tips on painting.)

· OTHER ITEMS

Specifications should also include all of the responsibilities of the contractor pertaining to permits, city inspections, and city approvals. There may be other items that do not fall under any of the aforementioned categories. Do not omit anything from the specifications. The purpose of specs is to describe, completely and accurately, the work to be done so that there can be no misunderstanding with contractor and workmen. It is your responsibility to make sure that plans and specs fulfill this requirement, no matter who prepares them. And some kind of specifications are needed for every job, no matter how small.

· DO YOU NEED AN ARCHITECT?

It is an architect's job to prepare construction documents (floor plans, detail drawings, and specifications), and if city approval of plans is required, the architect should obtain it. However, if you do not hire an architect, you must do this work yourself. If you are lucky enough to find a *highly* competent and reliable contractor and your renovation is a relatively simple job, he may be able to perform these services for you.

If there will be no wall changes, it is possible that you may not need a complete set of floor plans, but if the arrangement of kitchen and/or bathroom interiors is to be changed, there should be plans for these rooms. If you plan to get cabinets and appliances from a kitchen planning center or home improvement contractor, they can draw plans for you as part of their service.

You should understand all of the services an architect performs so that you can decide whether you need him or not.

An architect can be hired to do anything from a simple set of floor plans to handling the complete renovation job from planning through construction. How much work you require of him will depend on your budget and the complexity of the renovation. The complete basic services of an architect include:

1. Design development
2. Construction documents
3. Bidding
4. Administration of the construction contract

Design development includes conferences with you to discuss what you need and want in your house, followed by sketches of ways to handle the space. These sketches are discussed, and a conclusion is reached on the plan that works best for you.

Then work is begun on the construction documents. When floor plans and specifications are in order, the plans are submitted to the city for necessary approval.

When the plans have been approved, the architect will assist with the bidding, giving advice on the qualifications of prospective bidders and assistance in obtaining bids and awarding the construction contract.

During the construction, the architect will provide general administration of the construction contract, including periodic visits to the job to review the progress and quality of the work and to determine if the work is proceeding in accordance with the construction documents and contract. He will check on the contractor's applications for payment, determining the amounts due the contractor and issuing certificates for payment in such amount. If there are any changes to be made, he will prepare change orders asked for and approved by the owner. He will determine the date of substantial completion, turn over to the owner written guarantees provided by the contractor, and issue the final certificate for payment. At this point the renovation is complete, and the job of the architect is finished.

When hiring an architect, you normally sign a contract with him, setting forth the services he will perform and the amount of his fee. If you are contracting for all of the basic services just mentioned, the fee is based on a percentage of the construction cost, usually somewhere between 8% and 15% (but it can go as high as 20%). A schedule of payments to the architect will be set down in the contract, and usually is as follows:

An initial payment of 5% of the estimated cost, then:

Design development phase	35%
Construction documents phase	75%
Bidding phase	80%
Construction phase	100%

If you do not choose to use an architect for all of these basic services, you can contract for any one or several of them and negotiate a fee for the services to be performed. If you should decide not to use an architect at all, you must be prepared to perform all of his functions yourself.

Many cities require that plans be drawn by an architect (or licensed professional engineer). If this is the case in your city, you will have to hire an architect, if only to draw your plans. However, if the floor plan of your house is to be drastically changed, you will need the help of someone trained in design and familiar with local building codes and practices. No one quite fills the bill like an architect.

The complexity of building code regulations is one of the best reasons for hiring an architect. If he is experienced in renovation, he will be familiar with those aspects of the code dealing with alterations—which must be rigidly followed and which can be bent to solve a particular problem. A licensed architect not only has to pass a very difficult examination proving his knowledge of design, structure, mechanical and electrical engineering, heating, air conditioning, ventilation, and plumbing, but has also served an apprenticeship under a licensed architect. He may not have all the answers to your problems, but he is certainly far better equipped to handle them than you are.

· SELECTING AN ARCHITECT

The selection of an architect should not be taken lightly. You should not hire your best friend's brother or a social acquaintance unless he is truly qualified for your job. As with other professional services, it is often better to hire a total stranger with whom you have a purely business relationship than to have problems with hurt feelings when you treat a friend in a businesslike manner.

To quote from the American Institute of Architects' "Statement of Professional Services":

The selection of an architect is one of the most important decisions an owner makes when he undertakes a building program. In that decision, he selects a professional who is both a designer and an advisor who can translate his requirements into reality.

In hiring an architect, you are looking for a person who has the following qualifications:

1. He is experienced in renovation projects in your city.
2. His tastes are similar to yours.
3. He is willing and able to work within your budget.
4. He is enthusiastic about your project.
5. He has developed good working relationships with reputable contractors.
6. He continues to have good relationships with previous clients.

If you are only having the architect draw floor plans, all except number five are still important.

It is generally best to talk to several architects before making a selection. You will have some basis for comparison and the opportunity to get several points of view about your renovation. When interviewing an architect, you should talk to him about the services he can provide, what services he feels you need, his fee for those services, and whether he thinks your job can be done on your budget.

The selection of an architect should not be made on the basis of this interview alone. You should see some of his work and talk to the owners before making the decision to hire him. You are not interested in seeing the lovely office building he designed, because it is in no way relevant to what you are asking him to do. New construction and renovation are entirely different problems, and the architect right for one is not necessarily the choice for the other.

Here is what you should ask about any of the houses you see:

1. When was the renovation completed?
2. How long did it take from the time planning began?
3. How much did it cost?
4. Was there a budget for the job, and was it adhered to? If not, why?

5. Was the architect receptive to the owner's ideas and suggestions?
6. Who selected the contractor?
7. Were there problems during construction? If so, what kind?
8. Was the basic design of the house the owner's or the architect's?

All of these questions should be asked of both architect and owner, and their answers compared. In addition, you should ask the owner if he is happy with his house and if he would use the same architect again.

When looking at the houses, pay careful attention to the design. If an architect shows you only contemporary houses and you want a traditional house, he may not be the right architect for you. If you are planning to salvage much of the existing house and all the houses you are shown have obviously been gutted, beware. If the architect shows you only very expensive renovations and your budget is quite small, ask to see less expensive renovations he has done. If the architect shows you houses completed several years before, ask about his recent work.

Check the workmanship if the architect was responsible for assisting in the selection of the contractor and in administering the construction contract. If he was not involved in these phases, the responsibility for the workmanship lies purely with the owner. If you are planning to use an architect only to draw plans, the workmanship is less important. However, it would be a good idea to get the names of contractors on each job you see and make notes on the quality of the work they did. This list could be a good source when you are ready to get bids for your job.

The fee an architect charges will obviously be important, but the quality of the work you will receive from him is equally important. If you select an architect whose fee is lower but whose plans are bid far beyond your budget, you will have made a costly mistake. It would be far better to pay more to an architect who designs a house you can afford to build. You will live with and pay for the results of an architect's work for a long time, so you cannot take his selection lightly.

· WORKING WITH AN ARCHITECT

Hiring an architect does not mean you can turn everything over to him and forget about it. To quote once more from the AIA's "Statement of Professional Services,"

It should be noted that the architect does not "supervise" the work, but based on his on-site observations as an architect he endeavors to guard the owner against defects and deficiencies in the work of the contractor. The contractor, and not the architect, is solely responsible for construction means, methods, techniques, sequences and procedures, and for safety precautions and programs in connection with the work. The architect likewise is not responsible for the contractor's failure to carry out the work in accordance with the contract documents.

Understanding this, it behooves you to keep abreast of the work being done on your house and not rely solely on the architect to see that it is done properly.

Give an architect all necessary information before hiring him—the size of your budget, what kind of house you want and why, and any special features of the house you wish to retain. He needs to know as much about you as possible if he is to design a house to fit your requirements. Once you hire him, do not let him force his ideas on you if you do not like them or cannot afford them.

You must never lose sight of the budget you have set for yourself. Too many extra ten-to-fifty-dollar items can shoot your budget in a hurry. If an architect has a weak point, it is usually in matters of economics. This is why you should check his ability to stay within a budget. You must continue to ask the cost of everything you wish to add and never let the architect lose sight of your budget; if you have no regard for it, you cannot expect him to be concerned about it. You might be wise to include in your contract with the architect a clause stipulating that he must redraw the plans at no additional cost if bids for the work exceed a specified amount. You must be prepared to lose time if you invoke this clause; therefore, it is better to make sure that you hire a budget-conscious architect in the first place.

To quote from an interview with Pietro Belluschi, M.I.T. dean of architecture and planning, that appeared in *House & Garden* under the title "Why Hire an Architect":

Some architects can't help seeing their work as monuments to themselves. If yours seems more interested in monumental achievements than in translating your wishes into the environment you expect, you have the wrong man. The main cause of conflict, however, is not design vs. practicality but rather cost vs. financial ability. Almost every client wants more house than he is willing or able to pay for. Architects know this perfectly well, but too few have the courage to get tough about keeping the budget down. Their failure to build houses for a promised amount of money has given the architectural profession its greatest black eye.

An architect uses very detailed plans and specifications, because the amount of time he can afford to spend on the job is limited. Most architects plan to make a specified number of inspections of the job and may charge for additional ones if they are required. In addition, the architect's fee does not include the cost of printing plans. Printing is not expensive, but if many sets of plans are needed, the bill can mount.

Architects often do not specify flooring, cabinets and appliances, lighting fixtures, and hardware when getting bids, but specify fixed dollar allowances instead. This method of bidding gives the owner more flexibility in his choices, but the owner must make certain that the allowances set are adequate to supply what is needed.

If the architect is administering the construction contract, it is best to let him select the contractor (after you have thoroughly checked the contractor yourself), because the relationship between architect and contractor is all-important—there are bound to be problems when these two men do not get along well.

Remember that you are dealing with a professional whose time is limited. If you are unable to make a decision, constantly change your mind, or do not know what you want, the architect will lose interest in your job.

· TERMINATING ARCHITECTURAL SERVICES

Changing architects is both expensive and time-consuming. You want to avoid it whenever possible by proper selection in the first place. However, there are times when you find you have made a mistake. It is better to terminate the services of an architect than to continue with the wrong one. You will owe the architect money for the work he has done for you up to the time of termination even though the work may be worthless to you. This is usually a bitter pill to swallow, but it can be less expensive than continuing with the same man.

13 How the Work Will Be Done

THERE IS MORE than one way to get the renovation done. You can hire a general contractor to handle the entire renovation; hire several contractors, each of whom is responsible for parts of the renovation (subcontract the job); or hire individual workmen on an hourly, daily, or weekly basis. An occasional renovator who is a real glutton for punishment has done the entire renovation himself— though this is impractical and in some cases illegal. Many a renovation job has been a combination of two or more of the above methods.

The first thing to consider is time. If the house is vacant during construction, the faster the job is completed, the sooner you can utilize the house you are paying for. If, however, the house is in acceptable condition, you may want to move right in and do the renovation over an extended period of time so that you can pay for it gradually. In either case, you should get any rental units finished as quickly as possible so that income can be realized.

A renovation done over several years usually means subcontracting the job, since the work will be done in a piecemeal fashion. However, if time is important, a general contractor is usually the answer.

· WHY HIRE A GENERAL CONTRACTOR?

Hiring a general contractor (G.C.) has many advantages. One man is responsible for all phases of the job from start to finish. He supplies the labor and material, along with scheduling and co-ordinating the work of the various trades. He may hire subcontractors to do all or parts of the job, or he may have a full crew of men working directly for him.

In building, there is much overlapping of trades. Take the simple matter of a recessed lighting fixture. The carpenter must frame out the opening in which the fixture is placed, but the electrician must supply the wiring and install the fixture. A mess is inevitably made in the process, and neither electrician nor carpenter feels he has any responsibility to clean it up—that job requires a laborer, not a skilled craftsman. The general contractor supplies the laborer as well as making sure that the carpenter is present when the electrician needs him and vice versa.

Situations like this are repeated and compounded throughout a renovation. Scheduling (having men and materials on the job when needed) is vital and is basically the reason for the existence of the general contractor. For this, plus his knowledge and experience (something a renovator usually does not possess), you pay him a fee. Why pay a G.C. when you can subcontract the job and save his fee? is a question often asked by renovators. Here is a list of reasons:

1. He supplies and schedules all labor, guaranteeing that work will be done according to specification. He has more leverage than you do in hiring and getting a good job from workmen and subcontractors because of potential future employment.

2. He supplies all material (which he is able to get at a better price) and sees that it is on hand when needed.

3. He pays all bills, relieving you of all bookkeeping chores: You pay only once. He also pays all workmen's insurance and benefits.

4. He gets all permits and copes with city inspectors.

· SUBCONTRACTING THE JOB YOURSELF

There are many renovators who have subcontracted their own work quite successfully. The simpler the renovation plan, the easier it is to subcontract the job yourself. The more complex the job, the greater the need for a competent G.C.

There are two conditions under which subcontracting your own job is virtually mandatory: (1) if the job is to be done gradually over an extended period of time; (2) if the entire job is so small that no G.C. would be interested in it.

It is seldom advisable or even feasible to do your own subcontracting unless you are living in the house or can be on the job several hours every day. There is a constant need for co-ordination and supervision (what happens when the carpenter has not appeared and the electrician is waiting for him?). If you cannot be there, you should hire someone to be responsible as foreman—usually the head carpenter.

The only practical way of subcontracting is to hire subcontractors who will be responsible for each part of the work, supplying all labor and materials needed. Each subcontractor would have his own contract, his own set of construction documents, and would be responsible for city inspections of his part of the job and for insurance and benefits for his workmen. In short, he would be acting as a G.C. for a portion of the job. If you should have to supply materials, you would be involved in ordering and scheduling deliveries, credit with suppliers, record keeping, and many frustrations.

· HIRING INDIVIDUAL WORKMEN

Another way of getting the job done is to hire individual workmen instead of subcontractors. This usually involves supplying materials yourself and paying wages, including social security, workmen's compensation, unemployment insurance, and so on. You would also have to keep an elaborate set of books and, in essence, set up your own contracting firm. An occasional day laborer to help to do odd jobs is fine, but a steady crew of employees is not recommended.

The Stanforths were unintentionally dragged into such a situation when their contractor walked out and left them with a crew of unpaid workmen. They had a hard enough time meeting payrolls and were unaware of required workmen's benefits. When the job was finished, one workman applied for unemployment compensation. Neither the Stanforths nor the contractor had paid for unemployment insurance. Although innocent victims of a dishonest contractor, the Stanforths nonetheless were hounded by the New York State Department of Labor until they made a settlement (though the contractor got off without paying because he could not be found).

To avoid having this happen to you, hire workmen by the job, as contractors, so that *they* are responsible for workmen's benefits.

Will you actually save money by taking on the job of contracting yourself? Maybe yes, maybe no. Many people who feel they save money by contracting the job themselves fail to consider the time element, which in some cases can have dollar value. When a house is vacant during renovation, time is money. If it will take you a year to subcontract the job yourself when a G.C. could do it in six months, you must add the cost of paying for your current residence for an additional six months to the cost of the renovation. If you are paying two hundred dollars a month rent, using a G.C. would save you twelve hundred dollars.

Philadelphia architect Benjamin Kitchen did his own house, working evenings and weekends. It took him three years. When he finished, he realized that he would have been better off financially if he had saved for three years and hired a general contractor to do the work.

· DOING YOUR OWN WORK

Most renovators have a bit of do-it-yourself in them, and hardly one has failed to handle a hammer or paintbrush at some point during the renovation. People who had previously been all thumbs have learned to build cabinets and lay floors. Few, however, have been able to do all the work themselves.

Be realistic about what you can reasonably accomplish. Taking on more than you can do comfortably only leads to frustration. A renovation should be stimulating, not a drag. Select those jobs that you can do and still have time to talk to your wife (husband) or read to the children. Do-it-yourself projects are fun and rewarding when taken in palatable doses, but like too much liquor for too many days in a row, too many projects can give you a never-ending hangover.

Usually it is the finishing details that can be most practically and effectively done by the owner: special cabinet-work, flooring, painting, or wood stripping. Whatever you choose to do yourself, remember that it must be co-ordinated with the rest of the work so that you do not hold up construction if your job is not completed on schedule. Since someone will have to pay the men who are losing time, it may cost you more than you can save.

· WHICH METHOD WORKS BEST FOR YOU?

Hiring a general contractor does not mean that he must do all the work on the house or that the entire renovation must be completed while he is working. You can hire a

G.C. to do all the basic work, saving most of the finishing details to complete at your leisure.

Martha and Charlie Stamm have always used a general contractor because they did not want to be bothered with scheduling or dealing with building inspectors. However, they hire their own subcontractors for floor finishing and painting, supply such items as appliances and lighting fixtures, and do some of the finishing work themselves, thereby saving money in some areas while having the G.C. handle all of the tedious jobs.

The method you choose may be one or a combination of several. But regardless of which you use, you must plan for how the work will be done and who will be responsible for each task. The owner is the manager of his house. Even though he may do some or all of the work himself, he must have a clear picture of the project from start to finish, from purchase through planning and construction, if the renovation is to go smoothly and be completed to his satisfaction.

· OBTAINING BIDS FOR CONSTRUCTION

Before the construction documents are sent to contractors for bids, any necessary city approvals should be obtained. Sometimes plans must be amended in order to get city approval. If plans were sent out for bids prior to approval, amended plans would have to be resubmitted to all bidders.

The construction documents must be designed in accordance with the way the work is to be done. If you plan to do some of the work yourself or if you are subcontracting the job, the specifications must clearly state the responsibility of each party involved.

You should get more than one bid for the job (or for each phase in the case of subcontracting), so that you can get the best price possible. But getting bids is not a case of the more the merrier; the contractor must have assurance that he has a chance of getting the job if his price is right. Three bidders is the standard number.

A complete set of construction documents is sent to each bidder; all must have the same information if the bids are to be properly assessed. Remember, it takes time for contractors to make their estimates. You seldom receive a bid for a week after the construction documents are distributed, and two to four weeks is normally required.

Finding reputable contractors to bid on the work is not always easy. If you are using an architect, he is the logical source for competent contractors. Your local lumber dealer and plumbing supply house are good potential sources for names of reliable contractors. Renovators tend to band together into organizations, and these, along with individual renovators, can often provide information on contractors. Real estate brokers are another potential source of names. And if you saw houses in checking on architects and followed the suggestion to take the names of contractors, by all means use those whose work you have already seen. Friends, relatives, the building department, your local AIA chapter, even the Yellow Pages of the phone book are potential sources. But do a little checking on the contractor before allowing him to bid.

· Methods of Bidding

There are two methods of bidding: (1) *fixed price* and (2) *cost plus*. The method used depends on the individual contractor and the area in which you live. Fixed-price bidding is the most common, but because of the unforeseen difficulties involved in renovation, many contractors will not bid a fixed price.

A *fixed-price* bid means that the contractor has carefully studied the construction documents, estimated the cost to do the work, added his profit, and come up with a cost for the job to be done. Once the contract is signed, the contractor is obligated to perform the work specified in the contract for the price agreed upon. However, any change made in the construction documents after the contract is signed gives the contractor an opportunity to alter his price.

In a *cost-plus* job, the contractor also estimates what he thinks the cost will be, but he does the job on the condition that you agree to meet all of his costs plus an agreed-upon fee for himself (usually a percentage of the cost of the job). On payday he submits bills for his expenses since the previous payday, and you pay him that amount. Cost-plus contracting is sometimes referred to as "time and materials."

Sometimes it is possible to include an *upset price* in a cost-plus contract. This means that a maximum price is guaranteed for the job as specified. If the contractor's cost is below the upset price, the owner receives the savings; but if the cost is higher, the owner will pay no more than the upset figure.

There are obvious risks in hiring a contractor on a cost-plus basis; there is no incentive for him to keep costs down. The cost-plus contractor must be impeccably honest and reliable, because he could easily pad his expenses. However, a fixed-price contract with a dishonest or insolvent contractor is worthless, so the question is not really so much one of bidding method as of the contractor's dependability.

· WHAT IF ALL THE BIDS ARE TOO HIGH?

This is indeed a sad day in the life of any renovator, and we wish we could report that it did not happen often.

If all bids are too high, either the plan for the renovation was too elaborate for your budget, or the contractors who bid were too expensive for your pocketbook.

There are many contractors whose cost for the same job may be miles apart. Just because a contractor is expensive does not mean that you will receive value for the dollar.

Though you should always be wary of a bidder who is substantially below all others, an inexpensive price does not necessarily mean inferior work. There are factors other than labor and materials that may influence a contractor's bid. If he is very busy and does not need the work, he may bid higher than usual because the job would mean hiring additional men and more work for himself. On the other hand, a contractor may bid a job very close if he thinks it would bring repeat business or new customers. The same could be true if the job came at a slow time when it would mean the difference between keeping valuable men and laying them off.

The most obvious reason for the difference between bids is the overhead of the contractor and the wages he pays his employees. A contractor who hires union workmen is usually more expensive than one who uses nonunion labor. If the contractor actually works on the job, as is the case with many small contractors, his price will usually be lower than that of purely administrative contractors.

Talk to the contractors who bid, and ask them why their bids were higher than the budget you set. They might be able to make suggestions for alterations in the plans that will lower the cost. One might even be able to suggest a contractor who could do the job within your budget.

Before drastically altering your plans, try to get bids from less expensive reputable contractors. But do not panic and accept a low bid without properly checking on the contractor.

If you are unable to find a reliable contractor at the right price and are unwilling or unable to pay the additional cost of renovation, you must redraw your plans on a more modest scale. In redrawing the plans, try to make provisions for those things which can be added later.

· SELECTING A CONTRACTOR

Before hiring a contractor, you must check him thoroughly. The importance of checking a contractor applies to subcontractors as well as general contractors. The building business has its share of incompetents and even outright crooks. You certainly do not want to entrust your hard-earned money to either.

The contractor, like the architect, will be with you for a long time, and you will either live happily or unhappily with the results of his labor. As the AIA Statement of Professional Services says, "the contractor is solely responsible for the construction," and you are solely responsible for whom you hire to do it.

You cannot depend on the law to protect you from a dishonest contractor. A construction contract is only worth as much as the man who signs it. You and your property are readily accessible to liens and lawsuits, whereas the contractor operating under a corporate name can liquidate his corporation or see that it has no assets.

A corporation can be formed by filing the necessary papers with the office of the Secretary of State. It is a simple matter and the cost is usually minimal. The corporate laws do not require corporations to have financial stability, but they do limit the liability of officers and stockholders. Most businesses that operate under corporate names are legitimate operations in business to provide goods and services to make an honest profit. However, the corporate structure is also a haven for con men.

If the contractor you hire operates under a corporate name, it is the corporation you must petition or sue for redress of grievances. The contractor himself may have assets, but if the corporation has none, it will do you no good to win a lawsuit. Therefore, you must make as certain as is humanly possible that the man and his corporation have a record of honest dealings, reputable work, and solvency. You cannot depend on trust or assumptions, and you cannot rely on someone else to check for you. (Do not assume that you should not check the contractor because your architect recommends him, even if they have worked together before. Your architect's apology is small consolation if the contractor goes bankrupt or walks out on your job.)

Take the time to do a thorough check. No matter how pressed for time you think you are, you can lose more time and a great deal of money if you are careless in this investigation.

The truly amazing fact that emerges is that countless bright, intelligent people have employed architects and contractors without any indication of their qualifications.

When a family decides to purchase a washing machine, they go to a number of stores, study consumer guides, question repairmen, ask friends whether they are satisfied with theirs. And yet when they are going to spend thousands of dollars on their homes, few make any inquiry at all about past performance of contractors before signing a construction contract. Small wonder that disreputable contractors find such easy prey. A plumber, electrician, or roofer should be investigated at least as carefully as a washing machine.

Brooklyn homeowners Rik Pierce and David Shipman both admit that they were actually warned against the men they hired, and yet they hired them. The Pierces had bad experiences with architect and contractor. Shipman, who agrees that he should have known better, is involved in a lawsuit against his contractor (he used an architect only to draw plans for building department approval). A year or more later, his potentially handsome living room is still a shambles because he needs it as evidence in his case. The lacy plaster moldings that adorned his ceiling lie stacked in pieces around the floor, where they must remain to prove the damage done by the contractor. Shipman bought his Boerum Hill house after having the experience of restoring three houses on Cape Cod, and is so knowledgeable that he has meanwhile bought, designed, and completed a house across the street where he did the contracting himself (while running his own advertising business). Somehow he allowed himself to be conned by the contractor, even though he knew his house was being butchered. Shipman can tick off a long list of crimes the contractor committed: he did not insulate the outside walls; he put in door frames with just a few nails, taped sheetrock seams so badly that they split, reused old pipes and valves in the plumbing and did electrical work that did not conform to the code. When Shipman insisted that he do things properly, he was charged extra for each item. According to Shipman, the same man bought and resold a nearby house after installing new bathrooms on top of the old lead plumbing (fortunately, in this case, the victim was one of the contractor's business associates).

• HOW TO CHECK ON A CONTRACTOR

To avoid problems during construction, investigate any contractor before hiring him. Here is what you should check:

1. First, easiest, and most obvious—is he or his corporation listed in the telephone book? Does he have an office or merely an answering service or mail drop? Go and find out. (This is a good quick check on anyone who wants to do work for you. Fly-by-night con men seldom have offices and listed phones.)
2. How long has he or his corporation been in business? (If it is a new business or new corporation, check the background of the owner. What did he do before and whom did he work for?)
3. Ask for a list of several of his suppliers, including major ones such as lumber and plumbing supply dealers, and find out whether his credit is good and over how long a period of time. (Beware of a contractor who cannot get credit.)

4. Ask where he has his bank account, and find out how long he has had the account, whether he maintains a substantial balance, whether his checks bounce, and whether he has loans he is repaying. (This, of course, applies to corporate accounts if that is his way of doing business.)

5. The most important means of checking (and not to be omitted) is references from people whose houses he has completed. You should have at least three (the more, the better), and at least one that is recent. Do not merely telephone (they could be friends or family). Interview the owner, and see the house the contractor worked on. Look at the workmanship (not the design): is it done well? How extensive was the job? Does it compare in size to yours? (If it was a minor job, do not accept it as a bona fide reference.) Ask the owner if he is satisfied with the quality of the work. Does everything function properly? Were there any problems during construction? What were they, and whose fault? Was the work done on schedule? (It almost never is, so a short time beyond the schedule is not enough for disqualification.) Does the contractor stand behind his work, returning to make corrections or repairs? Were there many extra charges? Why, and for what? Were there any liens?

6. Have a check made through your lawyer or the bank that holds your mortgage to find out if there is any litigation pending against the contractor or his corporation.

We all look for bargains, particularly when dealing in thousands of dollars. But to do so can be a mistake. If a contractor is honest, he must make a reasonable profit in order to stay in business. He has to pay workmen and buy materials to produce a good job. As in any business, overhead and profit must be added to these costs. You cannot expect the contractor to cut the price below the level at which he can make a profit and still deliver a sound construction job. If you have reason to believe he is deliberately underbidding merely to get the job (without any reasonable explanation), beware.

This does not mean that some contractor's bids cannot be substantially lower than others; there can indeed be a very wide range of difference. But weigh all factors carefully, and make sure the lowest bidder has a solid reputation and record.

· THE CONSTRUCTION CONTRACT

Although many renovators have hired contractors with no agreement other than a verbal one, this is simply asking for trouble. Just as the contract for the purchase of property sets down the terms and conditions under which the property will be bought, the construction contract spells out the terms and conditions under which the renovation work will be done. Any agreement not incorporated in a contract is not binding on either side.

Lien laws protect the right of workmen (including contractors and architects) and suppliers to be paid for work and materials that go into property by enabling them to make claims (liens) against the property for unpaid bills. A proper construction contract is the owner's means of protecting himself against unjustified claims, because it specifies the work to be done, the price of the work, and the responsibilities of each party.

You should have a written agreement with anyone who is doing work on your house. How detailed this agreement should be will depend on the amount of work to be done. Any contract involving a large sum of money should be discussed with your lawyer, and it is best to have him read the agreement before you sign it. He may have some valuable suggestions to make, and he will certainly be able to tell if you are giving away your right arm without knowing it.

Any construction contract should contain the following:

1. Name and address of owner
2. Name and address of contractor
3. Address of property where work is to be done
4. Time of commencement and completion
5. List of construction documents (plans, specs, etc.) on which the work is based
6. The price of the work
7. A schedule of payment
8. Guarantee of the work
9. Proof of workmen's compensation insurance
10. Signature of both parties
11. No blank spaces that could be filled in later to the detriment of the owner

There should be two signed copies of the contract, one for the owner and one for the contractor.

The construction contract is the basis of any claims against the contractor, so it is important that the contract cover everything of interest to the owner. The AIA prints standard contracts that come with a set of general conditions stating the responsibilities of each party and procedures for terminating the contract. AIA document A-111 is used when the basis of payment is a stipulated sum (fixed price), and AIA document A-101 is used when the basis of payment is the cost of the work plus a fee (cost plus). These documents are available through an architect or from your local AIA office. If your construction contract is not an AIA one, it should still cover all items discussed in the AIA General Conditions.

Contracts are for the benefit of both contractor and owner, and your contractor should want one as much as you do. However, you should not wait for him to provide one but should discuss the contract when talking to him about the job. Construction contracts are standard procedure with architects who administer the construction phase and with most general contractors. However, subcontractors and independent craftsmen are often lackadaisical about written agreements. You cannot afford to be.

· COMMENCEMENT AND COMPLETION

Setting a date for completion of work in the contract usually has little meaning unless there is a lawsuit. However, it is possible to include a penalty clause for work not completed on schedule. (This clause is obviously binding only if the owner makes no changes in the plans and specifications.) The penalty is usually expressed in a dollar amount to be subtracted from the price of the job for each day beyond the deadline that work is not complete. Contractors are generally reluctant to agree to such a penalty in renovation work because so much is unknown until work actually begins. Often the contractor will agree to the penalty clause only if he receives a bonus for finishing ahead of schedule.

· LIST OF CONSTRUCTION DOCUMENTS

The plans and specifications must be a part of any construction contract. These documents should be listed in the contract as follows:

_____ pages of floor plans

_____ pages of electrical plans

_____ pages of specifications

_____ pages of detail drawings

To make certain that there is no misunderstanding about what is in each of these documents, the owner should have one complete set with each page initialed by both himself and the contractor.

- THE PRICE OF THE WORK

The price quoted in the contract is based on the work described in the construction documents. If work is not specified in the contract or if changes are made in the work specified, the contractor has the right to additional money. The construction contract should make provision for changes or additions to the work. (The AIA General Conditions make such provision.)

- SCHEDULE OF PAYMENT

Every job, no matter how small, should have an agreement on when and how payments are to be made. The payment schedule should be fair to both parties—the contractor should not be paid too much in advance, and the owner should not expect the contractor to finance the renovation.

Payments are normally made in stages as work progresses. If a construction loan is financing the work, payments to the contractor must be co-ordinated with the bank's takedown schedule, so that the owner is not obligated to pay out money he does not yet have.

The contract should specify that the contractor obtain any necessary approvals and certificates from the city and turn over to the owner all warranties for equipment before the final payment is made. The usual procedure is to hold ten per cent of the price until the job is completed, but the larger the final payment, the more leverage the owner has in getting the job completed to his satisfaction.

- GUARANTEES

All work should be guaranteed, and the terms of such guarantees spelled out in the contract. When dealing with a general contractor, you should have guarantees on the work of all subcontractors as well as a general guarantee from the G.C. A time limit should be specified for repair of any problem covered by the guarantees.

· WORKMEN'S COMPENSATION INSURANCE

You, as the owner, are responsible for injury to anyone on your property. To protect yourself against claims for injury, you carry liability insurance. However, liability insurance covers normal conditions and may not cover injury during construction. In such a situation a serious injury could wipe you out financially.

Special insurance (workmen's compensation) is available to cover injury to men on construction jobs. Most states require contractors to carry this insurance for their employees. However, you must be sure that any contractor you hire has a workmen's compensation insurance policy in effect. If there are men working on your house who are not so covered, you should take out a workmen's compensation policy yourself.

Every construction contract should contain any agreement made between you and the contractor. The more detailed the contract, the better protected you are in case of difficulty. However, no contract can protect you against problems with a dishonest contractor. The contract sets down rights and responsibilities, but enforcing the terms of the contract is another matter. The only protection you have against a disreputable contractor is not hiring him.

· PERFORMANCE BONDS

A *performance bond* is an insurance policy guaranteeing that work will be completed as specified in the construction contract. The bond is obtained and paid for by the contractor, but the cost (usually one per cent of the contract price) is included in the price of the work. The bond is provided by a surety company (bonding company), which must be satisfied that the contractor is experienced and financially sound enough to perform the work for the agreed price.

Usually only major construction jobs are so insured, because few small contractors are able to meet the requirements of the bonding companies and because the companies themselves do not find it worthwhile to check out contractors' qualifications for a small job. However, some FHA insured mortgages require a performance bond or other guarantee of completion.

A contractor who is "bondable" may refer to himself as a bonded contractor, though this only means that he is able to get a performance bond. If the owner wishes to have this insurance, he must so request and stipulate in the specifications. The bond itself should be incorporated in the construction contract.

Though a performance bond may appear to be the answer to all renovation problems, it has its drawbacks. Although the surety company is obligated to pay for completion of the work if the contractor should default on the contract, legal complications can cause lengthy delays, and the quality of the work may not necessarily conform to the owner's expectations. The cost of a performance bond is relatively small, provides protection against liens, and is worth the investment when it is available. However, it is no substitute for careful checking on the contractor and proper supervision of the job.

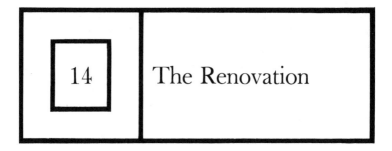

| 14 | The Renovation |

THE DAY THAT WORK finally begins is a milestone, one you thought would never come if you did proper planning in advance. If you have followed the recommended procedures and precautions, there should be no major problems from this point on. (If there are, you should be equipped to handle them.) This is not to say that you can go on vacation and return to the finished house. There are always problems in renovation, because you never are sure what you will find once you start tearing down walls. But the problems can be solved readily *if* you keep track of the job and have a good relationship with the contractor and workmen. You must use good common sense, being reasonable at all times without letting the contractor take advantage of you.

· HOW WORK PROGRESSES

You should understand the various stages of construction and the plans and specifications for your job in order to know whether work is progressing as it should. There are no hard and fast rules in renovation construction because at least some of the existing features of the house will remain. However, a logical order must be followed if work is to progress smoothly and rapidly; if new partitions are closed up before wiring, etc., is put in, you will have real problems.

Construction work falls into two general classifications: the rough and the finish. The *rough* encompasses everything hidden inside the walls and includes studs (the wooden framework that supports the walls), wiring, pipes, ducts, and flues. The *finish* begins with enclosing the walls and includes all work that must be done to finish the job.

Renovation work often begins at the top of the house and progresses downward (except for rough plumbing, where pipes must be installed from bottom to top). The reason for this is logical: Workmen carry their tools to the top, finish the work there, and move down to the next floor, so that when the top floor is complete it can be sealed off and not disturbed while work goes on below. (Were the process reversed, work completed could be damaged by workmen going through to get upstairs.) In a four- or five-story house, it is not unusual to find work at a different stage on each floor.

If work is being contracted by trades, each trade will want to finish its phase of the work at one time. A plasterer generally will not come to plaster only one floor at a time when there are several floors to be plastered; he wants to bring his men and materials to finish the job in one trip. However, when a contractor has men working directly for him, he has more flexibility in scheduling the trades and generally has workmen who are skilled in more than one trade. Therefore, the work of the various trades can progress at a different pace than when the trades are subcontractors; one floor can be almost complete with very little work having been done on another floor.

As soon as demolition is complete, the carpenter can begin laying out the new floor plan. (If the house is to get all new wiring, the electrician must provide temporary lines until the new electrical system is complete and usable.) As soon as all partitions are in place, the plumber and electrician can begin their work. Before partitions can be enclosed, all structural work, piping (for plumbing and heating), wiring (including prewiring for phones and cable T.V.), duct work (for heating, air conditioning, mechanical ventilation, and venting for dryers and stove hoods), flue work (for furnace and fireplaces), and insulation must be done. Changes or additions to the rough after the finish has begun require tearing walls open.

Before the finish is begun, the house should be sealed to prevent damage. This includes roofing and flashing, gutters and leaders, new windows and repair to existing ones, the closing of any holes or openings in the exterior, masonry repair to exterior walls, and any necessary waterproofing of the exterior. Exterior painting can be done then or later, but if masonry repair requires the use of scaffolding, it is best to have painting done at the same time.

The finish begins with enclosing new walls and patching of existing ones, and includes all items visible to the eye. The plumber and electrician will return to finish their work, other craftsmen will appear on the scene, and the carpenter(s) will be ever present.

How work will progress once walls are closed will vary, but certain work must be done first. Door jambs must be installed before moldings. New flooring goes in before baseboards. Doors are hung at the very end of the job so they will not get banged up or in the workmen's way.

In bathrooms, tubs are installed as part of the rough, because they must be in place before walls can be closed. Floor and wall tile are installed before the remaining fixtures are put in.

In kitchens, built-in sinks and appliances cannot be installed until cabinets and counter tops are in place. New flooring is put down before removable appliances are moved in.

Unfinished wooden floors can be laid early in the finish but prefinished wood flooring and tile (except in baths) should go in just before painting to prevent scratching and other damage.

The finish includes not only all new work but also the repair of existing features. All finish work, except floor finishing and installation of decorative equipment such as lighting fixtures, should be complete before painting is done if the paint job is to stay fresh and clean. The last item in renovation should be the sanding and finishing of wood floors. When the floor finisher departs, the renovation should be complete.

The finish will move rapidly at first and then slow down to a snail's pace toward the end. It is here that constant checking is mandatory to be certain that plans and specifications are being followed and that the quality of workmanship is acceptable. The rough might be considered the technical phase of renovation, where the basic elements for convenience and comfort are laid out; the finish, the aesthetic phase, where flaws that may frustrate you later become manifest.

· POSSIBLE PROBLEMS

Because renovation is a combination of existing conditions and new construction, it holds a degree of uncertainty that is not present in building a house from scratch. No matter how much planning has been done in advance, unexpected problems can arise. Plumbing that you thought could remain may suddenly spring a leak. A demolished partition may reveal a pair of old doors that you would like to use. When old plumbing fixtures are removed, you may find the beams beneath them notched and rotting. Beams may be located where ducts or pipes are to run.

As the owner of an old house, you must be prepared to be flexible should unforeseen trouble arise. A wall may have to be shifted slightly, causing some problems with the floor plan. There may be extra charges for replacing beams or repairing a ceiling that suddenly gives way.

As there are no hard and fast rules for how the work progresses, there are no pat solutions for handling problems that occur during renovation. You must just use good common sense, be prepared to compromise a little, and always keep your sense of humor. You too will find those trying times can make humorous anecdotes at cocktail parties in the future.

The problems that are difficult to cope with are caused by the following:

1. Inadequate construction documents
2. Lack of a proper construction contract
3. Failure to check the contractor before hiring him
4. Lack of communication between owner, architect, and contractor
5. Changes made after construction begins
6. Paying the contractor too much in advance
7. Contractor having underbid the job
8. Lack of skilled workmen and sloppy workmanship
9. Improper supervision

Most of these problems can be avoided.

· ADDITIONAL CONSTRUCTION CHARGES ("EXTRAS")

Most extra charges during construction occur because of inadequate construction documents, an inadequate contract, or changes made after work has begun.

The plans and specifications are your instructions to the contractor and his workmen. The more detailed the construction documents, the fewer problems that arise and the less supervision the job requires. You cannot expect the contractor to read your mind. He will know what you want only if you have told him. The instructions that are enforceable are those included in the construction contract.

If proper planning has been done, you will have taken care of all your needs and drawn up exact plans and specs for the job. There may be slight changes or additions during construction—extra shelves in a closet, another light for the bedroom, and so on—but these should be minor. With adequate plans and specifications incorporated into a detailed construction contract, there can be no additional charges for the work covered therein. There may be extra costs for unforeseen problems such as replacing a rotten beam or a ceiling that falls through no fault of the contractor, but if you have a reputable contractor and have been fair and reasonable with him, these costs should be held to a minimum.

Any changes made after construction begins can be costly. If you discover a change that must be made, get a price in writing before you have the work done. If his costs are running higher than he expected, even the most honest contractor has a tendency to charge more than the work is truly worth when the price is set after the fact. Get the price for everything before authorizing additional work, and keep a running record for yourself so that you are aware of the total—those small charges can add up quickly.

Some changes can be made for little or no extra cost if they are made in time. The location of a closet or other partition can be changed slightly in advance of framing. It usually makes no difference to the contractor if a wall is moved a foot or so in either direction, provided the work does not entail the replacement of a floor or ceiling that was to be retained. If, however, a closet is to be enlarged, requiring additional labor and materials, you should expect to pay an additional price. If changes involve work that has already been done, the contractor will be frustrated, his men will complain, and he will probably make you pay through the nose for it.

The more familiar you are with the job being done and the progress being made, the easier it will be for you to discover the changes you may want to make in advance of construction in that area. If you are reasonable and use some common sense when making changes, extra expenses can be kept to a minimum.

· WORKING WITH THE CONTRACTOR

By far the most serious problems that occur in construction are the result of the owner's failure to investigate the contractor before hiring him. The best contract and the most detailed plans and specifications are meaningless to a man who is unreliable.

The more you know about the man (men) you hire, the easier it will be to work with him. There is no such thing as a perfect contractor, because renovation work is difficult, particularly when there is much salvaging to be done, and the job of the contractor is a tedious and trying one. If you know that the man you are hiring has a tendency to be slow, you can begin prodding him to finish on schedule from the very beginning.

You must establish good communication with the contractor from the start. The contractor, not his men or subcontractors, is responsible for the job—you must tell *him* if something displeases you. How is the contractor to know if you are dissatisfied unless you say so?

You should meet regularly with the contractor to discuss the progress of work and any problems that have come up. (If your architect is administering the construction contract, he should deal with the contractor and you should meet with him regularly to direct all questions through him to the contractor. The contractor can have only one boss.)

The relationship between architect, owner, and contractor should always be kept on a reasonable basis. Raised voices seldom accomplish anything but anger.

Money is the only real leverage you have. It is the anticipation of payment that provides the incentive for the contractor to move ahead with the job. Do not let your contractor lose his incentive. Draw up a fair payment schedule, and then stick to it.

A contractor will often ask for money in advance, but an owner is unwise if he gives in. Contractors who are doing more than one job at a time often feed money back and forth from one job to another. You want to make sure that your money is being used exclusively for your work. Once it goes into someone else's job, the contractor may find himself in trouble and request additional money. Giving in only allows him to go further into the hole. If your contractor is in financial difficulty, the sooner you know about it, the better. When most of the money has been paid for a job that is less than half finished, the owner is in trouble. Terminating a construction contract is not easy, but it is best done at the earliest possible moment to avoid large financial losses.

- SUPERVISION

The more you know about the work being done on your house, the sooner you can detect any serious problems. Even if you are paying an architect to administer the contract, and even though you trust and respect him, you should check the progress and quality of the work yourself as often as possible. It is *your* money that is being spent, *your* house that is being renovated, and no one will be as concerned as you. If something is not being done properly, the chances are fairly good that you will find out about it by being there and observing carefully, even though you think you know nothing about construction. If you are not using an architect, you would be wise to check the job every day.

Even with detailed plans and specs, someone must see that they are being followed. Contractors and workmen can be particularly independent about what they install, feeling that if they put it in, it has to stay whether the owner likes it or not.

Tile men are notorious; there are innumerable tales of owners who found different tile installed than what they had chosen, and submitted meekly to living with the tile man's choice rather than their own. However, one such autocrat met his match in Dorothy Friedman.

Experienced as a hard-working interior designer, Dorothy knows what she wants and insists upon getting it. What she wanted for her children's bathroom was yellow fixtures and matching tile. Awaking one morning in her suburban Long Island home, she had a presentiment that something was going wrong in the renovation of her West Eightieth Street brownstone. Sure enough, when she arrived on the job there was a man standing in her yellow bathtub putting brown tiles on the wall. Dorothy's tirade of abuse produced the complacent assurance that the color was "fawn," not the four-letter word she called it, and that it was the very latest thing, the most popular shade. What's more, he refused to remove it. Satisfied that he had quelled the tempest, he was occupied in boasting to the contractor about his skill in handling homeowners when Dorothy returned with a screwdriver borrowed from the electrician. Stepping into the tub next to the workman, she began flicking off the offending tiles. As they fell shattering, the tile contractor lost his smugness. "Stop," he pleaded, "before you break them all so I can't even return them!" Needless to add, the Friedmans have a yellow bathroom.

The Stanforths arrived too late to avoid one disaster, and almost too late to prevent another. The small front parlor of their house had ornamentation that had convinced them to buy the house. The foot-wide plaster frieze just below the ceiling had every wreath, garland, and crossed torch intact. In the flat part there was only one small hole, where a sprinkler pipe had run through. Dozens and dozens of times the contractor and men had been warned not to damage the frieze. And yet when the plasterer got up on a ladder to patch the three-inch hole, he stripped off three feet of the canvas-backed frieze and threw it on the floor! It took Deirdre Stanforth weeks of striving and two unsuccessful attempts to make a mold from the remaining frieze to recast and patch the needless destruction.

To complete their apparently willful destruction of this one perfect room, the contractor's men almost succeeded in throwing out the incredibly elaborate fireplace. They were busy plastering up the opening when Deirdre and the architect arrived one day for a routine inspection. Apparently ignoring the plans, the workmen were under the impression that this fireplace was to be eliminated. It very nearly was, because most of the parts were rescued at the door, where they were awaiting removal by the rubbish truck. Not all could be found. Several pieces were broken off and missing from the sculptured, green-patinaed bronze sidepieces, one of the three sections of iron backing (made with wreaths to match the frieze) was gone, and the pink marble facing was cracked in several places. It all had to be painstakingly pieced back together again.

Supervision is essential to avoid these and other catastrophes. Even the most reputable and honest of contractors can make mistakes. A dependable contractor will rectify them, but the time wasted and the nuisance of having workmen in the house after the job is supposed to be complete are annoying and sometimes costly. There are even times when it is impractical to rectify mistakes after they have been made.

Progress of work should be checked regularly and the house thoroughly inspected on each visit. You or the architect should be on hand when the new floor plan is being laid out so that any difficulties can be solved immediately.

Finishing details in a house are particularly important. The most common problems are the faulty installation of moldings around windows and doors, improper placement of light switches and outlets, doors that open the wrong way or are hung improperly, small items omitted (such as locks on windows), substitutions made for items specified, and generally sloppy workmanship.

Poor workmanship is an all-too-common occurrence in renovation work as well as in new construction. The construction business often seems to train butchers rather than craftsmen. If poor workmanship is a problem in your renovation, discuss it with the contractor as soon as it first comes to your attention. Sometimes workmen are careless simply because they have not been properly trained. Getting to know the workmen and praising them when they do a good job can often work miracles. Many times workmen do not understand how a job is to be done, particularly in restoration work. A few kind words, genuine interest in the problem, and intelligent questions can often bring them around to your way of thinking.

If, however, a workman continues to make the same mistakes in spite of explanations and praise, insist that the contractor replace him with someone qualified to do the work. If you have a good contractor, he will be as concerned as you are with poor workmanship. When work must be done over, it costs the contractor money and eats into his profit. However, you should not expect perfection in a renovation; you are dealing with an old house that may have had flaws in it from the day it was built. A contractor cannot be expected to make an old floor absolutely level unless you are willing to pay him to rip it out and start all over again, from beams through subflooring.

When the finish begins, start making checklists of work done improperly and items missed. Give the list to the contractor at the beginning of each week. Continue until everything has been corrected. Keep a notebook and pencil in your pocket: Only if you write things down will you remember all of them when talking to the contractor. You might even make a list of things you want to check while at the job.

Do not issue final payment until the job meets with your approval: Trying to get a contractor back to rehang a door or change a faulty lock after he has been paid can be more difficult than making a child take bad-tasting medicine.

Occasionally an honest and dependable contractor will find himself in the awkward position of having underbid the job. This is a difficult situation for both contractor and owner, one that requires finesse and common sense.

If you are basically happy with the work that is being done and would like to see the contractor continue, you may have to be flexible about the cost of the job. Contractor and owner should discuss the problem to see if an equitable solution can be worked out. Point out that you had expected to pay only the given price for the work, which was the reason the contractor was hired. However, realize that in renovation there are sometimes unforeseen difficulties; you must either be willing to spend a little more or eliminate some items in order to get the job done. Changing contractors would probably mean going over the budget to finish the job, so if you are satisfied with the contractor, you might be better off continuing with him and paying him some additional money. If you remain rigid, demanding that the terms of the contract be fulfilled to the letter, the contractor may cut corners detrimental to your interest or walk off the job.

However, if you are unhappy with the contractor and his work is not acceptable and he is not following the construction documents and the contract, the only sensible solution is to get rid of him, and the earlier in the job you do it, the easier it will be.

- ### TERMINATING A CONSTRUCTION CONTRACT

It would seem a simple matter to get rid of a contractor who has not lived up to the terms of the contract, but it is easier said than done.

The termination of a construction contract can be likened to a divorce: The longer it is postponed, the more deeply involved the two parties become. The amount of debt to be settled at the time of contract termination is often difficult to determine, and the owner can be liable for the full amount of the contract under certain circumstances. If the owner has paid the contractor the full amount due at a given point but the contractor has failed to pay workmen and suppliers, these men can demand payment from the owner up to the full amount of the contract price. In such a case, the owner becomes involved in litigation that is costly and time-consuming.

It is generally easier to determine the value of the work completed in the early phases of construction than toward the end. The payment schedule provided in the contract is one basis for settlement when terminating the contract. By signing the contract, you have given the contractor the right to receive the amount of money specified at any given stage. (This is one reason for making sure the payment schedule does not provide too much money in advance of work completed.)

As an example, take the following payment schedule for a $20,000 renovation job:

$2,000 on signing of contract
$4,000 on completion of demolition
$6,000 on completion of rough plumbing and wiring
$6,000 on completion of plastering
$2,000 on completion of all work

Should the contract be terminated before any work has begun, the owner would forfeit the $2,000 he had paid on the signing of the contract. (A lawsuit could possibly recoup some of this money, but legal fees and court costs would probably be as much as could be obtained from a settlement.) If the contract were terminated at the end of demolition, the contractor would be entitled to an additional $4,000 by the terms of the contract. As work progresses further, it becomes more difficult to determine how much work has been done. Determining the amount owed to the contractor can thus become a hassle.

Besides making a financial settlement, the owner must get a signed *release* from the contractor to legally terminate the agreement. Unless there is a release, the contractor can tie up the property in legal actions and prevent work from being completed. In the release the contractor relinquishes any rights he has under the terms of the contract. Since he would still be liable under the terms of the contract, the contractor generally will not sign a release unless he receives a release from the owner giving up any claims he might have against the contractor under the terms of the contract. This means that the owner takes full responsibility for work already done; if work is defective, the owner must assume the burden of repair or replacement.

A release will enable the owner to get someone else to finish the job, but finding another contractor may be difficult. The new contractor will be responsible for another's work, which may not be satisfactory. The second contractor will often charge a premium price for finishing someone else's job. The less work that has been done, the easier it is for the new man. If work has progressed too far, the owner may have to hire individual workmen to finish the job. In this case, there is usually no guarantee of the work, and the owner must take the consequences if there are problems.

As you can see, getting rid of a contractor once you have hired him is far from simple. Hire only a reputable contractor so you can avoid the problem. However, should you hire a contractor who proves unsatisfactory, terminate the contract as soon as possible, discussing procedure with your lawyer in advance of any action. Always be sure that the contract you sign has provision for termination and that you are provided with maximum protection if the clause is invoked.

· LIENS

Even when the owner has a signed release from the contractor terminating the contract, workmen and suppliers whose materials and labor went into the work can come to the owner for payment of unpaid bills, although the contractor has been paid for the work. At any point during construction a man who has not been paid can place a lien on the property for the amount owed to him if he has been unable to collect. This puts the owner in the awkward position of being liable for bills he has already paid.

Placing a lien is usually a simple matter. For an owner to remove a lien he feels is unjustified is often not so simple. Lien laws vary from state to state. In New York, for example, a mechanic's lien stands for one year. At the end of that year the lien must be renewed. At the end of the second year the lien is automatically dropped if court proceedings have not been instituted to collect the debt. If an owner feels the lien is unjustified, he can sit out the two-year period and wait for the lienor to go to court. However, the owner may not be in a position to wait. If he has a construction loan, the bank probably will not issue further payments until the lien is removed. If the owner plans to refinance or sell the property, the lien usually has to be removed before either transaction takes place. To remove a lien, the owner must institute court proceedings, a costly and time-consuming affair, or pay it off.

Martha and Charlie Stamm had a lien for $750 placed on one of their properties, which probably would have been thrown out in a court of law. However, the Stamms were midway through a renovation project when the lien was placed, and the bank refused to issue another payment until the lien was removed. Indignant, they went to see their lawyer, who agreed the lien was unwarranted but told them they had no choice but to pay it if they wanted the house finished on schedule. The alternative was to shut down the job, institute court proceedings, wait the year or more it would take the case to come to trial, and pay a minimum of five hundred dollars in legal fees and court costs to have the lien dismissed. Their lawyer suggested negotiations for settlement, and the Stamms ended by paying the lienor five hundred dollars to remove the lien. Their lawyer called it legal blackmail.

The case of the Stamms was an unusual one. Most liens are the result of the contractor's failure to pay bills he owes, with the poor owner caught in a trap if he has already paid the contractor. If the owner keeps close tabs on the job from the very beginning, he will soon find out if bills are not being paid because the workmen will often tell him. Every owner should check with major suppliers and subcontractors before issuing a payment to the contractor. A clause can even be inserted in the construction contract requiring the contractor to provide *waivers of lien* from every subcontractor and supplier before a payment is issued. The waiver of lien relinquishes the right of the signer to lien the property for work done to that date.

If a workman, subcontractor, or supplier has not been paid, the owner cannot simply pay the man and deduct the money from the amount he pays the contractor. The owner has a contract with the contractor and must make all payments through him. If he makes payments to the contractor's employees without his permission, he is still liable to the contractor for the amount owed him.

James Greene had an unfortunate and infuriating experience with a contractor in his house in Manhattan's Chelsea. The workman failed to complete work contracted for, and Greene withheld payment. This contractor was in trouble with the Internal Revenue Service for nonpayment of back taxes. When they pressed him for payment, the contractor informed the IRS that, according to the contract, he was owed several thousand dollars by Greene. Three months later, the IRS came to Greene demanding that he pay to them the amount owed the contractor. When he objected on the grounds that the money was not owed because the contract was not fulfilled, the IRS agent said that since Greene had not filed suit against the contractor within ninety days, he had no legal claim against the contractor and must pay the contractor's debt or face penalties himself.

This too is an unusual story, but it did happen. It shows how important it is to know your rights and responsibilities.

· TIPS FOR RENOVATORS

Anyone who has ever done a renovation has advice to give beginners. Each has had problems he would like to warn others about or solutions he would like to pass along. The tips that follow are insignificant when compared to the preceding general information. However, where applicable, they may save you time, energy, and possibly money. And anything that makes renovation easier is always worthwhile.

· PROTECTING ITEMS IN THE HOUSE

Damage to things in the house (items to be salvaged and items already installed) is common during construction. Workmen can be totally insensitive in this area. They consider the house a construction site, where cigarettes are put out on the floor and walls are used to make notes about the job. They often forget to change their habits once the finish has begun. Following are some precautions you should take:

1. Before work begins, remove all mirrors, hardware, and whatever else you plan to reuse; they may disappear or get broken during construction.

2. If you plan to salvage some items and get rid of others, clearly label each item that is to remain, either with paint or felt-tipped pen: "SAVE," "REUSE IN MASTER BEDROOM," and so forth.

3. When tearing out moldings and other items which match those that will remain in parts of the house, save a few to use in patching what is to stay. This applies to flooring and all woodwork.

4. If you plan to use existing wood floors, see that they are covered with building paper from the very beginning of construction. Plumbers have a way of setting up their pipe-cutting and -threading machines in the middle of parquet floors, spilling oil on them. Plasterers drop wet plaster on floors, burning the wood. Even if the floor is to be refinished, a thin parquet can take only a limited amount of sanding, and on other floors, stains may be too deep for sanding to remove.

5. Cover all new floors as soon as they are laid. Use building paper, and see that it is taped down.

6. Quarry tile and other unglazed ceramic tile absorb liquids and dirt. Be sure that a sealer is applied immediately after installation, or stains may occur before renovation is complete.

7. Be sure all tubs are completely covered as soon as they are installed, because workmen will be climbing in and on them to plaster, paint, and install plumbing trim. Plumbers should do the covering by applying paper with a flour-and-water paste.

8. Protect your own tools, preferably under lock and key. Any tools left lying around may be used by a workman who may not be as careful with them as you would be, and often they will end up in his tool box.

9. Do not bring items such as hardware and electrical fix-

tures into the house until they can be installed; they could get damaged or misplaced. Burglaries in unoccupied houses under construction are also common.

10. When in doubt about damage to any item, cover it— and cover everything you do not want painted before the painter arrives on the job.

• PLASTERING

Most renovators are involved with plastering even if new walls are made of sheetrock. When old walls or ceilings are to remain, there is usually patching or repair to be done. Since lime, the base for plaster, must be soaked overnight, plaster cannot be mixed on a whim the way spackle can. For this reason, all plastering should be done at the same time. Here are some suggestions about plastering:

1. If part of a ceiling or wall is in bad condition, the workman can often knock out the bad plaster and replace it without having to replace the whole wall or ceiling.
2. New plaster will not adhere properly to old plaster, especially if it has been painted. However, there are bonding agents that can be applied to old surfaces before applying new plaster. These are usually available at large paint and hardware stores.
3. Decorative moldings and ceiling medallions are often missing or damaged. Plaster moldings can sometimes be duplicated by putting together various pieces of wooden moldings; when they are painted, no one but you will know the difference. Ceiling medallions are now available in a synthetic called anaglypta and can be used to replace missing ones. They are inexpensive and easily installed with glue.
4. Where small pieces of simple plaster moldings are missing or damaged, a simple mold can be made to duplicate them. The procedure is as follows:

a. The damaged molding is removed, and the plaster underneath is coated with a bonding agent.

b. A small section of good molding is coated with vegetable shortening. A handful of wet plaster of Paris is then run across the greased surface to make a mold.

c. After the mold has completely dried, the inside is coated with shortening.

d. Globs of wet plaster are applied to the area where the molding is missing. The mold is then run along this plaster to form the missing molding.

e. Any excess plaster is removed and the whole area smoothed with a wet brush.

It often takes several tries to make this method work. The end result may not be perfect, but when the whole room is painted, the new molding will blend into the old.

5. Be sure that the plasterer does not leave holes around electrical boxes that will not be covered by fixtures and switch plates. The same is true around windows, doors, and floors.

6. Be sure that all plastering is done before the plasterer leaves the job.

· FINISHING DETAILS

The finishing details in your house can make the difference between a good job and a sloppy one, both in terms of the items selected and the way they are installed. A cheap doorknob on a carefully refinished mahogany door stands out like a dirty face on a child in a velvet party dress. Pay attention to finishing details when planning the renovation, and then check the job constantly during the finish to make sure that work is being done properly. The following are a few suggestions:

1. Be sure that moldings around windows and doors in the same room are alike. If you are creating a new opening and cannot match the existing trim, rip it all off and replace it with new moldings.

2. If you would like to have built-in storage in your closets, plan for it when determining closet sizes. Inexpensive drawer units designed to be built into closets are available from Sears Roebuck and other places. These come in standard sizes, so you must plan the closets accordingly.

3. Do not forget about rods and shelves for closets. Galvanized plumbing pipes make excellent rods: They are heavier than those purchased at hardware stores.

4. Additional room for storage can sometimes be found in odd places. When bathrooms are wider than five feet, the space at the end of the tub is usually boxed in so the tub can be recessed. If this space is wider than twelve inches, it can be used for storage. If the space is too deep for your needs, it can be shortened.

5. Workmen have a way of making new ceilings eight feet, even if specified differently, because that is the standard ceiling height in new construction. Specify ceiling height, and then be sure the specs are followed.

6. Stock doors come in a wide variety of sizes and designs. Flush doors have either hollow or solid cores, with the former being the least expensive: Paneled doors are more expensive than flush doors. (Hollow-core doors should never be used for exteriors.) Standard door heights are 6′ 8″ and 7′ with thicknesses of $1\frac{3}{8}''$ or $1\frac{3}{4}''$. Exterior doors should always be $1\frac{3}{4}''$ doors.

7. Stock moldings can be applied to flush doors to give them a custom look. This applies to cabinet doors as well.

8. Many building codes require that entrance doors be equipped with one-way viewers (peepholes). This is a good idea even if not required, because it enables you to see who is at the door before opening it.

9. New straight oak flooring should be laid in the opposite direction from the flooring underneath for added strength. Flooring is normally laid lengthwise in the house, because beams run across the house. If your flooring is being put on top of existing floors, the floor man will probably lay it lengthwise from habit and because it requires less cutting. Flooring laid widthwise in a hall will make the hall seem wider. Specify the direction in which new flooring is to be laid—then be present when it is installed to see that specs are followed. Floor layers often ignore specs, particularly when it saves them work.

10. Improper floor finishing causes owners a great deal of grief. The floor must be properly sanded before the finish is applied, and all finishes except wax require steel wooling between coats to remove bubbles and other imperfections. Floors should have at least two coats of finish, and three coats are preferable. The newer plastic finishes such as Fabulon and polyurethane (used on bowling alleys) are extremely durable and can be cleaned with a damp mop. To be sure you are satisfied with your wood floors, select a floor finisher who knows his business and can advise you on the different kinds of stains and finishes available.

11. In bad weather your floors and carpets can get messed up by wet boots and shoes. Small mats for wiping feet are often ignored by children and delivery men. Try recessing a large cocoa mat in the vestibule, where feet will be automatically wiped when people walk across it. This can save innumerable hours of cleaning.

12. If there are balusters (spindles) missing from your staircase, don't panic. If they are to be naturally finished, you must search for matching ones in the same wood. However, if you plan to paint them, new ones can be turned out by a local woodworking shop for very little money.

13. Mirrors and towel bars combined with appropriate wallpaper can give elegance to an ordinary bath. Be imaginative and you can work miracles on a very modest budget. Old mirrors in decorative frames can replace institutional medicine-chest mirrors, and wooden drapery rods with pineapple finials make fine towel bars when painted.

14. The location and kinds of bathroom accessories must be planned. Two soap dishes at different heights are nice for the family that uses a tub for both baths and showers. Toothbrush and glass holders are not particularly attractive and can often be tucked away out of sight by mounting them on the inside of a vanity door.

15. Plumbing trim is chrome-plated brass. It is possible to have the chrome removed for the same effect as expensive gold-plated faucets for a fraction of the price— particularly effective on simple institutional-looking trim. When selecting faucets, you might look at the lines used by hospitals; they can give a lavatory a sleek, contemporary look.

· Wood Stripping

A favorite occupation with renovators everywhere, stripping woodwork can be quite an ordeal. The job is not done when the paint or varnish has been removed; the wood must also be sanded and finished. Be realistic about the amount of stripping you can do, and be selective about what you strip. Some woodwork actually looks better painted. In the Victorian era, oak and mahogany were sometimes used as pine and fir are used today: You may find oak or mahogany that was painted from its very installation.

Once you have selected those items to be stripped, finish one item before starting the next, or you may find yourself sick of stripping without a single finished product. Do not put off stripping stationary objects until your house is finished. Paint remover takes off new as well as old paint, and floor finishes too.

For those who have not been discouraged, here are some pointers:

1. Shellac and some varnishes can be removed with alcohol. Try alcohol before using paint remover.
2. Use thick remover (called paste) for paint, and thin remover (called liquid) for varnish and the final application on painted surfaces.
3. Varnish will often roll off the wood when liquid remover is applied properly. Use a brush loaded with remover, and lay (rather than brush) it on—varnish smears when brushed. To remove loosened varnish, use a putty knife, and scrape from top to bottom or wash it away with another application of remover.
4. Apply paste liberally to painted surfaces, and let it stand long enough to eat away the paint. If there is much paint to remove, you will have to make many applications.
5. Doors or other items that can be taken down should be placed in a horizontal position for stripping. The remover can lie on flat surfaces long enough to work well; it tends to roll off vertical surfaces.
6. Invest in two sawhorses, and lay items to be stripped across them. Be sure sawhorses are the proper height so you can work in a comfortable position.
7. Get the proper tools: an old aluminum saucepan to hold paint remover, putty knives of various sizes (be sure to get one small enough to fit all surfaces of paneled doors and other details—your hardware store can cut down a larger one to any size you need), cheap paintbrushes, steel wool, rags or paper towels.
8. If you are doing much stripping, buy paint remover by the case, and try to get a discount on each case. You will be amazed at how much remover is required just

to strip a door. You might want to buy paper towels by the case also, or start collecting rags from all your friends—you will never have enough yourself to supply the need.

9. Use rubber gloves—paint remover is disastrous to the hands. Wear safety glasses to protect your eyes, and work in a well-ventilated area.

10. Paint scrapers should be used first to remove any loose, cracked, or peeling paint. They are available at hardware stores in various sizes; be sure to get the ones with replaceable blades, and get extra packages of blades. Take as much paint off as possible with the scraper before applying remover.

11. Apply paint remover to a small area at a time. Paint remover dries up and becomes gummy if it stands too long. When working on vertical surfaces, start from the top and work down to keep stripped surfaces from smearing.

12. For the tiny grooves and crevices use nut picks (they resemble dental tools and come packaged with many nutcrackers) or long nails to scrape out paint.

13. After remover has stood long enough to soften paint, scrape the surface with a putty knife to remove both paint and remover. Wipe surface clean before next application.

14. Steel wool can be used to remove stubborn paint. Apply remover, let stand, and scrub with steel wool.

15. When the surface is free of paint and varnish, wash the whole area with liquid remover and wipe it clean with a clean soft rag or paper towel.

16. Once wood is stripped, cover it completely until you are ready to sand and finish it. Raw wood will stain and get dirty, so be sure the covering is taped down.

17. Small removable objects such as shutters can be dipped in a lye bath to remove paint and varnish. Automobile-radiator repair shops have vats of lye and will often dip

shutters—the cost is well worth it. You can also make your own lye bath in a metal garbage can in the back yard. Lye can burn wood, and water can warp it, so you must not soak objects too long. They should be hosed down immediately to wash off the lye.

18. We have recently used an electric paint-removing tool that is incredibly fast and effective. An open heating coil with a wooden handle, it becomes red-hot within a few minutes after being plugged in. When held near the painted surface, it quickly causes paint to loosen so that it almost falls away at the touch of a paint scraper, often in hand-sized flakes, even out of grooved areas. The dry residue can be swept up, unlike the sticky wet mess from paint remover that can ruin your floors as well as your hands. This tool (called the HYDElectric Paint Remover) is nowhere near as hazardous as a torch, or as likely to scorch your woodwork, but it should be used with reasonable care.

   If your local hardware store does not carry it, ask them to order it for you from Hyde Manufacturing Company, Southbridge, Mass. 01550. Or you may buy it from D. & R. Auslander, 123 Chambers Street, New York, N.Y. 10007; or Roxy Hardware, 469 Columbus Avenue, New York, N.Y. 10024. Both stores will accept mail orders.

19. Finishes for wood include shellac, varnish, linseed oil, and wax. If stain is to be used, it is applied first; but the wood should have a protective coating other than the stain. A stained varnish does both jobs at once.

20. Raw wood normally requires more than one application of finish. In the case of linseed oil, varnish, and shellac, the surface should be rubbed with fine steel wool before the second coat is applied, since these finishes often raise the grain of the wood. Wax or linseed oil finishes need additional applications periodically to keep the wood protected.

• PAINTING

There is more to painting than just wielding a paintbrush. Unless walls are new plaster, much preparation must be done before the paint is applied. If you hire a painter to do the work, watch him closely if you are at all particular about the way your house looks. Following are some suggestions about painting, whether you hire someone to do it or do it yourself:

1. Spackling compound for patching holes and cracks comes in powdered form or ready-mixed. The latter is more expensive but far easier to use.
2. Be sure all telephone wires, nails, and so forth are removed before painting is begun. Painters often paint right over them even if told to remove them.
3. Remove all hardware before the painter goes to work. No matter how careful he is, paint will surely get on doorknobs and other fixtures.
4. If light-switch and outlet plates are not to be painted, remove them. If walls are to be white, you can get white covers with baked-on finish, but you must specify them.
5. If possible, have all lighting fixtures installed after the painting is complete to avoid any chance of getting paint on them.
6. Take all naturally finished doors off the hinges and store them in another room while painting is being done. This is usually much easier than covering them.
7. All woodwork that is to remain unpainted should be covered and taped to be sure that no paint gets on the wood—this includes kitchen cabinets.
8. Be sure that all floors are covered and edges taped, even floors that will be finished after painting is complete. Removing paint from raw wood requires extra sanding and is particularly difficult around the edges.

9. Specify in your contract that the painter remove any paint from windows and mirrors.
10. Use ready-mix paint wherever possible. If paint must be custom mixed, the color can be chosen from a book of color chips that are carefully catalogued and can be duplicated at any future date so long as you keep the catalogue number. If you or your painter mix the color, you will probably be unable to match it later.
11. Use semigloss (satin) paint on wood trim and doors because you can wash it more easily than flat paint. You might even want to use semigloss on walls for the same reason—the finish dulls very quickly.
12. Using light colored paint in rooms that are dark makes them brighter. It's amazing what white paint can do for a room that gets little natural light.
13. If you are doing any painting yourself with oil-base paints, we would like to pass on to you a marvelous time-saving tip. When you must stop working before your job is complete, simply wrap your brush or roller in aluminum foil and put it in your freezer until you need it again. It will not affect the other contents of the freezer, and when you take it out and unwrap it, you will find it in exactly the same condition as when you put it there, except for being a trifle chilly! This enables you to do a bit of work whenever you have a spare moment without worrying about the nuisance of brush cleaning.

· LIVING IN A HOUSE UNDER CONSTRUCTION

Living amidst a renovation is not everyone's cup of tea. Most who do so act out of necessity. Being greeted by workmen when you awake and living with constant plaster dust are part of the ordeal, but life can be easier if a little advance planning is done. The following tips are for people contemplating residence in a construction site:

1. Have all good furniture put in storage. The cost may seem unnecessary, but otherwise your furniture may be worth nothing by the time renovation is complete.

2. Pack everything but the barest essentials in boxes and store out of the workmen's way until work has been finished. Too many "things" get in the way and have to be shifted constantly.

3. Set up housekeeping in an area where the least amount of work is to be done. That way you can achieve some feeling of permanence while renovation progresses and will not have to move constantly from one room to another as work is being done.

4. You may want to move out of the house for a week or so while plumbing is being installed. The plumber will not have to work around your plumbing needs, and the job can be done more quickly. The cost of a hotel room for a week is usually a small price to pay to avoid the inconvenience of no hot water, or no water at all.

5. Remember that it is just as difficult for workmen to work with people in the house as it is for you to live with the construction. When you are considerate of their problems, they will usually be considerate of yours. Let all contractors who are bidding on the job know that you plan to live in the house. Discuss with them how to schedule the work so there is a minimum of inconvenience to everyone.

15 Being a Landlord and the Alternatives to Renting

BEING THE LANDLORD of a house you live in is scarcely more difficult than maintaining the whole house for yourself. The owner has the same responsibilities whether he occupies the entire house or has tenants: The property must be maintained in compliance with the local building code, the sidewalk must be swept and snow shoveled, and garbage taken care of in accordance with local regulations. The landlord is, of course, responsible for maintaining the rental units and any public areas, but if he occupied this space himself, he would have the same responsibility.

The main burden of being a landlord is in renting the apartments, keeping good relations with tenants, and collecting the rent each month. When you consider that these tenants are helping you pay for your house, the work scarcely seems like much. If you do not wish to take on this job, a professional management firm can be hired to operate the house for you, allowing you to live there as a tenant yourself.

Most renovators choose to do their own renting and managing, and have seldom had difficulty with either. They normally design apartments in which they would be willing to live themselves and are often far more imaginative in planning rental units than the average real estate investor, who looks solely at the economics of the situation. There are myriad ways in which renovators have found their tenants (there are real estate brokers who will be glad to rent your apartments for you; and if apartments happen to be scarce, the tenant pays the broker's fee and it costs you nothing for this service), but the most common procedure is advertising in the newspaper.

· HOW TO RENT AN APARTMENT

Make the advertisement appealing to the type of tenant you are seeking, and list the price of the apartment (or you may spend the day turning away people who had not planned to spend as much as you are asking). A typical advertisement might read as follows:

> 1-bedroom apartment in renovated town house. Fireplace, modern bath, and kitchen. House lovingly restored by owner-occupant. $150/mo.

Such an advertisement describes the apartment and tells the prospective tenant that he will have the security of living in an owner-occupied house, often a plus in areas where renovation has just begun. It also lets the reader know that the owner cares about the apartment.

The advertisement should also state the area in which the apartment is located. You might even want to give the exact address and have an open house for prospective tenants. In any case, be sure to list a phone number where people can call to get information and make an appointment to see the apartment.

The condition the apartment is in can be all-important in renting. Even if the apartment is not complete when you begin showing it, be sure it is clean and neat. A dirty bathroom or unwashed windows can detract from its charm. You will expect your tenant to take care of your apartment—show him you care by having it in good condition when he first sees it.

The most important factor in renting an apartment is checking on prospective tenants. Remember, you are selecting a tenant, not making a lifelong friend. Your first concern is that he is able to pay the rent and has a record of prompt payment. Other concerns are his stability and reliability: You do not want a tenant who moves in today and out tomorrow. You also want him to take care of your apartment and not be a constant source of noise and annoyance. If an applicant meets these qualifications, you should have a good tenant.

Any interested person should fill out an application for the apartment and leave a deposit of one month's rent, refundable if the applicant is not accepted. Julius Blumberg, Inc., makes standard application forms (available from 80 Exchange Place, New York, N.Y., or at large stationery stores), or you can make your own application form. Here is the information you need:

1. Name and address of applicant
2. Name and address of current landlord
3. Name and address of employer and how long employed there
4. Name and address of bank(s).
5. Charge accounts or other credits references (at least two)

Check all references carefully. Investigating tenants in advance of accepting them will prevent problems in the future. You certainly do not want a tenant who has a record of bouncing checks or unpaid bills. If an applicant does not seem reliable, refund his deposit and look elsewhere.

In order to keep the relationship between you and your

tenant on a business basis, you should require both a lease and a security deposit before he moves in.

· SECURITY

Security (usually in the amount of one month's rent) is a deposit given to the landlord to cover damage to the apartment or loss of income if the tenant breaks his lease. The security is held until the tenant moves out and the landlord has an opportunity to inspect the apartment. It does not cover normal wear and tear on the apartment, but is for repairs that have to be made as the result of the tenant's carelessness or neglect. Under no circumstances should the security deposit be accepted as the final month's rent; it is refunded to the tenant after he has vacated.

· LEASES

Leases are for the protection of both landlord and tenant. They set down the rights and responsibilities of each party. Leases can be written for any length of time mutually agreeable, but two years is the term of a typical apartment lease. Standard-form leases are available at most large stationery stores or directly from Julius Blumberg, Inc.

Be sure that the lease you use does *not* contain a *sublet clause*. The sublet clause allows the tenant to move out of the apartment if he can find another tenant willing to sublet the apartment for the remainder of the lease. You may want to include a clause that provides for landlord approval of a sublet tenant, but the straight sublet clause allows your tenant to select the new tenant for you, causing you to lose some control over your house. If a prospective tenant is subject to transfer or feels that he may be unable to fulfill the term of the lease, you can give him the right to break the lease with thirty to ninety days' written notice and the forfeit of his security if no new tenant is found during this period. This method is far preferable to a sublet clause, but any such agreement must be incorporated in the lease.

The names and number of occupants of the apartment should be included in the lease. If the apartment is rented to two unmarried people, it is best to have the lease in both names so that both are responsible. And of course, you do not want to find out that the apartment you thought you were renting to one person is to be occupied by several. When selecting a tenant, keep in mind the size of the apartment. Too many people in too small a space are bound to create problems, such as excessive noise and abnormal wear and tear.

There should be two copies of the signed lease, one for you and one for your tenant. At the time the lease is signed, you should receive the security deposit and one month's rent in advance. At the same time, the tenant should be made aware of his responsibilities. The policy of garbage removal should be explained, along with any other rules and regulations. If the tenant is to pay his own utility bills, he should be told to contact the utility companies to make provision for the meters to be put in his name.

You should make clear from the very beginning what you expect of your tenant; do not hesitate to see that he lives up to the terms of his lease. On the other hand, be sure that you live up to your responsibilities as a landlord. You cannot expect to have a good tenant if you are not a good landlord.

· HOW TO BE A GOOD LANDLORD

There are no rules for being a good landlord, but if you treat your tenants as you would want to be treated, you should have no problems. Keep your house in good condition, and make repairs promptly. If a problem arises that you cannot solve immediately, keep your tenant informed. Most tenants are sympathetic and will be patient if they know you are trying to get the repair made.

The following is a list of things that good landlords do:

1. Keep public areas clean (halls and the front and rear of the house).
2. Promptly shovel snow from sidewalks and exterior stairs.
3. Have an adequate number of garbage cans (if you provide them), and see that the area where garbage is stored is kept clean.
4. Replace light bulbs in public areas as soon as they burn out.
5. Provide plenty of heat and hot water.
6. Always be pleasant to your tenants.

· THE ALTERNATIVES TO RENTING

There is another way to handle space that you do not plan to occupy yourself—rather than rent, you can sell it. This can be done in one of several ways:

1. By selling an interest in the property to one or more people who will live in the other apartment(s).
2. By converting the house into a cooperative.
3. By converting the house into a condominium.

These alternatives should be discussed thoroughly with a knowledgeable attorney who can explain them, advise you, and perform the legal duties of the transaction.

A complete discussion of these different forms of ownership is far beyond the scope of this book, but there are a few things you should know when considering selling rather than renting.

If you are the sole owner of the house, you have sole authority to make all decisions yourself; if not, when you sell, you must share the decision-making, that is, your partner(s) or co-owner(s) may not want to spend money to paint the exterior or you may differ on what color it should be painted. On the other hand, you have others with whom to share the responsibilities and liabilities.

When you sell rather than rent, you recoup some or all of your cash investment. In return, you must pay your fair share of the operating costs of the house. When you have rental apartments in the house, you should pay a smaller amount of rent for your apartment than your tenants do because you have a cash investment in the house and are responsible for operating and maintaining it. In selling, you lose this advantage, along with certain tax benefits available to owners of rental property. (See Appendix, page 389 for tax benefits.)

The decision to sell or rent is a purely personal one—there are advantages and disadvantages in each situation. Your financial status may determine the choice. If the amount of cash you have is small, selling may be the answer. And when the purchase and renovation of a city house is beyond your means, it is possible to buy a house with one or more people and make it a joint venture from the beginning.

Appendix

· INCOME TAX BENEFITS

Real estate owners are allowed income tax deductions for the following:

1. Money paid for real estate taxes and interest on mortgages
2. Expenses incurred in operating income property
3. Depreciation of income property

· REAL ESTATE TAXES AND INTEREST ON MORTGAGES

Whether the house is urban or suburban, a private home or an income-producing property, real estate taxes and the interest paid on mortgages can be deducted from your personal income for federal, state, and city income taxes *provided* the house is in your name. (If the property is in a corporate name, it is the corporation that derives these and all other tax benefits.) Your tax bracket will determine how beneficial these deductions are, but even those in a low tax bracket will derive some tax savings. For example, if you are in a 20% bracket, you will save 20% on all money spent for tax-deductible items—that is, you will not have to pay any tax on that money.

For single people, the income tax bite can be the major motivation for buying and renovating a city house. Single people who earn above-average salaries find the lion's share going to pay income tax. Investing in a house therefore represents a double saving to them: Their monthly rent goes partly into their investment (amortization on mortgages) and partly into tax-deductible interest and real estate taxes.

• OPERATING EXPENSES OF RENTAL PROPERTY

Income from property will raise the owner's personal income, but he can deduct from his rental income the expenses incurred in producing it. When figuring operating costs for tax purposes, mortgage amortization payments are not included. The following is a list of operating expenses that are deductible:

1. Heat
2. Utilities for public areas and for tenants' apartments *if* the owner pays utility charges
3. Water and sewer charges
4. Insurance
5. Maintenance and repairs (labors and materials)
6. Management costs, if paid to someone else

If the entire house is rented, all these expenses are deductible. However, if the owner lives in part of the house, he may not deduct the listed expenses for operating his apartment. In such a case, he may deduct a portion of these expenses commensurate with the amount of rented space—that is, if half of the house is rented, 50% of the expenses are deductible.

· DEPRECIATION

An additional bonus to owners of income property comes in the form of depreciation. The technical definition of depreciation is the loss of value in real property brought about by age, physical deterioration, or functional or economic obsolescence. This means that the value of the building may be taken as an expense over an extended period of time (what the Internal Revenue Service calls the reasonable life of the building). Depreciation is figured in a dollar amount deductible yearly from the value of the property for tax purposes; it is a noncash expense, or what is commonly referred to as a tax shelter. Here is how depreciation works:

An owner figures the cost of the property, exclusive of land. (Land is not depreciable because it does not lose value through age, deterioration, and so on.) Then he must estimate the percentage of the building that is rented if he occupies part of the house himself; the rented percentage becomes the *base for depreciation*. If 100% of the house is rented, 100% of the value can be depreciated; if half of the house is rented, 50% of the value can be depreciated. *An owner cannot depreciate that portion of the house in which he lives.*

Once the base for depreciation has been figured, the period of depreciation must be established; for an older renovated house it is usually twenty to thirty years. The base of depreciation is then reduced over the period of depreciation, with the amount of the reduction taken as a tax-deductible expense of the property each year.

Depreciation over a twenty-year period is taken at 5% of the depreciable base, and for thirty years is taken at 3-1/3% per year; it is called *straight-line depreciation:* taking the same amount of depreciation each year. Another kind of depreciation is *accelerated depreciation,* in which a higher amount is deducted in the first years, with the amount diminishing yearly over the depreciation period. Whether to use straight-line or accelerated depreciation should be discussed with your lawyer or accountant, but for the purpose of this book, we will deal with straight-line depreciation. The following is an example:

A property cost the owner $50,000 to purchase and renovate. The owner lives in half the house and rents the other half. The value of the land is $10,000, leaving $40,000 as the value of the house. Because half of the house is rented, $20,000 (50% of $40,000) is the base for depreciation. The house will be depreciated over twenty years, enabling the owner to deduct as an expense $1,000 (5% of $20,000) each year for twenty years.

The theory behind depreciation is that at the end of the depreciation period the value of the property will be substantially reduced and will require an extensive investment in improvements in order to return it to its original value. Whether you agree or disagree with the theory, be sure to take advantage of the fact. Depreciation deductions can save you a great deal of money.

However, you should be aware that depreciation will have a tax effect when you sell the property. How much the property cost you is established when you first take depreciation, and is reduced by the amount of depreciation you deduct. On the property mentioned above, the owner's cost of $50,000 is reduced by $1,000 each year. Thus, if he were to sell it five years after he bought it, his cost for tax purposes would be $45,000 ($50,000 less the $5,000 already taken as a reduction in value). Therefore, if he sold for $50,000, he would make a profit of $5,000 on the sale as far as the Internal Revenue Service is concerned. He must now pay tax on the $5,000, which he has paid no tax on before. However, he will have less tax to pay at the time of sale, because the money is now capital gains rather than regular income.*

---

* However, if he reinvests the amount, including his profit, in a similar property, the tax on the profit is postponed indefinitely.

· REAL ESTATE TAXES

The assessed valuation (*tax assessment*) on property is the value set by the city* as a base for determining real estate taxes. The city has a *tax rate* that is applied to the assessment to determine the amount of real estate taxes levied against each property. The tax rate is often expressed in dollars per hundred dollars of assessed value. If the tax rate were five dollars per hundred dollars of value, the tax rate would be 5% of assessed value.

The amount of real estate taxes an owner must pay is based on the property's tax assessment and the current tax rate. A rise in taxes could be the result of either an increase in assessment, an increase in tax rate, or both. It is important for an owner to know his assessment so that he knows whether a property tax increase is based on a change in rate or a change in assessment. An owner can do nothing about an increase in rate, but it is often possible to do something about the assessment.

There is no universal policy on tax assessments, and you may find that the policy varies in different areas of the same city. The tax assessor acts as an independent agent, and one assessor may be more diligent and conscientious than another.

Whether your property will be reassessed as a result of renovation will in part be determined by past practice, though this is always subject to change. Some cities, such as Chicago, tend to give the renovator a break and make it a practice to let the assessment stand for several years after renovation is complete. Other places, like Manhattan, go to the other extreme and raise assessments at the first opportunity. Wherever you live, there is a better than even chance that there will be a reassessment as a result of reno-

---

* Technically not the city but the assessing unit, which might be a village, town, city, county—any or all of them together or separately.

vation. A little research on your part should give you an idea of what to expect.

Tax assessments, a matter of public record, are on file at the tax assessor's office. A trip there might well be worth the time. If there is renovated property in the area, the prior assessments on this property will give an indication of whether it has been reassessed, when it was reassessed, and how much of an increase resulted. If renovated and unrenovated property have about the same assessment, then no reassessment has been made. When looking at the assessment records, make a note of the properties with exceptionally high assessments, and go by and look at them to see if you can determine the reason for the high assessment.

There are several general guidelines you ought to be aware of. Single-family homes normally have lower assessments than the same property containing rental units. Tax assessments often reflect the amount of income a property produces for the owner. A property that has been sold several times for an increased price will often have a higher assessment than one that has had the same owner for many years. If sale prices in an area have risen sharply, there is a good chance that all property in the area will be reassessed to reflect increased value. In some cities the assessment is broken down into land assessment and total assessment. If a reassessment is based on a renovation, the land assessment generally remains the same but the total assessment is raised to reflect the increased value of the house. If the whole area is reassessed because of a general rise in sale prices, it is often the land value that is increased. The assessment of land is based on the size of the lot, and the same standard is applied to all property on a given street or in a given area. In the case of building assessments, there is often a wide discrepancy in assessed value.

As an example of land and total assessment policy, let us look at a block of Manhattan's Upper West Side. On one side of the street, all lots are 102.2 feet deep, but the width of the lots varies from 16 to 20 feet. Land assessment policy is based on front footage to a standard depth. The standard applied is $1,500 per front foot. Thus a 16-foot property has a land assessment of $24,000, and a 20-foot property has a $30,000 land assessment. Yet total property-tax assessments vary greatly. Two houses that were built at the same time and are the same size may have vastly different total assessments reflecting the most recent purchase price, when and if a renovation has been done, how often the property has changed hands, and the number of dwelling units and the rent of each.

In some areas of New York City, property has not been reassessed in many years even though sale prices have risen and property has changed hands several times. This apparent immunity from tax assessment increase could end at any time.

• You Can Protest Your Tax Assessment

Many property owners are not aware that they can protest their tax assessment. Each city has its own procedure for protest, but they follow a general pattern.

Tax assessments are posted each year at a specified time. (You must find out when this happens in your city.) The tax assessor usually has a given period of time in which to make his reassessments. At the end of this time, an assessment for each piece of property is posted in the tax rolls. This is often done well in advance of the issuance of real estate tax bills; it is often too late to protest when the tax bill is received. An owner must go to the tax assessor's office to find out if there has been a change in assessment. If an owner feels that an increase is unjustified, he can obtain a protest form from the tax assessor's office, which must be filed with the city by the date specified on the form. The owner is then given a hearing in which to state his case. If the city offers a reduction that is acceptable, this new assessment is entered in the tax books. If, however, no reduction is offered (or the reduction is insufficient), the owner can go to court with the case. However, a form must be filed to leave the protest open or reject the offer that has been made.

A protest of tax assessment should be discussed with your lawyer. The procedures are often complex, confusing, and difficult to follow. In many cities there are attorneys who specialize in tax protests. They normally work on a contingency basis—that is, you pay them nothing unless they save you money. These lawyers are thoroughly familiar with local tax policies and know what arguments to use at the time of the hearing. These attorneys are usually more effective than an owner can be. Your own lawyer should be able to provide the names of tax protest lawyers.

You usually cannot protest previous tax assessments, so be sure to file a protest the year of increase or the year you purchase if you feel the assessment is too high. You automatically accept the assessment if you do not protest, and it is hard to convince the assessor to reduce it the next year, even though you were not aware of your ability to object. Check the current assessment of the property when you buy it (along with the dates for posting new assessments and protesting assessments), and discuss with your lawyer whether it is too high in relation to the price you paid. As a neighborhood declines, so do property values, but the tax assessor seldom reduces assessment unless there is a protest. Tax assessments in a deteriorated neighborhood may be higher in relation to sale price than in other areas of the city. You generally have grounds to protest assessment based on the price you paid for your house, if the relationship of assessed value to market value differs from the general standard in the area.

· PROPERTY TAX ABATEMENT AND EXEMPTION

Some cities have a policy of tax abatement and/or exemption under certain conditions, such as for veterans, the elderly, or as an incentive for providing certain kinds of housing. These programs vary so from city to city that it is impractical to give specific information about them. You should check to see if abatement or exemption is available and under what conditions. Find out in advance, because these programs may affect the kind of house you buy and the renovation you do. For instance, in New York City, tax abatement and exemption are available upon conversion of Class B (rooming houses) to Class A multiple dwellings (three families or more) but do not apply to private or two-family houses.* If you wish to take advantage of this program, you must create at least three apartments, including your own.

Availability of tax abatement and/or exemption does not mean you will want to take advantage of them. Ask your lawyer if such programs are available in your area, and discuss with him their merits and disadvantages.

· INSURANCE

The insurance that most homeowners need consists of coverage for fire and other damage to the house and its contents, injury to persons on the property (liability), and theft. All of this coverage is available to owners of one- and two-family houses in a package policy (*homeowner's policy*) at substantial savings. The same insurance for multiple dwellings (three families or more) is provided by several policies. *Rent insurance* to cover the loss of income and provide quarters for the owner-occupant if the property must be vacated because of fire damage can be added to the homeowner's policy (and other fire policies) for a minimal charge.

It is mandatory that you insure your house for the proper amount because of *co-insurance* requirements. To get a fair recovery in case of loss, you need an amount of insurance equal to 80% of the *reconstruction cost* of the

* Except under certain strict exceptions.

house, less reasonable depreciation. In computing the value of your house, do not include the land. If your house has less than 80% coverage, you may, in case of partial loss, get "depreciation recovery" rather than the full amount needed to cover costs—for instance, as little as $5,000 or $6,000 after a $10,000 fire.

The amount of insurance you carry should not be based only on what you actually spent on the house, but must also take into account increases in construction costs and property values. Consult an insurance broker in determining the proper amount of insurance to carry in order to avoid a co-insurance penalty.

Renovators sometimes have difficulty obtaining insurance on vacant houses and those under construction where there is added risk of fire and malicious mischief. A good insurance broker can solve many of these problems. However, in some renovation neighborhoods insurance is difficult to obtain regardless of the condition of the house. One Brooklyn renovator contacted the Human Rights Commission for help after many rejections by insurance companies that felt her neighborhood posed too high a risk; insurance coverage for fire and liability is now available from a "pool" similar to that for poor-risk automobile owners.

LISTED BELOW are organizations with permanent addresses that can supply further specific information.

Baltimore

> Commission for Historical and Architectural Preservation
> 402 City Hall
> Baltimore, Md. 21202

Charleston

> Historic Charleston Foundation
> 51 Meeting Street
> Charleston, S.C. 29401

Chicago

> Lincoln Park Conservation Association
> 741 Fullerton Avenue
> Chicago, Ill. 60614

New Haven

> New Haven Redevelopment Agency
> 157 Church Street
> New Haven, Conn. 06510

Newport

> Operation Clapboard–Oldport Association
> Box 238
> Newport, R.I. 02840

New York

> Brownstone Revival Committee
> 230 Park Avenue
> New York, N.Y. 10017

> Little Old New York Citizens' Committee
> 46 West 94th Street
> New York, N.Y. 10025

Philadelphia

> Redevelopment Authority of the City of Philadelphia
> City Hall Annex
> Philadelphia, Pa. 19107

> West Philadelphia Corporation
> 4025 Chestnut Street
> Philadelphia, Pa. 19104

Pittsburgh

>Pittsburgh History and Landmarks Association
>900 Benedum-Trees Building
>Pittsburgh, Pa. 15222

Providence

>Providence Preservation Society
>24 Meeting Street
>Providence, R.I. 02903

Richmond

>Fan District Association
>P.O. Box 5268
>Richmond, Va. 23220

>Historic Richmond Foundation
>2407 East Grace Street
>Richmond, Va. 23223

San Francisco

>San Francisco Redevelopment Agency
>939 Ellis Street
>San Francisco, Calif. 94109

Savannah

>Historic Savannah Foundation
>119 Habersham Street
>Savannah, Ga. 31402

Washington

>National Trust for Historic Preservation
>748 Jackson Place, N.W.
>Washington, D.C. 20006

Index

abatement, tax, 396–7
accelerated depreciation, 391, 392
Adams-Morgan section (Washington, D.C.), 98, 145
adequate-wiring survey, 277
adjustments, at closing, 259–60
adobes, tile-roofed, 29
air conditioning, 280, 281, 286, 291–2, 315, 319
alcohol, for wood stripping, 375
Alexandria, Va., 15, 264, 265
Alley Dwelling Act, 93
American Institute of Architects (AIA), 59, 327, 347, 349; Statement of Professional Services by, 327, 330, 342
amortization, defined, 223–4
Amster, James, 50
anaglypta, 53 *n.*, 370
Angle, Paul, 109
Ann Adams Carrington house (Richmond), 140
Annapolis, Md., 29
Ansley Park (Atlanta), 135

Anson, George, 137
Ansonborough (Charleston), 137
Antiques magazine, 43
apartment, factors in renting, 382–5
appliances, 304–5, 315, 322–3, 325
appreciation of property, 200
architect, 195, 211, 241, 291, 324–32, 343, 358; basic services of, 325; fees of, 326, 329, 331; house inspected by, 209, 210; qualifications of, 328; selection of, 327–30; terminating services of, 332; working with, 330–2
artifacts-retrieval program, 104
assessment, tax, *see* tax assessment
Association for the Preservation of Virginia Antiquities, 140
Atlanta, Ga., 130, 135–6
attic, 283
auctions, property, 192

Back Bay (Boston), 30, 32, 35
back-to-back plumbing, 271–2, 273
Bacon, Edmund, 72
balloon mortgage, 231–2, 239
Baltimore, Md., 10, 16, 82–91, 399
Baltimore Commission for Historical and Architectural Preservation, 88, 399
balusters, 373
banks, 219, 220, 221; commercial, 218–19; savings, 218
base for depreciation, 391
bathrooms, 171, 172, 176, 177, 272, 280, 284, 292, 296, 298, 300, 316, 325, 372, 374
bathtubs, 298–300
Bay Village (Boston), 30, 36
Beacon Hill (Boston), 30, 34, 36–7
bearing wall, 264 and *n.*
Bedford-Stuyvesant Restoration Corporation (Brooklyn, N.Y.), 68, 144 *n.*
Belluschi, Pietro, 331
Benefit Street (Providence), 37, 41, 42, 72, 130
Bernal Heights (San Francisco), 116–17, 119
bidding for construction, 338–41, 346; methods of, 339–40
bidets, 297
binder, 189
Birmingham section (Pittsburgh), 103
Blumberg, Julius, Inc., 383, 384
Boerum Hill (Brooklyn, N.Y.), 14, 23, 62, 64, 65, 69, 145, 146, 220, 343
Boerum Hill Association, 62
Bolton Hill (Baltimore), 62, 84, 85–7, 89

bonds, performance, 350–1
bookcase, custom, 313
Boston, Mass., 18, 30, 30–7, 60, 192, 201
Boswell, H. Curley, 96
branches (pipes), 267, 268
brass water lines, 207, 268
bricks, black header, 78
broker: insurance, 398; mortgage, 220, 221; real estate, 184–5, 188–9, 255, 339
Brooklyn (New York City), 18, 51, 55–70, 145, 210; landmark tours of, 70
Brooklyn Heights (New York City), 57–61, 62
Brooklyn Heights Association, 58
Brooklyn Union Gas Company, 290; house renovated by, 69
Brown, C. Dudley, 96
brownstone, 16, 19, 47, 50, 60, 61, 66, 70, 87, 206, 287
"Brownstone Grapevine," sponsored by Abraham and Straus, 70
"Brownstone Hunter's Guide, The" (Con Edison), 69–70
Brownstone Revival Committee (New York City), 147, 399
"Brownstoning," Brooklyn YWCA course in, 70
Brown University, 38, 40
Buckler, Helen, 62
building and loan associations, 218
building codes, 143, 266, 268, 276, 281, 291, 292, 293, 297, 306–10 *passim,* 327, 372
building inspectors, 310
building permits, 307, 308–9
bulbs, light, 281, 282
Bulfinch, Charles, 130

Bullock, Helen Duprey, 97
buzzer system, door, 286, 318

cabinets, 295, 296, 315, 325;
 kitchen, 296, 301, 304, 313, 323
cable television, prewiring for,
 288
Cadman Plaza (Brooklyn, N.Y.),
 60, 61
Caigan, Mr. and Mrs. Robert,
 158, 159, 168
Cannery (San Francisco), 121
Cape May, N.J., 29
capital-gains tax, 261
Capitol Hill (Washington, D.C.),
 62, 93–8, 147
Capitol Hill Restoration Society,
 94
carpentry: finish, 315, 316, 321;
 rough, 315, 316–17
Carrington house (Richmond),
 140
Carroll Gardens (Brooklyn,
 N.Y.), 65
carrying costs, 211, 212
Catonsville (Baltimore), 90, 91
ceilings, 173, 178, 182, 208, 281,
 282, 283, 294, 295, 370, 372;
 fiberglass, 282
cellar, 207, 209, 270, 274, 278,
 286, 293; lights for, 283
Central Park (Manhattan, N.Y.),
 170
certificate of occupancy (C.O.),
 310
Chace, Mrs. Malcolm G., Jr.,
 40
chandeliers, 283; gas, 275
Charleston, S.C., 7, 44, 121, 130,
 136–8, 399
Charlestown (Boston), 30, 34–5,
 37, 247

Charles Village (Baltimore),
 89–90
Chelsea (Manhattan, N.Y.), 50–1,
 55, 146
Cherry Street (Philadelphia),
 80–1
Chicago, Ill., 16, 106–12, 204,
 393, 399
Chicago Historical Society, 109,
 110
Church Hill (Richmond), 62,
 139, 140, 141
Cincinnati, O., 105–6
circuit, 277, 278
circuit breaker, 277, 278, 286
circuit-breaker box, 278, 286
Citizens & Southern Bank
 (Savannah), 130, 131
Clapboard, Operation (Newport),
 43, 44, 45, 399
clean-outs, 270
Clinton Hill (Brooklyn, N.Y.),
 57, 62, 64, 68, 69, 145
closets, 372; lights for, 283, 285;
 see also storage space
closing, 248, 249, 258, 259–60;
 adjustments at, 259–60; costs
 of, 260
Cloyd, Royal, 30, 32, 33, 34, 60,
 128
Cobble Hill (Brooklyn, N.Y.),
 61, 62, 65
Code Enforcement programs,
 245, 246, 247
coffin niche, 18
coinsurance requirements,
 397
Coliseum Square (New Orleans),
 128, 129
College Hill (Providence), 37, 40,
 42, 62
Columbus, O., 10, 104–5
combination mortgage, 235–6

Concentrated Code Enforcement
program, 245, 246, 247
conditional sale, 254
condominium, 386
Consolidated Edison Company,
69
Constant Annual Percentage
Table, 197, 198, 214
construction contract, 325, 326,
332, 342, 346–51, 356, 367;
and construction documents,
348; guarantees in, 349–50;
and payment schedule, 349,
364; penalty clause in, 348;
and performance bonds,
350–1; price quoted in, 349;
termination of, 359, 363,
364–6; and workmen's
compensation insurance, 350
construction documents, 315,
324, 325, 326, 338, 339, 340,
356; list of, 348
construction loan, 233–5, 236
Consumer Reports, 304
contract: construction, *see*
construction contract; purchase, 248; sale, 254, 257, 258
contractor, 163, 164, 165, 167,
297, 325, 333, 338, 339, 362,
363, 367; bids by, *see* bidding
for construction; checking on,
343–6; general (G.C.), 334–5,
336, 337, 338; house inspected
by, 209, 210; incorporated,
342; licensed, 309; release
from, 365; selection of, 342–6;
working with, 358–9; *see also*
construction contract
convenience outlets, 280
Cooke, Caswell, 19
cooperative, house converted
into, 386
copper water lines, 207, 268

Copp's Hill (Boston), 36
cost-plus bid for construction,
339, 340
counter tops, for kitchen
cabinets, 301
Creager, Bill, 95, 97
crime problem, 68, 145, 158

Davis, L. J., 62, 64
*Death and Life of Great
American Cities, The* (Jacobs),
144
decorating, 265, 305–6
Delaney, Edmund T. ("New
York's Turtle Bay"), 55 and *n.*
demolition: specifications for,
315, 316; by Urban Renewal,
243
Department of Housing and
Urban Development (HUD),
240, 245, 247
deposit, 189
depreciation, 391–2
Depression (1930's), 53, 58, 93
design development, by architect,
325
detail drawings, 313–14, 348
Dickeyville (Baltimore), 90
Dilworth, Richardson, 70, 72, 74
discounting, of second mortgage,
228–9
dishwasher, 274, 280, 286, 305
door buzzer system, 286, 318
doors, 293, 294, 295, 372, 375;
French, 162
Downtown Brooklyn Committee,
69
drain, house, 270
dryer, clothes, 274, 280, 286,
305
duplex apartments, 19, 35, 176,
177, 178, 201

earnest money, 189

East Side, Upper (Manhattan, N.Y.), 50, 157

East Village (Manhattan, N.Y.), 51, 55

electric box, 279, 281, 284

electric heat, 289–90

electric wiring, 208, 209, 276–88; and fixtures, 281–3, 284, 305, 318; and outlets, 280–1, 285; specifications for, 315, 318; survey of, by electric company, 277; and switches, 284–5

engineer: house inspected by, 209; plans drawn by, 327

equipment, as element of renovation, 265, 295–305

equity, defined, 225

escrow, for taxes and insurance, 237

Esplanade (Brooklyn, N.Y.), 59

Esplanade Avenue (New Orleans), 125, 126, 127

Estern, Neil, 59

estimate of renovation costs, 210–13, 222

evaluation of property, 205

Fabulon, 373

Fabulous New Orleans (Saxon), 121, 124

Fan District (Richmond), 11, 139, 141, 142

Fan District Association, 141–2, 400

Father, Son, and Holy Ghost house, 80

faucets, 297, 300, 374

Federal architecture, 40, 94

Federal Hill (Baltimore), 62, 84, 87, 88, 89

Federal Housing Administration, 241

Federal National Mortgage Association, 242

Federally Assisted Code Enforcement (FACE), in San Francisco, 117, 118, 119, 120

Feely, Hugh Patrick, 206

Fells Point (Baltimore), 84, 87, 88

Fetch, Frank, 104

FHA, 10, 97, 150, 218, 239–42, 351

financing, 194 *ff.*, 211, 212, 213, 218–47; primary, 227; secondary, 227–33; *see also* mortgage; operating costs; refinancing

finish construction work, 353, 354–5, 362, 371

finish schedule, 313, 314

fireplace, 275, 313, 361

Fishtown (Philadelphia), 82

five-story house, 201

fixed-price bid for construction, 339–40

fixtures: electrical, 281–3, 284, 305, 318; plumbing, 297–301, 318

floor plans, 172–6 *passim,* 178–81 *passim,* 265, 269, 273, 296, 308, 311–15, 325, 348; and detail drawings, 313–14; electrical symbols used in, 313; and finish schedule, 313, 314; information provided by, 312–13; scale rulers for, 312; *see also* room arrangement

floors, 208, 263, 265, 305, 369, 373; oak, 323, 373; parquet, 17, 173, 323; specifications for, 316, 323

fluorescent lighting, 282

forced-air heating, 288, 291
foreclosure, 192, 223, 227
Fort Greene (Brooklyn, N.Y.), 69, 145
four-story house, 178
Fox Point (Providence), 42
French doors, 162
French Quarter (New Orleans), 28, 121, 124–8 *passim,* 135, 147
French Second Empire architecture, 101
Friedman, Dorothy, 360
Friedrichs, Chris, 126, 127, 128
Friends of the Stockade (Schenectady), 45
furnace, 207, 267, 288, 289, 290
furniture placement, 295
fuse, 278; defined, 277

galvanized iron water lines, 207, 268
gambrel roof, 130
Garden District (New Orleans), 128, 129
gas furnace, 290
gas lines, 274–6, 318
General Neighborhood Renewal Plan (Chicago), 110
Georgetown (Washington, D.C.), 3, 7, 10, 55, 91, 93, 104
Georgian architecture, 40, 82
Germantown (Philadelphia), 82
German Village Society (Columbus), 104
Ghirardelli Square (San Francisco), 121, 135
glue job, in tile work, 322
Golden Triangle (Pittsburgh), 99
Gothic architecture, 108
grace period, and mortgage, 237

Gramercy Park (Manhattan, N.Y.), 134
Grandview Avenue (Pittsburgh), 104
Greek revival, 16, 40, 101, 129, 140
Greenwich Village (Manhattan, N.Y.), 47, 50, 51, 55, 57, 59, 146, 308
Guide to New York, 59
gutters and leaders, 209, 270, 319, 320

Hamill, Pete, 57
hardware, 296, 305, 316, 323, 369
heating coil, 267
heating system, 259, 288–91, 317; expenses for, 196, 197, 201, 202, 203, 204, 211, 214, 215; inspection of, 209; specifications for, 315, 319
heavy-duty outlets, 280, 286
Held, Barbara, 96, 97
Here Today, San Francisco's Architectural Heritage, 120
Highland Park (Boston), 30, 37
Hill, Lewis W., 110
Hillyer, Mrs. Hansell, 130
Historic Charleston Foundation, 131, 137, 399
Historic District designation, 88, 89, 121, 129
Historic Richmond Foundation, 140, 141, 400
Historic Savannah, 134
Historic Savannah Foundation, 129, 130, 131, 134, 400
Hoffmann, Mr. and Mrs. Bernhard, 29
home improvement loan, 236–7

homeowner's insurance policy, 397

hot-water heating, 267, 288, 290

Houlton, Peggy, 54

house drain, 270

House & Garden magazine, 331

house sewer, 270, 271

Houses-in-Process tour, Barbara Held's, 97

house tours, in Richmond, 142

Housing Act (1964), 247

HUD, 240, 245, 247

Human Rights Commission (Brooklyn, N.Y.), 398

Hyde, J. A. Lloyd, 43

HYDElectric Paint Remover, 377

Hyde Park–Kenwood (Chicago), 108

Italian Renaissance architecture, 108

Jackson Square (San Francisco), 120

Jacobs, Jane (*The Death and Life of Great American Cities*), 144

Jova, Henri, 135

Kitchen, Benjamin, 80, 284, 337

kitchen cabinets, 296, 301, 304, 313, 323

kitchens, 172, 176, 177, 262–3, 264, 272, 292, 296, 325

"kiting," 167

incandescent light bulb, 282

Income and Operating Summary Form, 214

income tax benefits, 389–92

incorporation laws, 342

Ingersoll, Mr. and Mrs. Jared, 74, 76, 78

Inman Park (Atlanta), 135

inspection of house, 207–10; professional, 208, 209–10, 263, 278

inspectors, building, 310

insurance, 189, 197, 201–4 *passim,* 211, 214, 215, 219, 397–8; escrow for, 237; and FHA, 239–42; title, 259; unemployment, 336; workmen's compensation, 336, 350

intercom, 285, 286

iron water lines, galvanized, 207, 268

ironwork, 315, 322

lamp: convenience outlets for, 280; gas, 275

landlords, 385–6

Landmark Architecture of Allegheny County, 99

Landmarks Commission (San Francisco), 120

Landmarks Preservation Commission (New York City), 61

Larimer Square (Denver), 135

Larkin house (Boston), 35

Larsen, Roy, 72

laundry equipment, 172

lavatories, 297, 300, 374

lawyer, 189, 195, 211, 241, 255, 258, 259, 367, 392, 396; hiring, 249–51

leaders and gutters, 209, 270, 319, 320

lead water lines, 207, 268

lease, 384

Lee, Richard, 46

Lefferts Gardens (Brooklyn, N.Y.), 69
L'Enfant, Pierre, 7, 93
liens, 225, 342, 346, 351, 366–8; waiver of, 367
lighting fixtures, 281–3, 284, 305, 318
Lincoln Park (Chicago), 108, 109, 110, 111
Lincoln Park Conservation Association, 109, 110, 111, 206, 399
Little Old New York Citizens' Committee, 54, 399
Little Rock, Ark., 29
Liverpool Street (Pittsburgh), 102
loan: construction, 233–5, 236; home improvement, 236–7; the *312,* 35, 247
log, gas, 275
Loop (Chicago), 106
Lowrey, Mark, 124
Lowrey, Mr. and Mrs. Walter, 124, 125

Magazine Street (New Orleans), 128, 129
maintenance, expenses for, 196, 197, 214, 216
Manchester (Pittsburgh), 102, 103
Manhattan (New York City), 46, 47–55, 57, 210, 393; and Stamms' renovation, 149–57, 366–7; and Stanforths' renovation, 157–70, 336, 360–1
Mansard roof, 18, 82, 108
mantel, 264, 275
Margolis, Richard, and Martin Schneider ("The 60's Belong to the City"), 60

Martin, Mrs. Walton, 50
masonry, 315, 317
master circuit breaker, 277
meters: electric, 277, 278; gas, 275
Meyers, Tedson, 98, 145
mirrors, in bathroom, 374
Mission District (San Francisco), 115–17, 119
Mobile, Ala., 29
Model Cities program, 103, 245, 246
moldings, 296, 321, 369, 370, 371, 372
Moore, Charles, 20, 23
Morgan, Anne, 50
mortgage, 189, 196–9, 202, 203, 204, 211, 212, 214–15, 217, 238; annual payments on, 197, 198, 214, 224; application for, 221–2; balloon, 231–2, 239; combination, 235–6; conditions of, 226–7; defined, 223; FHA-insured, 239–42, 351; first, 214, 219, 227, 228, 229, 230, 234; and grace period, 237; ideal, 222–3; interest on, 196, 197, 198, 215, 223, 224, 227, 229, 389; monthly payments on, 196, 197, 224; prepayment clause in, 226, 253; and principal, 223, 224; purchase-money (P.M.), 229–30, 251, 253; second, 214, 227, 228, 229, 230; self-amortizing, 223–5, 231, 238; sources for obtaining, 218–23; subordination clause in, 230–1, 253–4; term of, 223; third, 227, 229; transferability of, 226; twenty-year, 198; *see also* financing; property; purshase of house; refinancing

mortgage bond, 225
mortgage broker, 220, 221
mortgagee, defined, 223
mortgagor, defined, 223
Morton (Philadelphia), 82
Moses, Robert, 58, 59, 60, 68
Mount Adams (Cincinnati), 105, 106
Mount Royal Improvement Association (Baltimore), 86
Mount Vernon (Baltimore), 87
Mount Washington (Pittsburgh), 104
mud job, in tile work, 322

Natucket, Mass., 29
National Association of Real Estate Boards, 60
National Observer, 11
National Trust for Historic Preservation (Washington, D.C.), 97, 147, 400
Near North Side (Chicago), 108
New England, 15, 18, 43
New Haven, Conn., 19, 46, 192, 399
New Haven Redevelopment Agency, 399
New Orleans, La., 7, 16, 28, 121–9
Newport, R.I., 15, 43–5, 137, 399
Newport National Bank, 44
New York, N.Y., 10, 16, 46–70, 146, 147, 192, 395, 399; Housing and Development Administration in, 246; rent control in, 255 and *n.;* tax abatement and exemption in, 397
New York magazine, 57, 62
New York Telephone Company, 287

New York Times, 156, 220
New York Times Magazine, 55
Nitardy, Ferdinand, 58, 59
North End (Boston), 30, 36, 37
North Side (Pittsburgh), 99, 101, 102
North Side, Near (Chicago), 108

Oglethorpe, James E., 129, 130
Old Philadelphia Corporation, 74
Oldport Association (Newport), 45
Old Town (Chicago), 14, 108, 109, 110
Old Town Triangle Association, 108, 109
operating costs, 196–9, 201, 202, 203, 204; estimate of, on finished house, 214–17; of rental property, 390; *see also* financing
Operation Clapboard (Newport), 43, 44, 45, 399
outlets, electrical, 280–1, 285
oven, electric, 276, 280, 286

painting, 265, 305, 316, 324, 378; pointers for, 378–9
paint remover, 375, 376
paint scraper, 376
Park Slope (Brooklyn, N.Y.), 57, 60, 61, 66–7, 145, 146, 220
Parkway (Philadelphia), 81
parquet floor, 17, 173, 323
Pei, I. M., 73
Pepys, Mrs. Charles, 43
performance bonds, 350–1
Permastone, 65, 88
permits, building, 307, 308–9

Philadelphia, Pa., 10, 15, 46, 70–82, 399; Redevelopment Authority of, 72, 74, 76

Philadelphia City Planning Commission, 72

Philadelphia Redevelopment Authority, 399

photoelectric cell, 285

Piety Hill (Detroit), 62

Pittsburgh, Pa., 10, 16, 99–104, 137, 400

Pittsburgh History and Landmarks Foundation, 99, 101, 102, 103, 104, 400

Pittsburgh Housing Authority, 101

planning, importance of, 262–6

plans: city approval of, 307–8; drawing, 311–32 *passim; see also* floor plans

plastering, 234, 315, 320, 370–1

plastic piping, 268

plumbing, 207, 209, 263, 266–76, 374, 380; back-to-back, 271–2, 273; by licensed plumber, 309; new, 271–4; one line of, 271, 272; rough, 274; specifications for, 315, 317–18; stacked, 272, 273

plumbing codes, 266–7

plumbing fixtures, 297–301, 318

Point Breeze (Pittsburgh), 104

points, and construction loan, 235

polyurethane, 373

Portsmouth, N.H., 29

Powelton (Philadelphia), 82

Pratt, Charles, 57

prepayment clause, in mortgage, 226, 253

property: appreciation of, 200; and auctions, 192; bought in Urban Renewal areas, 243–5; condition of, when purchased, 255–6; evaluation of, 205; right of access to, 257; survey of, 259; and tax abatement and/or exemption, 396–7; title to, 248, 249, 257, 258; *see also* purchase of house

Prospect Heights (Brooklyn, N.Y.), 69

Prospect Park (Brooklyn, N.Y.), 57, 67

Providence, R.I., 15, 37–43, 400

Providence Preservation Society, 38, 42, 400

Prudential Center (Boston), 34

Pulaski Square–West Jones Street (Savannah), 131, 134

Purchase and Renovation Summary Form, 212, 214

purchase contract, 248

purchase money (P.M.) mortgage, 229–30, 251, 253

purchase of house, 248–61; cash needed for, 252–3; and contents of house, 256; and date for taking title, 257; down payment on, 256–7; negotiating, 248, 251–7; and right of access, 257; *see also* mortgage; property

Queen Village (Philadelphia), 80

radiators, 289

Rainbow Row (Charleston), 137

real estate broker, 184–5, 188–9, 255, 339

recessed lighting, 281, 282
record-keeping of expenditures, 260–1
refinancing, 200, 211; value of, 233
refrigerator, 274, 276, 305, 306
Reich, Bob and Barbara, 96, 97
release from contractor, 365
renovation, 352–80; basic elements of, 262–306; city regulations affecting, 306–10; as do-it-yourself project, 337; estimating costs of, 210–13, 222; and "extra" construction charges, 356–8; financing, 233–7; how work progresses in, 352–5; living amidst, tips for, 379–80; plans for, 311–15; possible problems in, 355–68; and protection of items in house, 368–70; supervision of, 359–63; tips for, 368–80; *see also* architect; contractor; construction contract
"renovation generation," 10, 24
rental income, 156, 168, 173–4, 198, 199, 201, 203, 204, 216, 217, 222, 261
rent control, 255 and *n.*
renting: alternatives to, 386–7; methods of, 382–5
rent insurance, 397
repairs, expenses for, 196, 214, 216
revolving fund, 137
Rhode Island School of Design, 40
Richmond, Va., 10, 11, 138–42, 400
Ridge Avenue (Pittsburgh), 99
risers, 267, 271

Rittenhouse Square, West (Philadelphia), 80, 82
Roback, Arline, 97
roof garden, 182
roofs, 182, 208, 209, 263, 283; flat-topped, 319–20; gambrel, 130; Mansard, 18, 82, 108; specifications for, 315, 319–20
room arrangement, 265, 293–5; *see also* floor plans
rough construction work, 353, 355
Roxbury (Boston), 30, 37

sale contract, 254, 257, 258
sandblasting, 324
San Francisco, Cal., 10, 16, 112–21, 400
San Francisco Planning and Urban Renewal Association (SPUR), 120
San Francisco Redevelopment Agency, 117, 118, 119, 400
Santa Barbara, Cal., 29
Sarah Mellon Scaife Foundation, 101
satisfaction piece, 225
Savannah, Ga., 129–35, 203, 400
savings and loan associations, 218
sawhorse, use of, 375
scale rulers, for floor plans, 312
Schenectady, N.Y., 45–6
Schenectady Historical Association, 45
Schneider, Martin, and Richard Margolis ("The 60's Belong to the City"), 60
search, title, 259
security, given to landlord, 384

SEFCO (South End Federation of Citizens Organizations), 33, 146

service line, for electrical power, 276, 277, 286

Seton, Mother, 87

Seton Hill (Baltimore), 87, 88

Seton Hill (Detroit), 62

sewer, house, 270, 271

sewer charges, 196, 197, 201, 202, 203, 204, 211, 214, 215, 259

Shady Side (Pittsburgh), 104

sheetrock, 315, 320, 370

shower body, 300, 301

sinks, 173

skylights, 319

Snell, Stephen, 45

Society Hill (Philadelphia), 62, 72–9, 81, 82, 130

soil lines, 268–71, 272

South End (Boston), 14, 30, 32–4, 246

South Side (Pittsburgh), 103

space, working with, 174, 176–8, 182

spackling compound, 378

specifications, 315–24, 338, 348, 356

Sporl, Louis, 128

sprinkler system, 317

Spring Garden–Greene Street area (Philadelphia), 81

stacked plumbing, 272, 273

stacks (pipes), 268, 269, 270, 271, 272

stairs, 172, 208, 373; circular iron, 177

Stamm, Charlie, 28, 55, 149, 152, 153, 221, 309, 338, 366

Stamm, Martha, 26, 27, 55, 144, 146, 149, 154, 221, 309, 338, 366

Stamms' renovation (Manhattan, N.Y.), 149–57, 366–7

Stanforth, Deirdre, 157, 158, 164, 166, 167, 361

Stanforth, Jim, 157, 158, 161, 164, 166

Stanforths' renovation (Manhattan, N.Y.), 157–70, 336, 360–1

steam cleaning, 324

steam heat, 288

steel water lines, 268

steel wool, paint removed with, 376

Stockade (Schenectady), 45

Stockade Association, 45

stoop, high, 47, 283

storage space, 171, 295, 372; *see also* closets

stove, electric, 276, 280, 286

straight-line depreciation, 391, 392

studios, 178

subcontractor, 333, 334, 335, 338, 367

sublet clause, in lease, 384–5

subordination clause, in mortgage, 230–1, 253–4

Sullivan, Louis, 108

Sutton Place (Manhattan, N.Y.), 3

switches, electric, 284–5

take-down schedule, for construction loan, 234, 235

tax: capital-gains, 261; escrow for, 237; real-estate, 197, 201, 202, 203, 204, 211, 214, 215, 259, 389, 393–7

tax abatement, 396–7

tax assessment, 143, 183–4, 215, 393, 394; protest against, 395–6

tax exemption, 396, 397
tax rate, 393
telephone, prewiring for, 287
telephone box, 288
telephone jack, 287–8
television, cable, prewiring for, 288
tenant relocation costs, 212, 213
312 loan, 35, 247
three-story house, 192, 203
tile work, 296, 315, 316, 321–2, 360, 369
title insurance, 259
title search, 259
title to property, 248, 249, 257, 258
toilets, 297, 300, 316
Towne Properties, Inc. (Cincinnati), 105, 106
transom, 294
trap (pipe), 268
Trenton, N.J., 29
triplex apartments, 176, 177, 178, 201
Trustee's Garden Village (Savannah), 130
Turtle Bay (Manhattan, N.Y.), 3, 4, 42, 50
two-family house, 174, 204
Tyson Street (Baltimore), 84, 86

Underground Atlanta, 135–6
Union Park (Boston), 32, 34
Union Square (Baltimore), 89
University City (Philadelphia), 81–2
Upper East Side (Manhattan, N.Y.), 50, 157
Upper West Side (Manhattan, N.Y.), 51, 53, 54, 55, 232, 394–5

upset price, in cost-plus contract, 340
Uptown Neighborhood (Atlanta), 135
Urban Renewal, 33, 34, 36, 40, 46, 53, 54, 55, 60, 79, 80, 82, 86, 97, 108, 118, 147, 149, 150, 242–5, 246, 247
utilities, 259; expenses for, 196, 197, 201, 202, 203, 204, 214, 215–16
utility outlets, 280

vacating of house, 254–5
Vanderbilt, Mrs. William K., 50
Vann, James E., 119
ventilation, mechnical, 292–3, 315
vent stack, 269, 271
Victorian architecture, 16, 17, 32, 33, 40, 43, 81, 82, 94, 98, 101, 104, 108; San Francisco, 114
Vieux Carré Commission (New Orleans), 121, 125
violations, building, 249, 256

Walkabout (Schenectady), 45
washing machine, 274, 280, 286, 305
Washington, D.C., 7, 16, 91–9, 147, 202, 308, 400
Washington Square West (Philadelphia), 79
Washington *Star*, 11, 93
water charges, 196, 197, 201, 202, 203, 204, 211, 214, 215, 259
Waterfront Renewal (Baltimore), 84, 88, 89
water lines, 207, 267–8

Western Addition (San Francisco), 115, 117–19, 120
West Philadelphia Corporation, 81, 399
West Rittenhouse Square (Philadelphia), 80, 82
West Side, Upper (Manhattan, N.Y.), 51, 53, 54, 55, 232, 394–5
West Side Urban Renewal project (Manhattan, N.Y.), 53, 54, 55, 149
Williams, Roger, 37, 43
Williamson, Reid, 131
windows, 208, 292; colonial multiple-paned, 18
Windsor Hill (Baltimore), 90
wiring, electric, *see* electric wiring
wood stripping, 337, 374–5; pointers for, 375–7

Wooster Square (New Haven), 19, 46, 118, 247
workmen, individual, hiring, 336–7
workmen's compensation insurance, 336, 350

Yale School of Architecture, 20
"Your Building Department" (LPCA), 111
"Your 'Where-to-Call' Guide" (LPCA), 111

Ziegler, Arthur, 101
zoning laws, 143–4, 206, 306, 310; in Charleston, 121; in San Francisco, 114; in Washington, D.C., 97

A Note on the Type

This book was set on the Linotype in a type face called Baskerville. The face is a facsimile reproduction of types cast from molds made for John Baskerville (1706–75) from his designs. The punches for the revived Linotype Baskerville were cut under the supervision of the English printer George W. Jones. John Baskerville's original face was one of the forerunners of the type style known as "modern face" to printers —a "modern" of the period A.D. 1800.

This book was composed and bound by The Colonial Press Inc., Clinton, Mass., and printed by Halliday Lithographers, West Hanover, Mass.